WOMEN ADRIFT

To Susan Lindee
with much admiration
and gratitude,
Noriko Horiguchi

Women Adrift

. . . .

The Literature of Japan's Imperial Body

Noriko J. Horiguchi

University of Minnesota Press
Minneapolis
London

The University of Minnesota Press gratefully acknowledges financial assistance provided for the publication of this book by the Japan Foundation.

A version of chapter 5 was published as "The Body, Migration, and Empire: Tamura Toshiko's Writing in Vancouver from 1918 to 1924," *U.S.–Japan Women's Journal*, no. 28 (2005): 49–75. A version of the Conclusion appeared as "Migrant Women, Memory, and Empire in Japan in Naruse Mikio's Film Adaptations of Hayashi Fumiko's Novels," *U.S.–Japan Women's Journal*, no. 36 (2009): 42–72.

English translations of Yosano Akiko's poetry first appeared in Steve Rabson, "Yosano Akiko on War: To Give One's Life or Not—a Question of Which War," *Journal of the Association of Teachers of Japanese* 25, no. 1 (April 1991): 56–72, reprinted with permission of the publisher and translator; and in Laurel Rasplica Rodd, "Yosano Akiko and the Taisho Debate over the 'New Woman,'" in *Recreating Japanese Women, 1600–1945*, ed. Gail Lee Bernstein (Berkeley: University of California Press, 1991), 175–98.

Published by the University of Minnesota Press
111 Third Avenue South, Suite 290
Minneapolis, MN 55401-2520
http://www.upress.umn.edu

Library of Congress Cataloging-in-Publication Data

Horiguchi, Noriko J.
Women adrift : the literature of Japan's imperial body / Noriko J. Horiguchi.
Includes bibliographical references and index.
ISBN 978-0-8166-6977-6 (hardback) — ISBN 978-0-8166-6978-3 (pb)
1. Japanese literature—Women authors—History and criticism.
2. Japanese literature—20th century—History and criticism. 3. Human body in literature. 4. Women in literature. 5. Fascist aesthetics—Japan—History—20th century. 6. Literature and society—Japan—History—20th century.
7. National characteristics, Japanese, in literature. I. Title.
PL725.H67 2011
895.6′0992870904—dc23
2011028097

Printed in the United States of America on acid-free paper

The University of Minnesota is an equal-opportunity educator and employer.

18 17 16 15 14 13 12   10 9 8 7 6 5 4 3 2 1

Contents

Introduction: Japanese Women and Imperial Expansion   vii

1. Japan as a Body   1
2. The Universal Womb   19
3. Resistance and Conformity   35
4. Behind the Guns: Yosano Akiko   51
5. Self-Imposed Exile: Tamura Toshiko   81
6. Wandering on the Periphery: Hayashi Fumiko   123

Conclusion: From Literary to Visual Memory of Empire   157

Acknowledgments   177
Notes   181
Bibliography   203
Index   227

Japanese Women and Imperial Expansion

WOMEN'S BODIES CONTRIBUTED TO THE EXPANSION of the Japanese empire. *Women Adrift* shows how discourses about women's bodies redrew the border and expanded, rather than transcended, the body of the empire of Japan. Instead of emphasizing women's transgressions of the borders of gender and the nation, I explore the national in the bodies of women who crossed the imperial borders of the Japanese empire. I trace the paradoxical relationship between women's resistance to and participation in the empire rather than emphasizing one more than the other. Within the predominant paradigm of Japan as a body in some of the influential writings of policy makers, intellectuals, and writers in modern Japan, women were imagined in bodily metaphors ranging from the arms and legs to the womb of Japan. In this historical and political context, I explore discourses on women's migrant bodies as the site of changes running the gamut from resistance to conformity with an imperial discourse that demarcated and expanded the border/body of Japan. Specifically, I examine women's relationships to the empire and colonized neighboring nations in their prose and poetic discourse on female bodies that move between *naichi,* the inner territory of the empire of Japan, and *gaichi,* the outer territory of Japan.

This study examines in particular female bodies in works of three prominent and influential female writers, Yosano Akiko (1878–1942), Tamura Toshiko (1884–1945), and Hayashi Fumiko (1904–51), as their fictional characters move in the context of the expanding body/border of the empire. I analyze, on the one hand, how Yosano, Tamura, Hayashi, and their heroines transgressed the state's prescriptions concerning gender and sexuality and rejected the state's ideological assignments that subjected their bodies to nation building in *naichi.* On the other hand, I explore how each actively participated in the expansion of the empire in *gaichi,* where female bodies are re-inscribed into the state's definitions of race/ethnicity and the universality of the Japanese body. By tackling the reasons for and processes of the connection and disconnection between migrant bodies of women and the expanding body/border of the empire, this project explains how Japanese women, despite their marginalization in Japanese society, emerged as active agents against and for the modern empire of Japan.

With this project, I come to a different conclusion from the preceding scholarship on women and their relationship to the empire. Historiographical research on the empire of modern Japan (1868–1945) has shifted its focus in recent years from the emperor, state bureaucracy, and military to the Japanese people themselves. In the field of "people's history" *(minshū-shi),* scholars tackle questions about the relationship between the ideology of the state and that of the people, as indicated in the roles the populace played in building and expanding the empire. In raising these questions, there has been a shift to investigate continuity rather than discontinuity between prewar and immediate postwar Japan.[1] In the attempts to understand the specific roles women played in the era of empire, scholars have presented four principal positions: Japanese women as (1) passive victims of the government and military, (2) sacred mothers or goddesses who protected and nurtured life and peace, (3) resilient strugglers at the social and economic margins of society, and (4) artists and activists resisting state-driven nationalism. These four positions have been represented in a variety of ways, but they all tend to smooth over analyses of the roles of those women who actively participated in the formation of nationalism as a discursive tool serving Japan's expansion as an empire and its colonial endeavors. This study exposes the continuity between women's bodies that move and the border/body of the empire that expands. Only by acknowledging the national elements in the transnational bodies that cross the imperial borders do we begin to understand both sides of women's stories that at once resist and re-create the Japanese empire.

A relative lack of scholarship on—and of popular interest in—Japanese women as active and sometimes aggressive participants in the formation of the empire may be attributed to the predominant ideas about Japan and its women. As Jan Jindy Pettman writes in *Worlding Women,* nations in international relationships are often represented as women (as in "the motherland," Germania, Italia, and other images) and as natural bodies susceptible to aggression and penetration from outside.[2] One may therefore argue that women in general are identified with the nation that must be protected, in contrast to men, who are identified with the state that attacks and penetrates other nations with military might, as in the "rape of Nanjing." Japan has often been represented as "masculine" because of its association with military actions under the imperial regime in the modern era (1868–1945), and also the shogunate rulers in the early-modern and premodern periods. Conversely, Japan has also been perceived as "feminine" (i.e., associated with refinement, restraint, harmony, and aesthetics), as in the predominant image of geisha. These prescriptions, rather than descriptions, find their way into both older and newer discourses, including the recent example of "Utsukushii Nippon" (Beautiful Japan), a slogan of the Liberal Democratic Party under the leadership of Prime Minister Abe Shinzō in 2006. The notion of Japan as beautiful evokes another powerful postwar example of re-creating Japan(ese) in the international forum by the novelist Kawabata Yasunari in 1968. In his Nobel Prize acceptance speech, "Japan, the Beautiful, and Myself," Kawabata claims that the tradition of a Japan that is gentle, harmonious, and aesthetic determines his works of literature. In keeping with these efforts to re-create the national image of Japan as feminine, "Japanese Woman" has come to be perceived as the essence of elegance, restraint, calm, harmony, and beauty.[3]

These depictions have helped foster the notion of Japanese women as passive victims of aggressors—be they men, the Japanese state, or Western imperial powers in the modern era. Conversely, it has become difficult to conceive of a "Japanese Woman" who has a voice, participates actively, or shows aggression. Along with being victims, there has also been emphasis on women as resilient and persevering strugglers at the fringes of society. Another powerful example of a modern representation of Japanese women is the phrase coined by the Education Ministry in the late 1890s, "good wives, wise mothers."[4] The mother as a nurturer of life and peace overshadows the fact that she was re-created as the reproductive source of soldiers for military aggression and the atrocities of the empire. When women have been depicted with agency instead of passivity, it is the resistance of women as rebels against men and the state that has traditionally been celebrated.[5]

Studies of Japanese women's history until the 1970s, and analyses of Japanese women's literature even today, predominantly adopt schemas that present women as victims, idealize them as protectors and nurturers of peace, celebrate their resilient struggles at the margins of society, or cast them as rebels who fight against men and the state officials. As Suzuki Yūko points out, it was in the 1970s and the 1980s that a transition in the studies of women's history took place; the paradigm shifted from viewing women as victims to exposing them as aggressors when the following question was raised: Why did notable feminists such as Hiratsuka Raichō, Ichikawa Fusae, and Takamure Itsue make a commitment to imperialism?[6] Since then, scholars of women's history have argued the value and effects of exposing the support of female artists and intellectuals for imperial war efforts. For example, Suzuki investigates female intellectuals' activities during the prewar and postwar periods and challenges what she characterizes as the long-established framework that has uncritically vindicated the responsibility of the aggressors.[7] Against Suzuki, who deems female artists and intellectuals aggressors accountable for the atrocities of war, sociologists such as Chizuko Ueno characterize Suzuki's approach as a historical perspective of "accusation" (kokuhatsu) and "a transcendental view of history" (chōetsu-teki shikan):[8]

> Suzuki criticizes Ichikawa Fusae's inability to see through the entrapment of "nationalization" and Hiratsuka Raichō's ignorance for idealizing tennōsei [the emperor system]. What lies behind Suzuki's criticism is the absolute view that "nationalization" and tennōsei are evil. The reason why Suzuki's women's history is often called a historical perspective of "accusation" is because of her transcendental standard of judgment, which she advocates by standing in the so-called vacuum area of history.[9]

Ueno suggests that women's decisions and actions in support of imperial Japan were determined by the historical and political contexts of the time. The charge that their deeds were evil may only be possible from a postwar perspective that ignores the contexts of the time in which women lived.

This research wishes to contribute to the continuing debate on national history and add another perspective on the discursive forces that made possible the wartime actions committed in the name of Japan. In tackling questions of nationalism and empire in modern Japan, I recognize that female writers and intellectuals were not simply either passive victims or active participants, but played both roles simultaneously. Affirmation of women's ignorance or innocence not only prevents us from seeking knowledge but also ignores the effects of power generated by women's discourse. The celebration of women as the transgressors of the nation smooths over the ways some women tried to improve their status and negotiate a larger role in society both by resisting and by incorporating nationalism and the empire. Raising questions about women's engagement in the imperial discourse does not amount to an accusation against past historical figures, nor does tackling the issues of these female writers' participation in the imperial discourse constitute an apology for their decisions and deeds. This study, however, deems them responsible for the effects generated by their writings. Their active participation in the discourse, practices, and institutions of the empire was not inevitable. There were several options for writers during the war, including silence, resistance, cooperation, or returning to/re-creating classics and tradition. The writers who acted upon the discourse on the empire are held morally accountable in this research.[10] By raising historical and political questions about works of modern Japanese women's literature as discourse, I join the continuing debates on women's participation in, and responsibility for, the formation of the empire.

While recognizing the significant contributions of scholarship on women in Japan to date, *Women Adrift* proceeds from a different point of departure by examining the works of three highly acclaimed women writers that construct women as active and sometimes aggressive participants in the creation of empire. Yosano Akiko, Tamura Toshiko, and Hayashi Fumiko have heretofore received popular and critical attention mostly as resilient strugglers, protectors of peace, courageous fighters against male oppression and the state, and/or outsiders vis-à-vis the system of gender and the nation. Most scholarship has highlighted their move away from the nationalist discourse on women. To this picture I add another point of view by analyzing the contradictory ways in which these three writers, as the marginalized in society, because of their gender, class, ethnicity, or race, envisioned and experienced the modern empire of Japan. In my study, the three writers and their literary characters do not exclusively fall into either the category of active participants/aggressors or the category of victims, but emerge as both.

These three writers—and their female characters—refused to live domesticated lives as wives and mothers and instead became wandering travelers and migrants. By moving within Japan, Japan's colonies, the West, and its occupied territories, and by refusing to act as ideal national subjects, Yosano, Tamura, and Hayashi and their characters deviate from the norms of a united Japan. This book explores the process by which these prominent women writers and their characters in the inner and outer territories of modern Japan refused the ideological assignments that subjected their minds and bodies to nation building, and yet became part of the force that created the empire of Japan.

The paradox in the three writers' resistance to and participation in the empire results from the dynamics of "the triple principle of control of class, women, and . . . ethnos *(minzoku)* that connects one to another inseparably and constitutes the principle of the modern nation-state," as Wakakuwa Midori points out.[11] When Yosano, Tamura, and Hayashi and their heroines tackle the problems of survival, liberation, and empowerment, they focus on the questions of gender and/or class when they are in *naichi.* Whereas the identity of the nation-state is perceived to be secure in their eyes, it is their selves, determined by gender and/or class, that are threatened and insecure in *naichi.* To become active agents instead of accepting a position as passive observers or victims, they find importance in resisting the nation-state or in being outside it. Yosano, Tamura, and Hayashi and their heroines criticize or stand outside the system of the state that protects and controls Japanese women when they are in *naichi.*

When they move or shift their concerns to *gaichi,* however, they become conscious of the self that is insecure and threatened, not only because of their gender and class, but also because of their race and ethnicity, as created by the nationalist and imperial discourses. As a result, when their physical bodies move to the fringes of the Japanese empire, they come to participate in the central discourse of the state that constructs Japan. They re-create their agency by protecting, strengthening, and serving the nation-state. They incorporate the story of the nation-state's independence, power, and liberation into their stories of women's independence, power, and liberation. Women's discourse becomes part of the forces of aggression and atrocity of Japanese imperial expansion. By at times resisting and at other times supporting the state's designation of women for reproduction and production of the empire, women as the marginalized sought to articulate, analyze, and overcome their marginalized experiences. By exposing not only discontinuity but also continuity between the migrant female bodies and the expanding borders of the empire, I show that the three writers and their characters were at once the victims and the aggressors of the Japanese empire. I shed light on this neglected aspect of their writing and trace the reasons, processes, effects, and responsibility inherent in their paradoxical participation in the empire.

Literature

For this study, I focus on three of the most prominent female writers from modern Japan and review their texts for articulated hierarchies of meaning that revolve around empire and women. I not only offer analyses of intra-textuality of their works but also trace the affiliations of inter- and extra-textuality. I investigate how works of literature rearrange meanings of women and empire that are otherwise prioritized in accord with the state discourse on them. I attempt to place literary and "nonliterary" texts—including legal documents such as the Civil Code (1897) and the Imperial Constitution (1889), educational documents such as school textbooks and *Kokutai no hongi* (The essence of the national polity, 1937), and different media such as magazines, newspapers, and films—on the same plane, subject them to the same analytical tools, and investigate them in relation to the same contextual landscapes. By being especially attentive to the political effect of the text, which shapes its lines of enunciation, I situate modern Japanese literature as the object of scrutiny in the institutional and legal realms. As a result of viewing a literary text as part of other social and political texts, institutions, and practices, modern Japanese women's literature emerges as an effect of these texts and contexts of the prewar era.

In connecting literature with history and politics, I analyze how literature—as well as other discursive means, institutions, and practices—creates status and the role of both the Japanese Woman as a concept and women as active agents in modern Japan. This study examines how works of modern Japanese women's literature negotiate state discourses (such as laws, regulations, and textbooks written by intellectuals and policy makers) and re-create women and empire in Japan. Instead of universalizing the conditions and conflicts of women as the timeless predicaments of "people," "human existence," and "inner selves," I articulate how discourses and institutions mold women differently than they do men. Japanese female intellectuals—mainly literary artists—articulated the ways in which women construct their selves and experience the world differently than men do. Representations of social and political power relations are based on differences. By casting a critical eye on the *bundan's* (literary establishment's) predominant focus on male writers and protagonists, I attend to gender particularities. This study sheds light on marginalized women's experience—their undomesticated and subversive characteristics as well as their servitude to the nation-state—in woman's writing.

Although I focus on three women writers, I do not search for each author's intention or vantage point as the basis of the literary interpretation. In other words, the author is not an authority who is the exclusive determinant of the meaning of the literary text. I also question the concept of "representation" that presupposes a transparency of language, and that identifies the rational subject as the one who stands above and outside the representation. This approach is a response to Michel Foucault (1926–84), who challenged and changed many academic methodologies for literary and historical studies, including modern Japanese literature, with his politically and epistemologically radical concept of "discourse." In his rejection of the logic of representation, Foucault contends that it is not the conscious disposal of the author but the language of the text, or discourse, that creates the literary subject. Foucault displaces the knowing subject with the concept of discourse and proposes a synchronic analysis of statement, or enunciations, in any discourse.[12]

Body

As a site of analysis in discourse, I focus on the bodies and borders of empire and women. This research finds the body in discourse important as a site of analysis because the nation-state as the body was a predominant concept in some of the influential writings by intellectuals, policy makers, and writers in modern Japan. *Yūkitai kokka ron* (the organ theory of the nation-state) prepared the debates on *kokutai* (literally, "the body of the nation"). Whether it was a biological or cultural body, a literal or metaphorical body, or a combination of the two, Japan as a body was noteworthy in the modern discourses. Within the discourse of Japan as a body, the subjects of the emperor were defined as the empire's body parts. For example, the *Imperial Precepts to Soldiers and Sailors* (1882) defined soldiers as the arms of the emperor. As an extension of the ideology of "good wife, wise mother" created by the Education Ministry in the late 1890s, a government slogan, *kodakara butai* (childbearing corps), from the late 1930s, defined women as the womb of the empire. Concepts of Japan as a body and people as its body parts determined masculinity and femininity, ethnicity and race, and social classes. By acting on the discourses that created the notions of the bodies of modern Japan and its subjects, state officials and the people participated in the forces that created, expanded, and eventually destroyed the empire. The discourse on Japan as a body directly affected the bodies of individuals who lived and died for the cause of empire.

Women Adrift therefore examines the political and institutional tools with which intellectuals and policy makers drew the boundaries of Japan and women and disseminated the various notions both of Japan as a body and of women's bodies. Although the body of Japan was used as a metaphor and/or as a part of nature by thinkers and policy makers, the body in this study is defined as discourse—and more specifically as a boundary and surface of inscription that constructs Japan and women. I concur with Judith Butler, who contends that "the body is not a 'being,' but a variable boundary and surface whose permeability is politically regulated, a signifying practice within a cultural field of gender hierarchy."[13] According to Satomi Kishio, *kokutai* "is a conceptualization of the essence or the substance of the nation-state."[14] The body of the nation-state in this study is configured as having no essential or ontological existence. I neither presuppose nor celebrate the existence of the essential and ontological womanhood. It is the discursive means that manufactures and sustains the fabrication of the essence or identity that can be expressed. Thus my analysis of the female body in relation to the body of Japan takes an antipodal position to the idea of an essentialized identity of woman and of the nation-state. In contrast to biological and geographical determinism, this book explores the body of Japan and of women in antiessentialist terms, as a surface and boundary of inscription in legal and institutional documents and in works of literature. This study explores the changing dynamics of the discursive forces that delineated the expanding body and borders of women and of the empire.

Moreover, this project examines the bodies of Japan and women as the enactment of the inscriptions of the bodies of the empire and its subjects. In other words, living individuals come to enact (practice) Japanese and women's bodies based on the discursive means. As a result of enacting the discourse, Japan as the empire and its women became embodied, dismembered, and reconstructed as agents in reality. In the sense that these texts create the roles and positions of both the "Japanese Woman" as a concept and "women" as active agents, discourse—including laws, regulations, and literature—is performative insofar as its power creates identity. My position on the body as a result of enactment is guided by Judith Butler's theory on gender, which, she contends, seems to be essential and ontological but actually "proves to be performative."[15] Therefore, gender is neither a substance nor a static cultural marker, but a signification that the body performatively enacts. By contending that the body is a boundary and surface of inscription and a signifying practice that constructs gender, Butler equates the performativity of language with the performativity of the body. The power of performativity creates identity and reality. The body is itself affected and sustained by discursive means.[16] Women as both concepts and living realities are interrelated.

In analyzing the relationship between women and the empire, this study builds on the hypothesis that Japanese authorities from the late nineteenth century to the early twentieth century enacted a microphysics of disciplinary power, extending throughout the social landscape. Therefore, I explore the ways in which state officials configured the female body in legal and educational documents and institutions. This study first looks at how imperial Japanese documents define women as loyal subjects and as body parts of the nation (i.e., as reproductive bodies of mothers and wives and/or productive bodies as workers). In Foucault's schema of discourse, the body is constructed as a surface of inscription and events to legitimatize different regimes of domination. In an oft-quoted passage of *Discipline and Punish*, Foucault claims:

> The body is . . . directly involved in a political field; power relations have an immediate hold upon it; they invest it, mark it, train it, torture it, force it to carry out tasks, to perform ceremonies, to emit signs. This political investment of the body is bound up, in accordance with complex reciprocal relations . . . ; it is largely as a force of production that the body is invested with relations of power and domination; but, on the other hand, its constitution of labor power is possible only if it is caught up in a system of subjection (in which need is also a political instrument meticulously prepared, calculated and used); the body becomes a useful force only if it is both a productive body and a subjected body.[17]

In my analysis of Japanese women in modern discourse, it is the body as a force not only of production but also of reproduction that is invested with relations of power and domination. Thus I look at how the state discourse subjugated women as loyal subjects of the empire and politically prescribed and used their bodies as instruments for building and expanding the empire. According to legal and educational documents of the nation-state, the female body becomes a useful force only when it is a subjected body that is reproductive and/or productive.

The points of contestation that surround Foucault's theories also define the directions of this research. His critics point out his overestimation of the normalizing and repressive effects of disciplinary forms of power. In elaborating his statement on the reciprocal relations of power, Foucault claims that repression and resistance are not ontologically distinct; rather, repression produces its own resistance.[18] However, Foucault's investigation of power and control seems one-sided, because it is the perspective of the centralized institutions, not of those subject to power, that he adopts in examining power.[19] In addition, his view that disciplinary methods produce "docile bodies" conflates power with domination. In his agenda of emancipating individuals from modern forms of control, Foucault understands discipline as a prohibitory and repressive power controlling the docile bodies of individuals. His reduction of social agents to "docile bodies" has the effect of imposing passivity and silence on the individual people who cultivate the possibilities of articulating and overcoming their marginalized experiences.[20] His emphasis on the effects of power placed upon the body tends to align power with domination and leads to his denial of the potential for self-determination and agency. He does not explain how individuals can act in an autonomous way.

With consideration of the points of contestation surrounding Foucault's theory on the body, this study not only explores how the state exerted its control over its subjects but also how individual people—especially authors of literature, who are the objects of state control—inscribed the body as the unfinished field of contest in the modern empire and sought to transcend the overreaching political and social constraints of prewar Japan. If power creates resistance, as Foucault claims, we shall see how these three women writers' discourses fought against the state's designation of their bodies. Based on the notion that the female body is enmeshed in the power relations of the era, and thus is the site of politics and history, I examine how these three writers inscribe the gendered bodies of their characters within nationalist and imperialist texts, and contexts, of power and prohibition in creating the self and society.

Women's bodies had to be subjugated, productive, and reproductive for the purpose of building and expanding the empire. With this awareness, women writers of literature in modern Japan chose to focus on women's bodies. Noriko Mizuta explains that "expressions with themes of women themselves and their bodies . . . were the primary characteristics of women's literature in the twentieth century"[21]:

> Women, who became new objects of protection and control [of the state], had no choice but to face their own bodies, which were also reorganized as the bases of identities of women themselves. What these women chose as the means of self-expression was nothing but the genre of literature.[22]

As for the reasons that women's literature centered on the body, Mizuta writes:

> [Women's] self-independence could only be established by discarding motherhood; motherhood could only be accomplished by being protected and controlled [by the state]. This relationship of contradictory dichotomy of independence and motherhood directed women's self-consciousness and self-expression toward their own bodies, the sex that gives birth.[23]

Furthermore, "women's bodies were not only the ones that give birth. New discourse was sought on women's sexuality and body that does not rely on giving birth but also that chooses not to give birth and does not rely on the womb."[24] For women writers, the description of bodies functioned as a discursive strategy through which the writer and readers might liberate and empower themselves.

Of women writers from modern Japan, this study focuses on Yosano, Tamura, and Hayashi because they in many ways challenge women's bodies that are defined, controlled, and protected by the nation-state. Their works question the notion that all women base their gender identity on their biological ability to give birth. Therefore, I examine the different ways female bodies in literature enact, or refuse to enact, the nation-state's inscription and prescription of their roles and positions. I also explore these three writers because they describe themselves and characters that move in *naichi* and *gaichi*. In the modern period, when the nation-state seems to exert the central, dominant, and normalizing force in forming one's identity, I argue that the ideas, discourses, and practices of female bodies that move within and outside Japan are especially important because they sometimes support, and at other times challenge, the state-driven nationalist discourse on women. In the first half of the twentieth century, when migrant bodies carried money, materials, and information with them, mobility could mean the dissemination of or dissent against the modern state discourse and capitalist economy.

As the cultural and geopolitical boundaries of the Japanese empire expanded during the prewar era, the migrant bodies of female characters in works of literature showed that women could transgress the discursive and political boundaries that the modern Japanese nation-state drew for them. The works of women's literature *Women Adrift* explores disconnect the personal female body and the political body of the nation-state. However, women's bodies also become connected with the body of the nation-state and play their part as a microcosm of Japan. Thus female bodies in modern Japanese women's literature both challenge and conform to the nation-state's inscription of and prescription upon them. This study shows how and why women become participants in the imperial expansion while claiming their independence from it, and raises awareness of the different discursive ways in which Japanese women could be seen to embody what was considered to be "Japan" and "Japanese."

Chapter Summaries

Although discourse on the nation-state as the body could already be seen in the early modern period (1603–1868) in Aizawa Seishi's *Shinron* (New theses, 1825), Japan as a body in the modern era (1868–1945) has its source in the organ theory of the nation-state (*yūkitai kokka ron*) that was imported from Germany. Beginning with Katō Hiroyuki's *Kokuhō Hanron* (1875), a translation of J. C. Bluntschli's *Allgemeines Staatsrecht* (1852), which introduced the organ theory to Japan, the use of body as metaphor became a point of discussion among lawmakers and led to the re-creation of *kokutai* (the body of the nation-state). Whether it was a metaphorical or literal body, cultural or biological body, or a combination of the two, Japan as a body was a predominant concept in some of the influential writings by academics, policy makers, and writers in modern Japan.

Departing from the scholarship by Ishida Takeshi (*Nihon kindai shisōshi ni okeru hō to seiji*, 1976), Fujitani Takashi (*Splendid Monarchy*, 1996), and Tessa Morris-Suzuki (*Re-Inventing Japan*, 1998) on Japan as the body, and drawing on primary sources, chapter 1 examines the changing dynamics of the discursive forces that delineated the expanding body and borders of the modern Japanese national empire. More specifically, this chapter examines *not only* how the organ theory of the nation-state and the theory of the body of the nation-state became the political tools used to draw and expand the borders of Japan *but also* how concepts of Japan as a body and the people as its body parts shaped femininity and masculinity, ethnicity and race, and the social classes of Japan. By exploring some of the important concepts of Japan as a body that contributed to the formation and destruction of the empire, chapter 1 provides the readers with the theoretical and historical context that prescribed women as body parts of Japan.

Within the changing concepts of *kokutai*, notions of female bodies varied from domestic(ated) bodies of wives and mothers at home and laboring bodies outside the home to migrant bodies inside *(naichi)* and outside *(gaichi)* the homeland of Japan. Women engaged in reproduction and/or production and functioned as the womb and/or arms and legs of the body of Japan, depending on their socioeconomic class and the historically changing demands of industry and the military of the empire. For many state officials, women's bodies were functional and meaningful only when they materialized the wealth and strength of the empire.

Extending scholarship such as that of Kathleen Uno (*Passages to Modernity*, 1999) on how women from different socioeconomic classes played their reproductive and productive roles for the empire, chapter 2 describes how women's bodies were expected to act in publicly prescribed roles, which changed in accordance with different interpretations of how race and ethnicity constituted the Japanese body. This led to the following set of contradictions in the perception of women's roles: In a "multiethnic empire," a concept that justified the colonization and assimilation of the neighboring nations, mothers were expected to raise and educate more biological or adopted children so that they could expand the family and family empire. In a "homogeneous empire," an ever more dominant concept in the late 1930s, mothers became equated with the womb that would reproduce not only more but also purer human resources. It was also the case, after the 1930s, that mothers became equated with the universal womb of the community of human beings to justify the universality of Japanese empire. By exploring how the state discourse subjugated women as loyal subjects of the empire and used their bodies as an instrument to build and expand the empire, chapter 2 informs readers about the political context and the texts within which the bodies of Yosano, Tamura, Hayashi, and their heroines operated.

The analysis of bodies as inscribed in discourse is important because state officials and people acted in concert with this discourse and participated in the forces that formed, expanded, and eventually destroyed the empire. Chapter 3 problematizes how commentators and critics in postwar Japan have styled most prewar Japanese women as passive victims, nurturers of peace, or rebels against the state, while underrepresenting women who were active/aggressive participants in the formation of the empire. I examine how some of the writings and activities of leading women who were defined in the postwar era as maternalist, liberal, social, or anarchist feminists not only challenged the state discourse on Japanese female bodies but also incorporated the state discourse on the liberation, empowerment, and independence of Japan into their stories of the liberation, empowerment, and independence of women's bodies. Chapter 3 shows how the state-driven nationalism in the prewar era presented both possibilities for and limits to Japanese women, including Yosano, Tamura, and Hayashi.

This chapter further explores the applicability to Yosano, Tamura, and Hayashi of the concept of "the migrant . . . whose consciousness is that of the intellectual and artist in exile" (Edward Said, *Representations of the Intellectual,* 1996). These three writers are "decentered" and unsettled migrants who exert "exilic energies" for liberation as an intellectual mission. I argue that the authors and their characters, who reside at the periphery but move in and out of the central discourse of the state, create the possibility for the writer and reader both to envision a transcendence beyond the body and borders of Japan, and to act on that vision. Yosano, Tamura, and Hayashi and their female characters rejected the state's mandate for women to live domesticated lives as wives and mothers, and instead became and inscribed the bodies of wandering migrants. By moving within Japan, Japan's colonies, and the West's occupied territories, their literary characters refuse to act according to the dictates of ideal Japanese women's bodies, and thus deviate from the norms of a united, organic body of Japan. Through my exploration of the importance of the concept, practice, and representations of migrant bodies in modern Japan, the reader is prepared to enter the literary worlds of Yosano, Tamura, and Hayashi.

In the international scholarly community and among the general reading public in Japan, Yosano Akiko enjoys enormous prestige as a pioneer of modern Japanese poetry (*shi* verse and *shintaishi*) and as a representative Japanese female writer of the twentieth century. The somewhat limited number of approaches to her life and works, however, betrays an ongoing desire of her readers to cast her as (1) an innovator of modern poetry who challenged the tradition of Japanese poetry; (2) a woman writer who expressed the truth, freedom, and beauty of the modern self and womanhood; (3) an individualist or liberal feminist who challenged the state's glorification of motherhood and women's slavelike acceptance of the state's protection of their reproductive capacity; and (4) a promoter of peace who resisted militarism. Among the few scholars who have explored the politics of her poems—especially their support of war efforts—Steve Rabson, for one, argues that her poems conformed with militarism after her trip to Manchuria and Mongolia in 1928.

I step back from the celebration of Yosano's originality and independence and depart from a chronological interpretation of the change in her writing from resistance to support of war. Chapter 4 examines Yosano's concept and practice of mobility and the female reproductive body as the contradictory source of the strength and superiority of Japanese women and of the empire. Yosano once urged women to "awake and move" away from men and the state's prescription and protection of women's reproductive bodies. However, she celebrates the female reproductive body not only as the source of production of her poems but also as the site of reproduction of the empire. When woman attains agency, her body as the womb, the Japanese empire, and the world become connected on a universal scale, as we see in her poems. It is her re-creation of the female body that mobilizes the bodies of soldiers and people "behind the guns" that operate in unison with the state discourse on *kokutai*. Central to the paradoxical politics of resistance against and support for the empire is Yosano's description of bodies that give birth to, occupy, and move through the spaces of empire of Japan.

Tamura Toshiko was the first Japanese professional female novelist whose achievement in prose equaled Yosano's accomplishment in poetry.

The academic assessment of her various achievements can be summarized in four statements: She was (1) a representative of the "New Woman" who advocated women's financial and emotional independence from men; (2) a sensual writer who expressed the essence of womanhood; (3) a loner who was no longer a writer after she left Japan for North America in 1918 and died in China in 1945; and (4) a cosmopolitan who lived outside the framework of the nation-state and continued on the international scene to urge for the unity of workers and women after she left Japan in 1918.

Chapter 5 focuses on Tamura as a female migrant worker in self-imposed exile whose body moves from Tokyo (1908–18) to Vancouver (1918–35), to Los Angeles (1935–36), back to Tokyo (1936–38), and then to Shanghai (1938–45), demarcating a woman's shifting relationships with the expanding body of the Japanese empire. In contrast to the position that Tamura transcended the framework of the nation in her efforts to unite female workers, I expose the discursive force of the Japanese empire in the bodies that cross the imperial borders in Tamura's writings. In the context of Japan's contest with Western imperial powers and the racial discrimination against Japanese workers in North America, Tamura moved to Vancouver and engaged in creative activities to rebuild the bodies of female migrant workers and mothers who were aware of Japan's inferior position in "the world" and therefore needed, in her view, to redouble their efforts to elevate their own status and thus the status of Japan as empire. This chapter also explores Tamura's description of the female bodies of Japanese immigrants situated within the competing discourses of the state-driven nationalism of the Japanese empire and of the United States. Finally, chapter 5 examines Tamura's writings on the Japanese female workers as the arms of Japan while in Tokyo during the late 1930s, in her attempts to elevate the international status of Japan. I reveal this neglected aspect of her writing through examination of the poems and essays she contributed to the newspapers *Tairiku nippō* (Continental daily) and *Rafu shinpō* (Los Angeles news), aimed at Japanese immigrants in Vancouver and Los Angeles between 1918 and 1936, her short story, "Kariforunia monogatari" (California story), and her essays written in Tokyo between 1936 and 1938, before her departure for Shanghai.

Hayashi Fumiko is among the three most critically acclaimed female writers in twentieth-century Japan along with Yosano Akiko and Higuchi Ichiyō. As a self-proclaimed wanderer, Hayashi grew up with no stable home, job, or relationship. She wrote outside the cognizance of the general public and literary establishment, yet became one of the most critically acclaimed and financially successful writers of the century. Evaluating Hayashi's acclaimed writings of the 1930s and 1940s, critics sometimes label her "proletarian" or "anarchistic," but more often "personal" and therefore "apolitical." When addressing gender politics in her writing, critics most often see Hayashi and her characters as single women wandering at the economic and social peripheries and therefore residing outside the system of Japanese women and the nationalist discourse on race and ethnicity that contributed to the expansion of the empire.

Chapter 6 explores the migrant bodies of Hayashi and her heroines that move not only in *naichi* but also between *naichi* and *gaichi* in the context of the expansion of the border/body of the empire. I offer an intertextual analysis of her novel *Hōrōki* (Diary of a vagabond, 1928), through which Hayashi became an instant success as a writer, and *Hokugan butai* (Northern bank platoon, 1939), which she wrote after serving as a war reporter in China. In *Hōrōki*, the heroine, who is homeless in her native land and is thus decentered from the nation-state, identifies herself with the sexually, economically, and racially exploited female bodies of prostitutes, Manchurians, and aborigines *(dojin)*. As one of the marginalized in society, she lives in a state of fear and insecurity, and wishes for the explosion *(bakuhatsu)* of the society that confines her body, envisioning a utopia outside Japan. In *Hokugan butai,* the heroine as war reporter physically advances to *gaichi* and toward the central discourse of the state and marches with Japanese soldiers as their nurturer. Through identifying herself as the Japanese body that makes "progress," in contrast to the Chinese body that degrades, this heroine attains a euphoric sense of confidence, "sublime beauty," and security as part of the Japanese empire.

My analysis of Hayashi's *Ukigumo* (Floating clouds, 1949–50) shows how the heroine's body draws and expands the border of *kokutai* and therefore functions as part of the expanding body of the empire. I underscore this point by exploring how the heroine's sense of wealth, liberation, and power is experienced by an agent who acted at the behest of the colonization policies of the Japanese empire. Although the female bodies that move from the center of *naichi* to the margin of *gaichi* may appear to advance outside the empire, I argue that this movement of migrant bodies toward the margin supports the central discourse of *kokutai* of Japan as an expanding empire.

The conclusion of this book examines how visual technologies and metaphors used in the filmic adaptations of novels reframe the female migrant bodies in the language of space and time, and how the visual narrative functions as the medium of memory to re-create the Japanese imperial past in the present. Specifically, Naruse Mikio's adaptation films of Hayashi Fumiko's novels *Meshi* (Repast, 1951, novel and film) and *Ukigumo* (Floating clouds, 1951, novel; 1955, film) provide viewers and interpreters with the images of migrant female bodies that move through the space of the home to a place outside the home and then on to the fringes of Japan in the prewar and the immediate postwar periods. The popular and scholarly interpretations of Naruse's visual representations of migrant female bodies recirculate the narratives and ideologies that focus on the problem of gender and class in *naichi* (the inner territory) and smooth over the problem of women's participation in the Japanese colonization of neighboring nations in *gaichi* (the outer territory). By exposing both continuity and discontinuity between the female body in motion and the geopolitical borders of the empire that expand and shrink, the conclusion of this book brings the reader's attention to the representations of both women's marginalized experiences and their participation in the central discourse of the state. Migrants enable the audience/reader to envision and reenact movements that make it possible to transcend the borders of the empire and become free of nationalist and imperialist confines. Our focus on liberation also enables us, however, to envision and reenact movements that help us forget that female migrants' bodies sometimes redrew the borders that violated the lives of the peoples who were invaded by the Japanese empire. It was within the expanding body of Japan, which mobilized its subjects, that women who lived outside the institutionalized Japanese constructions of womanhood explored the possibilities of their personal freedom and empowerment. The knowledge of the national in the crossnational bodies that traversed the imperial borders helps us understand the contradiction of migrant women who at once cross and redraw the borders of the Japanese empire.

CHAPTER 1

Japan as a Body

THE BODY HAS BEEN A USEFUL ANALYTICAL SITE that developed in gender studies, postcolonial studies, cultural studies, and film studies, among others. Before the body became important in Western literary theory, especially after the 1960s, some thinkers and policy makers in modern Japan (1868–1945) vigorously discussed and questioned the body as the site of history and politics. Although it was not always represented in terms of the body, the nation-state of Japan as a body was a dominant idea that regained currency among some intellectuals and state officials, especially after the 1880s. Discourses on the body influenced the formation of the empire and its people/subjects. To tackle the question of how the bodies of empire and of women were created in modern Japan, I begin my analysis in this chapter with *yūkitai kokka ron* (the organ theory of the nation-state) and *kokutai ron* (the theory of the body of the nation). *Kokutai,* combining two Chinese characters meaning "nation" and "body," has been translated variously as "the national body," "the mystical body of Japan," "national entity," "national polity," and "national essence." Although *kokutai* could mean any of these, the notions of *kokutai* invariably contributed to the creation, expansion, and eventual destruction of the empire. Discourses on *kokutai* also directly affected the bodies of individual people who lived in modern Japan and its neighboring nations.

Before the dawn of the modern period, Aizawa Seishisai (1782–1863) used the term *shintai* (the body) to describe *kokutai* in his *Shinron* (New thesis, 1825). In his exploration, each of the five limbs of the physical body corresponds to a part of the archipelago of Japan. Douglas Slaymaker explains that Aizawa "construed *kokutai,* or what is essential to a nation, as the spiritual unity that makes a territory and its inhabitants a nation."[1] Although such discussion of the nation-state as a body can be seen as early as in the Edo period (1603–1868), the debates that focus on this project developed in the modern period, especially after the 1880s.

What prompted the debate on *kokutai* in the modern era was Japanese thinkers' and policy makers' reinterpretation of the organ theory of the nation-state that had developed in Germany. Japanese modifications of this theory led to two different understandings of Japan as a body: (1) the usage of the body as an analogy to conceptualize the empire, and (2) the notion of Japan as a literal body. Ishida Takeshi contends that the latter distinguishes the ways in which the nation-state as a body developed in Japan from those in Germany.[2] The change in interpretation from the nation-state as the metaphorical body to the natural body ignited the debate on *kokutai*. Eventually, the family empire and patriarchal imperial line were essentialized and viewed as facts of nature instead of metaphors.

In this chapter I examine how debates on the body of Japan developed into two strands of theory, both of which contributed to the creation, expansion, and destruction of empire. This prepares the reader to explore in chapter 2 how women were expected to play their roles as physical parts of the family empire.

The Body of Japan as a Metaphor

The organ theory in Germany that was important for the development of *yūkitai kokka ron* in Japan is presented in J. C. Bluntschli's *Allgemeines Staatsrecht* (General constitutional law, 1852), which compares the nation-state with the living body.[3] When this theory reached Japan, Katō Hiroyuki (1836–1916), a legal scholar and the president of Tokyo Imperial University, translated it in *Kokuhō hanron* in 1875. In the notes to *Kokuhō hanron* he explains: "Each department of the government, legislature, and judiciary is like each function of the living body. Therefore, the nation-state is compared to a living body."[4] According to the organ theory of the nation-state that was imported from Germany, the nation-state is analogous to the living human body.[5] In interpreting Kato's translation, legal scholars such as Ichimura Mitsue and Minobe Tatsukichi understood the body as a metaphor. In 1914 Ichimura wrote:

> The recent idioms in the studies of national laws, such as "the head of state" and "the organ of the state," were all influenced

basically by the organic body theory of the state. . . . As long as the organic body theory of the state exists as a metaphor to explain the reality of the life of the state, we [I and the like-minded] do not dare attack it.[6]

Ichimura thus interpreted the organ theory of the nation-state that developed in Germany and compared the nation-state of Japan to a human body. He rejected the discourse of the organic body of the nation-state as a theory of law but conceded that it could be used as a metaphor.[7]

In agreement with Ichimura, Minobe Tatsukichi (1873–1948), a professor of constitutional law at Tokyo Imperial University from 1900 to 1934, developed *tennō kikansetsu* (the organ theory of the emperor) in his *Kenpō kōwa* (Commentaries on the constitution of the empire of Japan, 1912) and compared the state with the human body and the highest institution with the head/brain. Thus the emperor was compared with the head/brain of the body of Japan, and the people with other parts of the body.[8] In *Gikai seiji no kentō* (Examination of congressional law, 1912), Minobe wrote:

> Article VI of the Constitution clearly states that the emperor is the "head of state." This means that if the nation is likened to the human body, the emperor occupies the position of its head. . . . Needless to say, the brain is just one of man's organs, but it is the pivotal and paramount organ. In other words, the emperor-organ theory is identical in meaning with the Constitution's statement that the emperor is the head of state. . . . The idea of a nation prospering or progressing assumes as its basic premise that the nation is a vital, dynamic entity comparable to a living body. The emperor is its head and occupies the position of its paramount organ.[9]

Minobe's theory that the emperor was analogous to the head and the people to different parts of the body was attacked by those who argued that Japan was the body itself and that the emperor constituted the entire body of the nation, rather than just the head. Although this strand of theory can be seen as early as in the 1880s, during the debates about the sovereignty, they erupted in the mid-1930s. The theory Minobe had been exploring since 1912 came under vigorous attack by his opponents when he rearticulated it in the mid-1930s in the debates about *kokutai*. Minobe's defense of his theory highlights the points of difference between him and his opponents and helps us understand the elements being contested. Minobe disputed the identification of the emperor with the entire body of Japan in his *Gikai seiji no kentō*:

> It is plain that the idea that the ruler *is* the nation cannot be accepted in its literal sense. Since the foundation of the Japanese state there has been only one Japan; one and the same nation has been in continuous existence. Yet from Emperor Jimmu to the present emperor, there have been 124 rulers. How, then, can one say that the ruler and the nation are identical? The nation is a community of the ruler and the people; both the ruler and the people are together the main elements that constitute the nation. If the people were all eliminated, how would it be possible for the ruler alone to constitute the nation?[10]

Against the idea that the emperor *is* the entire body of the nation, Minobe argued that the nation consists of both the emperor and the people. He likened the emperor to the head and the people to other parts of Japan as a body.

The Body of Japan as Nature

As a counterargument to the position held by scholars like Ichimura and Minobe, who disputed the idea that "the emperor is the nation," a different strand of the organ theory emerged that postulated the emperor as identical with the nation and Japan as a natural body in "its literal sense." During the Meiji 15 (1883) debate about the sovereign, the organ theory in Bluntschli's *Allgemeines Staatsrecht* that compares the state with the body metamorphosed into the theory that the nation-state *is* the body itself in Japan. In emphasizing the difference between the body as a metaphor in Germany and as nature in Japan, Ishida Takeshi wrote in 1976 that in Carl Schmidt's exploration of the topic, "the organic body as a metaphor rises . . . as a concept and as an abstract image of the state. . . . In the theory of law at the time of the nineteenth century [in Europe], . . . there is no way of conceptualizing the relationship of the organic body [of the state] as a real body."[11] Japan, however, came to be equated with the body as nature itself in writings by some political theorists and policy makers. As a proponent of Japan as a literal body, Hozumi Nobushige wrote in 1886 that "human society is an organic matter."[12] He further wrote, in 1889, "The study of law is part of sociology. Sociology is part of biology."[13] Kaieda Nobunari stated in his "Schtein's Lecture" that studies of the nation-state examine the development of the organic body that constitutes the nation-state.[14] More explicitly, Kato Fusō stated in *Nihon kokutai ron* (1892) that multiple cells of the organic body constitute the nation-state and claimed that the body of the nation-state was nature itself.[15]

The theory of the nation-state as the human body itself led to the debates on *kokutai*. When the body of the nation-state is equated with a natural, literal body, this connection becomes one of the conditions to essentialize the nation-state as a family and the emperor as the patriarch who inherits the unbroken and pure imperial line from ancestors. For example, Hozumi Yatsuka's *Kokumin kyōiku aikokushin* (1897) explains the nation as a body itself (i.e., *kokutai*) and the emperor-patriarch (*zokufu*) as a natural fact of the family nation-state.[16] Whereas the metaphor of the organic body contributed to the ideas of a lawful nation-state and of the protection of the legal right of the sovereign, the notion of Japan as a natural body essentialized the emperor as a patriarch.[17] In other words, by the late 1890s these were no longer matters of metaphorical comparison but facts of nature. Thus the theory of the organic body in Japan was the foundation on which the essentialized concept of a family-state and the emperor as the patriarch stood.

The notion of *kokutai* as a literal body is tied to the idea that the unbroken and therefore pure blood of the imperial line flows in the body of the emperor. Oguma Eiji points out that "the notion of *kokutai* as a family of the same and pure blood was tied to the social organic theory of the body."[18] What distinguished the *kokutai* of Japan from other national bodies politic of the world was, allegedly, the unbroken and sacred line of the imperial family. For example, to clarify *kokutai* for the German advisers, Minister of the Right Iwakura Tomomi demanded in 1883 that a book of guidance be compiled: "The basis of the national polity [*kokutai*] [is] the Imperial line unbroken for ages eternal, and the customs which date from antiquity."[19] Iwakura's position was reaffirmed in 1889 with the promulgation of the constitution (1889), which claimed the unique qualities of *kokutai* as follows:

Article I. The Empire of Japan shall be reigned over and governed by a line of Emperors unbroken for ages eternal.

Article III. The Emperor is sacred and inviolable.

The continuous succession of the imperial lineage was supposedly unparalleled in the world and unique to Japan.

This unbroken blood flowed from the ancestors to the emperor, or so it was understood. Thus it was the unbroken and therefore pure blood that maintained the body of Japan. For example, Hozumi Yatsuka argued in *Kokumin kyōiku aikokushin* (National education: Patriotism, 1897) that "the specific system that is particular to the Japanese people" is "a group based on blood" *(kettō dantai)*. Conversely, "the imperial bloodline supports people sharing the same ancestors" *(kōtō wa minzoku dōso)*.[20] The emperor and the people share the same bloodline and therefore the same ancestor. Thus it comes to be understood that the Japanese are descended from a common bloodline whose original branch was the imperial family. Conversely, the idea that the emperor and subjects share the same blood supports the notion that they share the same body. Therefore, the strand of *kokutai ron* in which the nation-state is the organic body itself as nature and the emperor is the one who inherits blood from divine ancestors underscores the concept that the emperor and the subjects are identical in their body. Hozumi argues this thesis in his *Kokumin kyōiku aikokushin*.

The notion of the unbroken bloodline of the family empire also went hand in hand with the idea of the eternal spirit of Japan. Hozumi argues that the emperor is the site where the spirit of heavenly ancestors resides. Even when the body perishes, the emperor becomes the site that inherits the spirit of the ancestors for ages eternal. The emperor is the spirit and soul of the people. Accordingly, the spirit becomes an abstract idea that supports the notions of an unbroken line inherited by the emperor and the unity between the emperor and the people. The two ideas of unbroken-bloodline-as-nature and spirit-as-metaphor, which connect the emperor and people to the same ancestors, also become conflated. *Manshū Teikoku Kyōwa kai* (Manchurian Imperial Concordia Society) asserts that Japanese people "hold the spirit of unity of people in the blood."[21]

The idea of the emperor and people/subjects as one body is further carried out in *Kokutai no hongi*, published by the Ministry of Education in 1937. As the culmination of the movement for the enunciation of *kokutai*, this document emphasizes that the emperor becomes "one in essence" or "of one august body" with the imperial ancestors, and implicitly also with the sun goddess herself, through rituals such as the *daijōsai* (Shinto great food-offering ceremony).[22] Moreover, what is stressed is the role of people who are tied to the emperor, who in turn embodies *kokutai*. The introductory section of *Kokutai no hongi* states:

> The relationship between the emperor and the subjects is not an artificial relationship. . . . An individual is an existence belonging to a State and her history which forms the basis of his origin, and is fundamentally one body with it. . . . Our relationship between sovereign and subject is by no means a shallow, horizontal relationship . . . but is a relationship springing from a basis transcending this correlation, and is that of "dying to self and returning to [the] One," in which this basis is not lost. . . . In our country, this great Way has seen a natural development since the founding of the nation.[23]

This introduction postulates the identification of the body of emperor and people/subjects as a natural unity. The concluding section contrasts Western ideas and Japanese national polity to emphasize this point: "Hence, whenever this [Western] individualism and its accompanying abstract concepts developed, concrete and historical national life became lost in the shadow of abstract theories."[24] Thus Japanese nation/empire emerges as possessing a concrete life of the body instead of abstract ideas. The energy of a living body derives from the identification of the will of the emperor with that of the people/subjects:

> To serve the emperor and to receive the emperor's great august
> Will as one's own is the rationale of making our historical "life" live
> in the present. . . . To walk this Way of loyalty is the sole Way in
> which we subjects can "live," and the fountainhead of all energy.[25]

Furthermore, Japan and its subjects as natural bodies essentialize the empire as family. The section of *Kokutai no hongi* titled "Filial Piety" states, "The relationship between parent and child is a natural one. . . . Our country is a great family nation, and the Imperial Household is the head family of the subjects and the nucleus of national life."[26]

Borders and Body Parts

I have offered a brief overview of how the idea of Japan as the body developed. The debates on *yūkitai kokka ron* and *kokutai ron* operated not only within Japan but also in the context of an international competition for power and prestige among empires. What was important for many leaders and thinkers of Japan was to build and use the body of the nation-state as a family empire that was strong, liberated, and prosperous, both metaphorically and literally. For example, the strong body of Japan meant equipping the government with strong muscles (military might). Liberation of the Japanese body meant that the country should stand on its own feet (be free of the threat of Western imperial powers). A prosperous Japan meant a larger body (industrial development, capital buildup, and material riches). The expanded Japanese body with longer arms and legs meant the extension of geopolitical borders and territories.

Although ideas and policies aimed at creating, maintaining, and expanding the body of Japan changed throughout the modern period, the idea of *kokutai* as a family nation-state and empire continued after the 1890s. The notion of Japan as a family also raised questions about the race, ethnicity, and class of Japanese in the world: What constitutes Japanese blood, spirit, muscle, and skin? What should Japanese bodies wear? How should Japanese bodies behave and move in *naichi* (the inner territory) and *gaichi* (the outer territory)? How should Japanese bodies produce and reproduce the empire?

To strengthen, liberate, enrich, and expand the body/borders of Japan as an empire, state officials implemented laws, regulations, and censorship that protected, controlled, and (ab)used the bodies of Japanese people/subjects. The ideas of *kokutai* as the body of the family nation-state therefore affected the people's/subjects' practices of marriage and of bearing, adopting, and rearing children. These became concerns of the empire as a family, and also of the individual family as its microcosm.

The Mixed Blood of the Multiethnic/Multiracial Body of Japan

To strengthen, liberate, enrich, and expand the body/border of Japan, some intellectuals and state officials asked exactly which race and ethnicity constituted the body of Japan. Oguma Eiji has shown in *Tanitsu minzoku shinwa no kigen: "Nihonjin" no jigazō no keifu* (The origin of the myth of ethnic homogeneity: The genealogy of "Japanese" self-images) that competing ideas of homogeneity and hybridity coexisted in modern Japan. Although Japan is predominantly known for its homogeneity, especially in the postwar era, Oguma argues that ideologues of *kokutai* came to support the idea of Japan as a multiethnic nation by the 1920s.[27] Tessa Morris-Suzuki explains that "the Japanese people were of mixed racial origins and frequently identified this hybridity as the source of national strength and of claims to imperial power."[28] She continues: "The uniqueness of the Japanese was seen as lying, not in their racial purity, but in their unmatched ability to mold such disparate elements into an organically united society."[29] The idea of Japan as a united, organic body of multiethnic and multiracial constitution contributed to the expansion of empire. With the purported superior ability to assimilate foreign elements as a justification, the empire expanded by colonizing Taiwan, Karafuto and Kwangtung, Korea, Manchuria, China, and Southeast Asia from the 1890s until the early 1940s. Japanese imperial conquests began first by identifying their bodies with Western bodies.

To demonstrate to the Western imperial nations that Japan had become strong, independent, prosperous, and therefore an equal to the Western powers, officials in Japan embarked on a modernization process in the 1870s that included a measure to re-create the Japanese body as ethnically and racially Western. In facing the Western encroachment on Asia and Japan, and the threat posed to its sovereignty, the initial response of the leaders of Japan in the late Edo period (1603–1868) was in the vein of "repel the barbarians."[30] Gradually, however, equipping the nation with military power and acquiring material riches by using the West as a model came to be viewed as the way to ensure Japan's territorial security and acquire status on the international stage of power politics. Hence the Meiji government slogan "Rich nation, strong army" was instilled in the minds of many state officials and people/subjects. According to "Imperial Precepts to Soldiers and Sailors, 1882," soldiers were defined as the emperor's limbs, which move in unison with his body to strengthen the military might of the empire in the face of Western imperial powers:

> Soldiers and Sailors, We are your supreme Commander-in-Chief.
> Our relations with you will be most intimate when We rely upon
> you as Our limbs and you look up to Us as your head. . . . If you all
> do your duty, and being one with Us in spirit do your utmost for

the protection of the state, Our people will long enjoy the
blessings of peace, and the might and dignity of Our Empire will
shine in the world. . . . Remember that, as the protection of the
state and the maintenance of its power depend upon the strength
of its arms, the growth or decline of this strength must affect the
nation's destiny for good or for evil.[31]

As part of the effort to check the encroachment of Western powers, leaders had to manufacture the nation Japan and its people/subjects as unified
Japanese bodies that fight for the empire. The authorities embarked on a
campaign to draw and expand the body/boundary of Japan with the united
and healthy bodies of its subjects. The imperfect, unfinished body of Japan
had to be rebuilt to be equal to the Western body, and ultimately to super-
sede it. These efforts to re-create Japanese bodies by assimilating what was
perceived to be Western bodies are evident in government officials' rigor-
ous attempts to Westernize in the 1870s and 1880s. The modernization of
Japan included physical changes to the emperor and people/subjects.

The major concern for government officials was the abolition of extra-
territoriality in the 1870s. In his attempt to solve the unequal treaties imposed upon Japan, Inoue Kaoru, a member of the Meiji oligarchy, wrote
about the necessity of transforming Japan into a Western-/European-style
society in the late 1880s:

> Let us change our Empire into a European-style Empire. Let us
> change our people into European-style people. Let us create a
> new European-style Empire on the Eastern Sea. Only in this way
> can our Empire achieve a position equal to that of the Western
> countries with respect to treaties. Only thus can our Empire be
> independent, prosperous, and powerful.[32]

Westernization was meant to make Japan autonomous and wealthy as an
empire that could stand firmly on its own feet against the Western imperial powers. Fukuzawa Yukichi, the proponent of Japan's Westernization,
earlier wrote about the independence of the individual person but by 1882
asserted the independence of the empire: "We value the independence of
Japan, and our life-aim is focused on national autonomy."[33]

To make a European-style empire of Japan and its people, the naked
bodies of its subjects had to be covered and adorned in a Western manner.

As seen in the government's mandate of 1871, day laborers were required to keep their bodies covered.[34] Stylistic changes to re-create Japanese bodies as ethnically Western were made in clothing, hair, facial hair, and accessories. New dress codes geared to change clothing styles from Japanese to Western are apparent in the government proposal from the early 1870s to prohibit Japanese clothing.[35] As Donald H. Shively's studies have shown, beginning in the early 1870s the emperor wore a Western military uniform; men in official settings appeared in European attire; officials grew mustaches and beards in the style of European diplomats; men changed from the topknot to Western haircuts; people wore rings and watches in the Western style and carried umbrellas.[36] The movement of Japanese bodies was also prescribed in an attempt to be recognized as Western and modern. At Rokumeikan (Deer Cry Pavilion), a building completed in Tokyo in 1883 and dedicated to housing foreign dignitaries and hosting soirées, many high-ranking Japanese were introduced to Western manners. This moved one Japanese participant to declare that he had "danced for the sake of the country."[37]

The extent to which some state officials made attempts to re-create Japanese bodies as both ethnically and racially Western also can be seen in Sugiura Jūgō's criticism against the government policy:

> Current education is a matter of plastering Western civilization
> on one's person—and not merely plastering, either, for they are
> not satisfied until the body itself changes into that of a Westerner.
> Moreover, we have reached the point where some people
> advocate not only changing the body into that of a Westerner, so
> that in the end all human races will change into Western races.[38]

It was desirable for Japanese to become racially Western if they could change the color of their skin, hair, and eyes. Officials' attempts to change Japanese bodies in this way provoked a satirist to write: "Some ladies crimpled their hair with curling irons in the attempt to look like Westerners, and lamented they could not dye their eyes blue or whiten their skins."[39]

In the 1880s the oligarchs further discussed ways to transform Japanese bodies into a Western race by intermarriage. Takahashi Yoshio wrote in 1884 that the Japanese, "with their weak minds and bodies," are no comparison to the Caucasions; any attempt would only exhaust and weaken the Japanese bodies further. The only way to strengthen the race would be through intermarriage with "superior Caucasions."[40] Intermarriage with Caucasians was recognized as a positive force to re-create the bodies of Japan and its subjects as strong, independent, and prosperous. The idea of Japanese bodies as interethnic and interracial encouraged the state officials and people/subjects to identify themselves with the Western imperial powers in the 1870s and 1880s.

To become a stronger imperial power, the ethnically and racially hybrid body of Japan had to expand its borders. Some officials concluded that the expansion of Japan was possible by increasing its territories and multiplying the population of mixed-blood people. Tatebe Tongo, holder of the chair in sociology at Tokyo Imperial University, wrote in 1914 that for Japan to become a strong country in the world, expansion of the territory and "a billion Japanese people *(minzoku)*" were necessary. He added, "a billion Japanese people may not prevent some mixed blood."[41] Tatebe asserted the necessity of creating "more" Japanese people/subjects that included other ethnicities and races. From the beginning, the Japanese empire expanded by conquering people who were considered to occupy different spaces and times.[42] After controlling "backward" Ryukyuans in the south and Ainu in the north of the Japanese archipelago, the modern empire expanded when Japan won the First Sino-Japanese War (1894–95) and colonized the Taiwanese people in 1895. When Japan colonized Korea in 1910, the total number of Taiwanese and Koreans was ten million, that is, one third the population of the Japanese empire. With the colonization of Taiwan and Korea, Japan expanded its body as a multiracial and multiethnic empire with interracial marriages and mixed-blood children. As the empire expanded, Taniguchi Kōnen, an anthropologist, stated in 1942 that "not only ethnographers from all countries but also Japanese experts equally acknowledge that we Yamato people are an ethnic group with mixed blood."[43]

The ways in which the idea of Japan as a mixed-blood but united body contributed to the expansion of empire are especially clear in the Japan's colonization policies and practices vis-à-vis Korea. *Nikkan dōtai* (Japanese and Korean, the same body) is an example of the imperial multiethnic and multiracial discourse. Minami Jirō, who assumed the position of army general in Korea in 1936 and contributed to the Japanization of Koreans, stated that Korea and Japan "must become one body with form, heart, blood, and flesh."[44] The concept *Naisen ittai* (Japan and Korea, one body) also promoted the notion of Japan and Korea as one in body in 1941.

Some policy makers asserted the similarity/identity of Japanese and Korean bodies using evidence drawn from the social sciences. Kurashima Itaru stated in 1942: "According to the physical anthropological studies in our country, the island people from the middle of Korea are extremely similar to the people in the Kinki region [the southern-central region of Japan's main island Honshū] of *naichi* in several points."[45] Thus Kurashima used the geographical proximity of Japan and Korea to assert the similar/identical constitution of the bodies of Japanese and Koreans.

For "the embodiment of Japan and Korea as one," Minami Jirō promoted the Japanese government's policy of intermarriage between Japanese and Koreans beginning in 1937.[46] Intermarriage was understood to be a natural practice inherited from the ancestors and imperial families who had united Korean and Japanese bodies. With the notion of *nikkan dōso* (Japanese and Korean, the same ancestry), Japanese and Koreans were considered to be united at the level of ancestry and, furthermore, at the level of imperial families. The position that the Japanese imperial family came from Korea was supported by, among others, Yasuda Yojurō, who wrote in 1938 that "the mother of Emperor Kōmu" was "from the royal family of *kudara* [one of the first dynasties of Korea]."[47] The notion that the Japanese family empire shared the same ancestors as Koreans contributed to approval of the practice of marriage between the Japanese and Koreans.

To justify the expansion of empire, some thinkers and government officials also used the notion and practice of adoption. Oguma points out that the argument that the Japanese always adopted peoples from other nations, as a family adopts children, justified the family empire's colonization of neighboring nations as extended family members who did not compromise the core lineage of the Japanese. Colonization was seen as a practice of adopting neighboring nations as a part of Japan's extended family.

In mixing the body of Japan with the bodies of neighboring nations, the government adopted policies designed to foster assimilation. In marriage, schools, industry, the military, and sex slavery, the Japanese government forced colonized nations to assimilate to Japanese ways. Koreans were made to adopt Japanese names, learn the Japanese language in school, work in Japanese factories, fight in the Japanese military, and serve Japanese soldiers sexually.[48] The forced assimilation effort from 1937, called *kōminka undō* (the transformation of the peoples into Japanese imperial subjects), which became a full-fledged movement in 1938, reinforced the view that the Taiwanese, Koreans, Chinese, and Southeast Asians were all part of the Japanese family empire.[49]

The Pure Blood of the Homogeneous Japanese Body

Along with the idea of the mixed blood of the multiethnic and multiracial Japanese body, another strand of *yūkitai ron* and *kokutai ron* contributed to the expansion of the empire. Viewing the emperor as the direct descendant of the unbroken and therefore pure bloodline of Emperor Jinmu supported the notion of the Japanese body as homogeneous. The idea of Japan as a pure and unique national body was first emphasized in the xenophobia of the late 1880s, when fierce opposition from the leaders against mixing Japanese bodies with foreign elements emerged. The opponents of the Westernization of the Japanese body argued that Japan's strength, independence, and wealth could be attained through Japan's uniqueness and purity; it would be compromised if Japan became a copy of the West. The promulgation of the Imperial Constitution and Educational Rescript in 1890 promoted the idea that the emperor and his subjects are based on the natural unity of the unbroken, pure, and homogeneous bloodline.[50] This sense of Japan's uniqueness derives from and leads to the definition of Japan as a natural body. When it is understood that the emperor is the entire body and/or the embodiment of the pure spirit of Japan, then the bodies of Japanese people uniting with the foreign elements are perceived to compromise the pure and unique essence of Japanese body. Thus intermixture of the Japanese people with colonial subjects was understood to dilute the body of Japan and therefore had to be avoided.

Another powerful example of the attack on the idea of mixed blood and a multiethnic Japanese body came from proponents of the theory of eugenics. They asserted the necessity of creating a Japanese family empire with pure blood. Theories of eugenics can be seen as early as the 1920s, but it was in the 1930s that they came to postulate mixed blood specifically as a crisis for the empire, and gained force in opposition to the idea of the Japanese body as multiethnic/multiracial.[51] For example, the Japan Association of Racial Hygiene (Nihon Minzoku Eisei Kyōkai), a eugenic lobby group established in 1930, called in 1939 for the improvement of "the quality of the Nippon Race from the standpoint of racial hygiene, thereby to contribute to the prosperity of the state and the welfare of society."[52] In the early 1940s, the Japan Hygiene Association (Nihon Eisei Kyōkai) increased its study on the mixing of Japanese blood with the Ainu, Chinese, South Pacific Islanders, Europeans, and Indians, and its journal stated that "as a nation, mixed blood is a problem that must be avoided in every instance."[53] In 1942, the Council *(shingikai)* of the Greater East Asia Co-Prosperity Sphere claimed the importance of maintaining the pure blood of the Yamato people. Kiyono Kenji wrote:

> From the standpoint of politics and eugenics, too, the Japanese must guide the co-prosperity sphere by increasing the number of Japanese themselves. . . . [We] must avoid mixed blood and increase the Japanese race purely, and make efforts to create the Greater East Asia Co-Prosperity Sphere.[54]

Therefore, the emphasis was on re-creating and maintaining both "more" and "purer" Japanese bodies for the expansion of the family empire.

In re-creating, maintaining, and multiplying Japanese bodies with pure blood, the government, especially the newly established Ministry of Health and Welfare, discouraged intermarriage between the Japanese and people from the neighboring colonized nations. The members of the Association of Eugenics became the officials of the Ministry of Health and Welfare and influenced the report on the global role of the *Yamato minzoku* (Yamato people) in 1943. This report criticized intermarriage with what was considered to be other races.[55] By preventing interracial marriage and the birth of mixed-blood children, who were considered to be inferior and sickly offspring, Japan could ensure the expansion of the empire with not only more but also purer children, who would become the strong and superior next generation of Japan.[56]

Furthermore, the proponents of eugenics came into direct conflict with the assimilation policies of the colonial government and instead implemented separation policies. Whereas the discourse on the mixed blood of multiethnic/multiracial Japanese bodies forced colonized subjects to become assimilated, the discourse on the pure and homogeneous empire separated the colonized nations from the Japanese. To maintain the purity of Japanese blood and body, Japanese colonizers were encouraged to take their spouses with them to the colonies so that they would not intermarry with the natives. Bodies of mixed-blood children were stigmatized as individual, disease-ridden, and bereft of national spirit, in contrast to the notion of the collective, healthy, and patriotic spirit of the pure Japanese.[57] The Japanese were disconnected, in theory, from their colonized subjects in neighboring nations in marriage, school, the military, and in sexual encounters.

Whether the body of Japan was understood as mixed blood and multiethnic/multiracial or as pure blood and homogeneous, Japan's imperial expansion was understood as the extension of the blood kin of the family empire. In articulating and forming Japanese nationalism and empire, the central ruling power employed the notion of blood and spirit as a discursive tool in creating and expanding the Japanese race. As Louise Young has explored in *Japan's Total Empire: Manchuria and the Culture of Wartime Imperialism,* the discourse on sacred Japanese in the late 1930s depicts the empire as an extended biological family with the emperor as the paternal head of this national household, and the inhabitants of Japan's colonies as relatives of the family empire.[58] Japan's economic and political conquest of its peripheries was understood as a sacred mission to extend the family's kin. Furthermore, the Shinto ideology of the divine ancestry of the Japanese people served to explain their invasion and dominance as a divine mission to plant the colonies with the spirit of the ever-prosperous, dynamic living body of the family empire.

Although Japan expanded the borders of its body by colonizing other nations, state officials constructed Japan not as an aggressor but as a benevolent leader who would bring about advancement for Asia, with Japan at its center. By incorporating blood/spirit as a doctrine into the Japanese imperialist discourse on the body of family empire, Japanese people/subjects were cast as superior siblings who must lead the populations of Japan's colonies as their inferior brothers and sisters. "Investigation of Global Policy with the Yamato Race as Nucleus," prepared by the Population and Race Section of the Ministry of Health and Welfare Research Bureau from 1942 to 1943, explicates the destiny of the Japanese as the "leading race" in Asia and, implicitly, the world.[59] As Young points out, the Japanese as the central and superior race prescribed the duty of Japanese settlers to "lead and enlighten" *(shidō keihatsu)* and "guide" *(yūeki)* the people under the Japanese occupation. The Japanese family, and specifically brothers and sisters in a superior position to guide the inferior siblings, supported the administration of the Co-Prosperity Sphere and justified Japanese efforts to colonize the Manchurians and Chinese. It was the correlating discourses of the Shinto glorification of Japanese sacred mission and Confucian idealization of holding to one's proper place in social hierarchies that justified the invasion of the bodies and borders of Asia.

The discourse of hierarchy and the putative civilization gap between Japanese and the colonized encouraged the Japanese people/subjects of *naichi* to identify themselves as parts of the body of the family empire, to immigrate to *gaichi,* and to extend the borders of the Japanese empire. The elevation of the status of Japanese in the colonies served to involve them in state-led colonialist endeavors. Japanese entered the colonies with measures of progress and liberation for both their own bodies and those of the colonized. Medical theorists and practitioners diagnosed the bodies of the colonized and prescribed standards of personal and public hygiene.[60] They worked to prevent the causes of disease so that illness would not spread in the bodies of the colonized and of the empire.[61] As healthy and strong body parts of the empire, Japanese factory owners and workers labored based on the ideology of heightening the level of material resources among the native populations in occupied territories. The conception of Japan's superiority and advancement led bureaucrats to evaluate and lead the technological and economic development of the colonies. Elevated from poor and underprivileged villagers to rich and privileged colonists, farmers planted the seeds of Yamato in the expanded garden of the Japanese household.[62] As Young argues, despite the atrocities committed by Japanese soldiers, the self-image of the imperialist was a positive and peaceful one. As parts of the ever-prosperous and dynamic body of the family empire, the bodies of Japanese people/subjects moved from *naichi* to *gaichi,* expanded the borders, and operated to liberate and strengthen the imperial body.

CHAPTER 2

The Universal Womb

How did the changing dynamics of discourse in the laws, regulations, and policies of the Japanese state system define, shape, and mobilize women's bodies? How were women's bodies assigned their roles in serving the body of the empire within the boundaries of home, school, workplace, and brothel? These questions must be tackled in relation to the overarching problems of how state discourses defined women as loyal subjects, and how ideas and practices of female bodies changed in accordance with the shifting concepts of Japan as a body.

Beginning in the late 1890s—when the idea of the family nation-state (*kazoku kokka*) became intertwined with the organ theory of the nation-state (*yūkitai kokka ron*) and the modern theorization of the national body (*kokutai ron*)—bureaucratic agencies of the Japanese state developed a centralized national policy that spelled out the public roles women were expected to play as physical parts of the Japanese empire. Within the changing concepts of *kokutai* (national body), female bodies were assigned various roles, including (1) reproductive, domestic(ated) laboring bodies of wives and mothers at home, (2) productive laboring bodies inside and outside the home, and (3) migrant bodies outside the Japanese homeland. Women were seen as engaging in reproduction and/or economic production, depending on their socioeconomic class and the historically changing demands of both industry and the military. In addition, women's bodies were expected to act in accordance with shifting interpretations of which race and ethnicity legitimately constituted the Japanese body. Expected roles for women's bodies shifted depending on whether Japan was conceived as a multiracially, multiethnically diverse empire or a homogeneous one. Despite the differences, the recurrent theme throughout the modern period was the state's (ab)use of women's bodies for the purpose of continuation and development of individual households and the family empire. Because state authority over women as daughters, wives, and mothers was exercised through the agency of the individual family, women of all classes and regions were expected to play their respective roles in building the body and expanding the borders of the wealthy and strong family empire of Japan. From the perspective of state officials, women's bodies were meaningful and functional only insofar as they enhanced the wealth and strength of the empire. Women were deemed useful only when they were subjected, reproductive, and productive bodies.

State Discourse on Female Bodies in Japan

As political, economic, and historical conditions changed and the demands of government, industry, and the military shifted, the manner and pace at which the state appropriated women's bodies varied, too. There were inconsistencies within gender; indeed, "no uniform or monolithic conception captures the diversity of women's experience in early twentieth-century Japan."[1] Women from the middle and lower classes engaged in reproductive and/or productive labor in distinctly different ways. The roles of women's bodies also differed depending on whether Japan was viewed as a multiracial and multiethnic body or as a homogeneous one. Nevertheless, it is still possible to discuss the dominant ways in which the state appropriated the bodies of women in building and expanding Japan.

To strengthen and enrich the body of the empire and extend its borders, the state deliberately approached education for women as a large-scale project designed to reconfigure womanhood and women's bodies. Debates on the organ theory of the nation-state led to the modern theorization of the national body in the 1880s. In the late 1890s, the concept of the family nation-state furthered this development, and as a result, state officials' discussion on women's roles intensified. This coincided with the industrial takeoff of the 1890s and swelling national pride following Japan's victory in the Sino-Japanese War (1894–95), which further intensified state officials' rhetoric about women's bodies. Riding on the Meiji slogan of a "rich nation, strong army" (fukoku kyōhei), Japan colonized Taiwan in 1895. In this context, the leading architect of Meiji education, Mori Arinori, proclaimed, "The foundations of national prosperity rest upon education; the foundations of education upon women's education."[2] The term ryōsai kenbo (good wife, wise mother), coined by Nakamura

Masanao, became the core of Mori's program and the basis of women's education at the end of the nineteenth century.

Motherhood was refashioned in modern Japan when the government commanded women to engage in activities for the benefit of the empire, both physically and materially. Although it is difficult to say how thoroughly the slogan "good wife, wise mother" impinged on the everyday life of women,[3] both middle- and lower-class women gradually recognized and incorporated the values encapsulated in the phrase, and this contributed to the capitalist economic buildup of the empire and to Japan's military conquest of neighboring nations as well. State conceptions of motherhood gained currency among the populace, especially after the 1920s, and eventually became the ideal of many Japanese women.[4]

"Wise Mothers" of the Empire

The slogan *ryōsai kenbo,* propagated by the Ministry of Education, both derived from and supported the notion of women's bodies as parts of the body of the family empire. In accord with the concept of *kunmin ittai* (the emperor and people as one body), articulated in *Minsen giin setsuritsu kenpakusho* (Demands for the establishment of a representative assembly) in 1874, women's bodies were expected to function in unison with the body of the emperor. Nakajima Kuni explains that "individual, private situations were ignored. The [state's] focus was given only to what uniformly answered the nation-state's demands, what cooperated with it, the part that became one body with [it]."[5]

The state-driven nationalism in modern Japan reconstructed women primarily as objects of state control and protection, referring to them as "mothers of the empire." From the 1870s on, a continuing diffusion of new conceptions of womanhood, especially for educated middle-class women, emphasized the centrality of the mother in nurturing infants and older children.[6] Maternal duties did not necessarily involve bearing children but definitely included rearing them. By giving women the job of raising the emperor's babies *(sekishi)* to become Japan's future leaders, workers, and soldiers, the connections among the family empire, individual households, and Japanese women were cemented. The idea was that a woman only became fully maternal by nurturing her children, her husband, and her in-laws as *sekishi* of the emperor. As wise mothers, women provided physical care so that both children and adults were fed, clothed, bathed, and nursed according to evolving standards of nutrition and hygiene.[7] Based on education according to modern scientific principles, women as mothers also socialized the subjects/people of the empire by instilling Japan's national and imperial values in them.[8] By teaching their children and the emperor's *sekishi* the Japanese language, manners, and academic and vocational knowledge, women played a key role in assimilating subjects from various economic and political backgrounds into a unified Japanese body politic.

This new responsibility for the children of the family empire, given to women as "wise mothers," was specifically modern. In the early-modern period in Japan (1603–1868), as Kathleen Uno has explored, the biological mother was *not* normalized as the primary provider of education or care to the children she bore.[9] Instead, women were stigmatized as biologically inferior and thus unfit for such a serious role as rearing a disciplined and moral child.[10] In the late nineteenth century, young mothers still lacked authority over child rearing in families both urban and rural, rich and poor. It was the male household head or older family members who made important decisions about the education and care of children. Older siblings, and even full- and part-time apprentices and servants, could also play determining roles in nurturing infants and toddlers. Thus the internal division of labor in the home was rather fluid, and women were not seen as the sole bearers of reproductive work in the nineteenth century.[11] However, new and changing conceptions of womanhood in the modern era positioned married women, especially in the educated middle class, to assume increased responsibility for rearing the children they bore.[12]

The Maternal Body

Mother's bodies held crucial significance for the empire. As Sumiko Ōtsubo's studies indicate, male leaders such as Naruse Jinzō, the founder of Japan Women's College, emphasized the usefulness of physical education for women.[13] Naruse stressed the importance of providing women with proper scientific knowledge about health, to help them become physically fit for bearing and rearing strong and healthy children. Active exercise would increase the size and capacity of the relatively small and weakly built bodies of Japanese women.[14] For a "rich nation, strong army," it was important for women to bear healthy children who would grow up to work and fight for the empire. By being elevated to the important role of educating the children of empire, women also gained stature as a major source of national strength.

This new conception of fertile female bodies was also a symbol of the state. As Miyake Yoshiko explains, "The Japanese government . . . promoted population growth not only to assume a supply of soldiers and colonists for imperialist expansion, but also to associate ideas of fecundity and productivity with the power of the state."[15] The fertile female body literally bore children of the empire and metaphorically represented the power and growth of that empire: when Japan was understood as a metaphorical body, the emperor was analogous to its head, while women were analogous to the womb of the body of the empire; similarly, when the emperor was conceived of as the entire body of Japan (discussed in chapter 1), women could be considered to be the womb that bore his babies *(sekishi)*.[16] State discourses avoided using the exact term "womb" to describe women's function within the body of the empire, however.

The Maternal Body of a Multiethnic Japan

Women's ability to bear and/or rear children assumed different meanings in accordance with shifting ideas about the ethnic and racial constitution of the body of empire. The idea of the body of empire as multiethnic and multiracial implicitly demanded that women bear "more" but not necessarily "purer" Japanese. As mentioned in chapter 1, Tatebe Tongo wrote in 1914 that "a billion Japanese people" would be needed, and that this might well involve some "mixed blood."[17] In his wish for Japan to become a strong empire in the world, Tatebe therefore emphasized the quantity allowed by racial diversity over the quality of so-called racial purity. Within this notion of Japan as a multiracial and multiethnic empire, "purity" was thus synonymous with health and strength.

The function of the female body to bear and rear children of the multiracial and multiethnic body of empire must also be explored in the context of intermarriage. As shown in chapter 1, government officials encouraged intermarriage between Japanese and colonized populations during the period when the empire was conceived of as diverse. For example, the government encouraged marriage between Japanese and Koreans by emphasizing that they shared the same ancestry *(nikkan dōso)* and the same body *(naisen ittai)*. After the annexation of Korea in 1910, marriage between Japanese women and Korean men was a common practice.[18] It was thought that husbands from Korea and the children of these unions could be educated and assimilated to become Japanese thanks to their "good wives, wise mothers," whose task it was to turn their charges into loyal and diligent subjects of the emperor even when their biological heritage was not "purely" Japanese.

As long as the objective was to create more children, rather than racially/ ethnically pure children, the state also used adoption as a metaphor. Colonizing other nations was equated with adopting their citizenry as family members of the multiethnic and multiracial empire. When the body of Japanese empire expanded by adding neighboring Asian peoples to the core family of Japan, the government's assimilation policies encouraged and sometimes even mandated that Japanese and the colonized be united in school education, marriage, and sexual encounters (chapter 1). Adopted children could be socialized/assimilated by wise mothers to become Japanese. Use of the metaphor of adoption may well have been tied to the state's emphasis on the socializing role of women as wise mothers, as well as to its lack of emphasis on a "natural" biological mother's bodily function of bearing the children of the natal family.

This is also suggested by the fact that adoption practices, which had varied throughout Japanese history, continued in the modern period for the survival of the *ie* (household). As Tessa Morris-Suzuki notes, from the late nineteenth to the early twentieth century, "the maintenance of the household name was more important than biological blood ties so that the adoption of heirs, who would take on the family surname, was a common practice."[19] It was not unusual for children to be raised and trained as apprentices or servants outside their natal households by persons other than their biological parents.[20] And because households were created and sustained by the family name and institution rather than by "pure," homogeneous bloodlines, adoption was not only accepted but encouraged. The notion and practice of adoption at the level of individual nuclear families may thus be linked to using the metaphor of adoption in the state discourse that justified the expansion of the multiethnic and multiracial family empire. By not depending solely on the body of the married Japanese woman to bear children, the empire could both extend its lineage and expand its territory by adopting children from other nations—that is, by colonizing neighboring Asian nations.

The Maternal Body of a Homogeneous Japan

There was, however, a countercurrent in Japanese society to the urge to assimilate ethnically "non-Japanese" populations and make the children of such unions Japanese by enculturation through the agency of mothers. I offer here the argument that this had important consequences for how women's bodies were viewed. Expectations about women's bodies seem to have shifted when it began to be thought that the ethnic/racial constitution of the body of Japan needed to be homogeneous and "pure."

The idea of a homogeneous family empire gained proponents especially after the mid-1880s, during the rise of antiforeign sentiment, and after the late 1930s, with the growing influence of eugenics. As explored in chapter 1, in some of the discourses among Japanese intellectuals and policy makers, the idea that the emperor and his subjects shared the natural unity of an unbroken, pure, and homogeneous bloodline led to the definition of Japan as a natural body. By the early 1940s, the Japan Hygiene Association (Nihon Eisei Kyōkai) stated that "as a nation, mixed blood is a problem that must be avoided in every instance."[21] Hence marriage between Japanese and colonized peoples became a problem for the eugenics theorists.

In this context, women's physicality, as part of the body of Japan, gained renewed importance. Mothers became seen as fertile bodies that would bear not only more new subjects but also racially and ethnically purer members of a homogeneous empire, in addition to their established role of socializing their children to become loyal Japanese subjects. For example, in the late 1930s, the government's initiative to create more Japanese was reinforced by the slogan *umeyo fuyaseyo* (give birth and increase [the number of children]). Another phrase from the same time, *kodakara butai* (the childbearing corps), used military terminology to describe the female body as "a human incubator" that would provide more soldiers for the empire.[22] In 1940, the state also issued a mandate, "Outlines for Establishing Population Growth Polity," designed to impel women to redouble their efforts to bear more children for the empire.

In 1938 proponents of eugenics gained dominance in the Ministry of Health and Welfare and issued two crucial mandates. The National Eugenics Law (Kokumin Yūsei Hō, 1940) made it mandatory for women to be sterilized if diagnosed with a hereditary disease. The same law prohibited the use of birth control for women deemed healthy. Citing a housewife's statement in 1942, Nakajima Kuni explains, "The child is not my child, but the nation's child. It is our mission to nurture *(sodateru)* well the nation's children who have received good blood."[23] In the context of the eugenics theorists' increasing focus on the homogeneous racial constitution of Japan, "good blood" meant not only healthy and strong but racially "pure" blood.

It is reasonable to postulate that in this paradigm, children could no longer be adopted but had to be born of the "natural," biological mothers of Japan. Thus the bodily function of the womb of the biological mother gained greater prominence, alongside the role of a wise mother who nurtured and socialized children. At this historical juncture, segregation policies were also promoted to distinguish the Japanese people (with their "pure" blood) from people in the colonized neighboring nations.

The Maternal Body and Spirit of Japan

In the emerging view of this period, a women's body functioned to improve the quantity and quality of Japanese children as body parts of the empire. In addition, the maternal body that bore and reared children was understood to connect the bodies of the emperor and his subjects by passing on the spirit of the ancestors, and thus instilling this spirit in Japan's soldiers. A document produced by the state-sponsored Greater Japan Women's Association for National Defense (Dai-Nihon Kokubō Fujinkai) in 1943 stated:

> It is the mother, not the father, who is the true spiritual center of the household. The mother is the one who experiences the pain of childbirth and raises children. It is therefore no exaggeration to say that in fact the Japanese spirit is maintained and passed on by splendid mothers.[24]

By bearing and rearing children, the mother's body transmitted the spirit that descended from the ancestors to the emperor and then to the soldiers. Thus the maternal body functioned as a medium to connect the body of the emperor and the bodies of his people/subjects.

The notion of Japanese women as the bodily resource of the empire ultimately led to the explicit concept of Japanese women as the universal womb of the community of human beings. Mori Yasuko wrote in 1942,

"Structurally the family community is the motherly womb *(botai)* of the history of human beings. Furthermore, the motherly womb of the family community is the mother herself."[25] Thus the woman in modern Japan, as the bearer of domestic reproductive duties, not only functioned within the body of the Japanese empire but was further elevated to a universal level of importance in the context of all-out war after the late 1930s.

As already mentioned, maternal duties included giving care and socializing/assimilating children to become loyal, healthy, and strong body parts of the empire. They also included bearing the *sekishi* (babies) of the emperor. Women engaged in production as well as reproduction, however, thus functioning as arms of the empire both outside and inside the home. As Nakajima Kuni puts it, "The demand for the mobilization of workers and fertility needed the ideology of the one body of the emperor and the subjects."[26] Women therefore worked with their bodies in accordance with the shifting social and political demands of the state.

Bureaucratization and industrialization had created a division of labor by separating home and workplace for the middle class in the late 1890s. In the late 1930s on, however, the division for middle-class women became blurred. In its total mobilization for the war effort, the Japanese state demanded that middle-class women work as both reproductive and productive bodies. During the Pacific War (1941–45), the state needed to increase production of wartime necessities at a time when supplying soldiers for the battlefields was draining the male labor force from the factories. Middle-class women were therefore mobilized as laborers outside the home, facing the virtually impossible demands of (1) functioning as pillars of households that had lost their fathers to the battlefield, (2) reproducing the next generation of human resources, and also (3) producing munitions from material resources.[27] Nakajima points out that the ideology of "good wife, wise mother" became stronger at this time precisely because Japanese women's ability to fulfill its injunctions had broken down. The lack of a male labor force in the 1940s mobilized mothers to work outside the home, and as a result, the ideal image of a woman as a "good wife, wise mother" within the domain of home collapsed.[28]

Laboring Female Bodies

I have analyzed the concepts and practices of "wise mothers" and their physical functions within the Japanese empire. In addition to being mothers and/or wombs, women worked as "good wives" within the border of the home in modern Japan. As Kathleen Uno explains in *Passages to Modernity*, motherhood and wifehood are neither static nor synonymous. As wives, women engaged in both reproductive and productive work for the household and for the family empire.[29] Uno writes: "While an heir was necessary to maintain continuity, family values as practiced in daily life stressed hard work for the sake of the household and obedience to coresident in-laws rather than child rearing or child bearing as the essence of a young wife's role."[30] Rather than devoting most of their time to child rearing, young married women engaged in work that required skills and bodily strength and endurance.[31]

Good wives' unpaid domestic, productive work included cooking, cleaning, washing, sewing, frugal management of household finances, and consolidating the relationships among children, husbands, and in-laws.[32] Women as wives thus contributed to the nutrition of healthy and strong bodies of children, hygiene for the prevention of disease within the body of empire, saving for the economic growth of the household and family empire, and consolidating the relationships of family as a microcosm of the family empire.[33] The work of a "good wife" in the modern period was formed by the state's implementation of education in science and household management within the family empire.

In the minds of some thinkers, protection of the bodies of wives was important for the empire. As Otsubo's study points out, the "eugenic significance" of the law proposed by Hiratsuka Raichō and Naruse Jinzō in the 1920s was that "the protection of housewives and their children would improve the quality of the nation *(kokumin)* and strengthen national power *(kokuryoku)*."[34] Leading architects of the modern state fostered acceptance and protection of the unpaid and paid productive labor of wives, especially those from poor and lower-class Japanese families, due to their overarching consensus that these women's labor was beneficial to the nation's industries. Within the paradigm of women's unselfish devotion to the family empire, lower-class women were subsumed by the state's need for cheap labor. Women from poor and lower-class families (including many merchant and farm families) engaged in paid productive work in handicrafts as pieceworkers, petty entrepreneurs, and wage laborers. Thus they participated in both the reproductive housework and productive family trade. Young married women from wealthy families served their husband or in-laws, supervised apprentices and servants, tended wardrobes, and oversaw inventories of family possessions.[35] Women's laboring bodies were class specific in the capitalist society, but both lower- and middle-class women's labor was used to advance the interests of the empire.

Outside the home, women from poor and lower-class families made up the majority of the labor force in textiles, the first significant mechanized industry to develop during the 1880s. In her study of Meiji peasant workers in their teens, Sharon Nolte explains that a woman would tolerate poor dormitory and factory conditions and minimal wages because she was bound by contract and debt, and also out of filial piety.[36] Thus women's labor outside the home was not an alternative to family but an inherent part of it. Women from the poor and lower classes worked for both the individual household and the family empire under financially and physically excruciating conditions.

As the modernizing Japanese state made enormous demands on women, the bodies of peasants and the urban poor were exploited for long working hours at minimal wages, and housed in dormitories under poor conditions. Patricia Tsurumi's study found that some female textile workers' song lyrics compared the textile factory to a brothel where they sold their bodies like prostitutes, but with even lower economic compensation and status.[37] By abusing women's bodies engaged in production, the industry of the Japanese empire grew economically powerful.

The health of female workers was important to state officials to the extent that women were the mothers of future recruits. Vera Mackie points out that policy makers debated improving working conditions for women, asserting that this would advance both the national interest and the advancement of export industries. By defining female workers as the future mothers of the empire, state officials drafted the protective provisions of the Factory Law (1911). Interestingly, the factory legislation assumed that it was necessary to implement policies directed solely at women with children. By grouping women and children in the same category, the legislation implied that women were physically vulnerable and therefore in need of the state's protection.[38]

Prostitution in modern Japan illustrates another aspect of the relationship between the body of empire and the bodies of women. The political authority in the Meiji period reorganized the licensed prostitution system, which abused lower-class Japanese women as well as women in the colonies. Fujime Yuki contends that "domestic class control and Asian aggression were the fundamental causes of prostitution for Japanese women in Japan proper and overseas."[39] Massive numbers of women turned to prostitution as the result of an economic crisis caused by the enormous government expenditures devoted to the Russo-Japanese War (1904–5) and a postwar recession. In some cases, the Japanese military forced women to become prostitutes.[40] Women's bodies were thus used as sexual objects as a consequence of the state's efforts to strengthen and expand the body of empire.

Despite the fact that women were sexually and economically (ab)used as a direct consequence of state efforts to elevate Japan's status as a military industrial power, it was prostitutes who were stigmatized as being "antisocial," "carnal," and "dirty." Mori Ōgai—a civil and military physician who wrote a blueprint for the Factory Law in 1911, and a literary authority who penned the novella *Youth* in the same year—re-created the discourse on two types of women in modern Japan. In *Youth*, the "prostitute type" appears in opposition to the "maternal type." It is important to promote the maternal type because these women contribute not only to the continuation of human kind in general but also to the sovereign state. "The maternal type [who] desires only to breed" contributes to society because such women reproduce sources of national strength.[41] According to *Youth*, it is crucial to educate and increase the number of women of the maternal type because the nation includes the antisocial prostitute type as well. They are antisocial because "the prostitute type has only carnal desire" and no desire for reproduction.[42] In *Youth*, the carnal desire of the prostitute is defined as a disease that saps the energy of men who should be devoting their healthy and strong bodies to strengthening the empire.

Borders

Women who were defined by and confined in certain categories, such as mothers, wives, laborers, and prostitutes, were understood to occupy different spaces, such as the home, factory, and brothel, for which boundaries were delineated in the state discourse. The Civil Code (1897) defined home as the proper domain in which women were to engage in public duties for the empire. In other words, women's laboring reproductive bodies were confined within the borders of domestic space of each individual family as a microcosm of the family empire. Similarly, factory laws drew the borders of factories and dormitories and defined the conditions in which the female bodies operated for the growth of industry and military. Last but not least, the legality of prostitution justified the Japanese military's establishment of "comfort stations" in *gaichi* (the outer territory of Japan), where women's bodies were abused sexually by Japanese soldiers.

The line between inside the home as "private space" and outside the home as "public space" was often blurred, however. Women's bodies often functioned within the home as a public space rather than a private haven (since it was there that they nurtured the empire's future workers and soldiers), while women in factories remained bound by obligations to the household (for their sense of filial piety as daughters was invoked to induce them to tolerate poor working conditions and minimal wages, as we have seen). In addition, sexual and economic abuse of female bodies in brothels was legally sanctioned by Japan's "family empire," which did not hesitate to provide women's bodies to Japanese soldiers as the empire expanded its territories. Women were often confined, whether in the home, factory, or brothel, and the borders that distinguished one from the other were hazy and overlapping. However, although the boundaries that delineated the bodies of women were in flux, according to the state discourses, women were designed to function solely within the borders of empire.

A stagnant and bleak economic future caused many Japanese to leave their homeland and cross the imperial border in search of better lives abroad. The uneven capitalist development most affected the rural peripheries of the Japanese empire. The collapse of household finances and village structure there has been attributed to a decrease in rice and silk prices as well as to crop failure, bad weather, and overpopulation.[43] As Louise Young writes, "Faced with the emergence of a politically organized working class demanding social reform, entrenched political elites [i.e., Socialists and Communists] promoted the social and economic benefits of colonial expansionism as a potential alternative to social welfare policies."[44] Japanese social imperialism emerged with the greatest force in the rural areas. Emigration was thus promoted by government sponsorship, social networks, and advertising. Prefecture and government associations prepared books, pamphlets, posters, and lectures, and they encouraged many Japanese in the agrarian villages to leave *naichi* (the inner territory of Japan). As a result, many emigrated to Taiwan, Korea,

Manchuria, North America, and South America. The mass emigration of village farmers to Manchukuo in 1937, under the financial sponsorship by the Ministry of Agriculture and Forestry, is an example of institutionalized state-sponsored social imperialism.[45]

Among the emigrants were many women who, though they had moved away from *naichi,* were still expected to obey proclamations declaring the Japanese state as the center and the people as its subjects. Female migrant bodies engaged in both reproduction and production within the shifting discursive framework of the racial/ethnic constitution of the Japanese empire and its relationship to Western imperial powers and the Japanese colonies. Female migrant bodies and their relationships with Japan, the United States, Canada, China, and French Indochina are explored in the following chapters, as described in the writings of Yosano Akiko, Tamura Toshiko, and Hayashi Fumiko.

Women's bodies were mobilized for industrialization and militarization of the empire, but the women themselves were unable to exercise control over their lives as citizens without suffrage in *naichi* and *gaichi.* Japanese governmental laws and censorship deprived women of political rights both inside and outside the home. The Civil Code of 1897 deprived a married woman of her right to act as a head of household in financial and legal transactions. As a microcosm of the body of family empire, the status of head of the individual family was conferred upon the father (i.e., the patriarch). Thus women could not own or manage property. The state also prohibited political activities of women outside the home. By 1890, when the Meiji Constitution went into effect, the state had deprived women of their rights as voters, elected officeholders, and bureaucrats. By being deprived of suffrage, women were unable to exercise their legal rights to determine their roles and positions, as well as the functions of their bodies within the empire.[46]

The confinement of female bodies to home, factory, and brothel—not to mention women's exclusion from political agency—were, of course, in the interests of the industrialization and militarization of the family empire. The state justified women's political exclusion by citing their special duties and place within the family empire. Male architects of the modern Japanese state forbade women to make political demands or even to present views opposed to the state-driven nationalist discourse on women. For example, press laws aimed at stopping women from advocating betterment of their position and role in society were one way state censorship countered disturbing elements in the family empire. The Home Ministry banned a number of feminist publications, including *Seitō* (Bluestocking, 1911–16), for presenting feminist, erotic, or socialist views. In addition, the government stigmatized women who raised their voices against the state discourse on women. In 1925, Kira Motoo, a member of the Diet, declared that women in the suffrage movement were as unchaste as beasts.[47] Wives and mothers were understood to be chaste and reproductive resources for the body of empire, in contrast to unchaste and unreproductive whores. When women acted as feminists, they came to be regarded as promiscuous and even contaminated nonhumans acting against or outside the body and border of Japanese women. In 1921, Baron Fujimura Yoshirō explained the state discourses on Japanese women since 1890:

> It is not a very good thing for [women] to engage in political movements on their own. First, speaking both physiologically and psychologically, this violates the laws of nature. Second, if we speak also of women's duties and mission *(honbun shimei)*, it is not proper for women to take an active part along with men in political movements, in particular. Women's duties are in the home and in education and social work. Furthermore, when women do step out into society and engage in political movements, the results have been terrible. . . . Finally, permitting women in these political movements would run counter to the family system, the basis of social organization in our country.[48]

To subvert and co-opt feminist activities, the Home Ministry organized a national feminist organization called the Women's Alliance (Fujin Dōshi-kai, 1930). Self-governing feminist groups were seen as a political threat to the state, whereas the government-run feminist group was deemed a social service to the public. When the state used women as body parts of *kokutai* for the fulfillment of imperial goals, women were understood to carry out not political but "social" duties. Women were deemed political when they opposed the state, precisely because by doing so they violated the borders set by the prevailing political discourse.

The state deemed the control and protection of female reproductive and productive bodies necessary to strengthen the body and extend the borders of empire, both literally and metaphorically. Women's bodies in the service of the empire were defined differently at different times, depending on shifting economic and political demands as well as changing perceptions of the racial/ethnic constitution of Japan as a body. Within the family empire, women as parts of *kokutai* constituted (1) reproductive laboring bodies, which were inscribed into the home; (2) productive laboring bodies inside and outside the home; and (3) migrant bodies outside the homeland of Japan. Women as mothers and wives labored to provide strong and healthy bodies of the subjects who would equip the body of empire with military arms and industrial muscle. In particular, the maternal body as the womb of the empire gave birth to the emperor's *sekishi* (babies), who would become patriotic, efficient, and strong workers and soldiers. Productive bodies worked as the arms of the empire. Migrant bodies expanded the borders of the empire. Whether as domesticated bodies of wives and mothers or as undomesticated bodies of workers and migrants, women's bodies were subjugated as parts of the body of empire by the dominant state discourse of modern Japan.

· CHAPTER 3 ·

Resistance and Conformity

D ID WOMEN ASSUME NO AGENCY over their own bodies when the state discourses of modern Japan defined, controlled, and protected the female bodies within the body of empire? Had the disciplinary power of the Japanese imperial state from the late nineteenth to the mid-twentieth century permeated society completely, the enforcement of repressive laws and censorship would have been so effective as to make any resistance from women impossible. Kathleen Uno reminds us that "despite the visions and powers of states and elites, it is unwise to assume that their initiatives were monolithic or invariably successful; pursuit of contradictions and failures can be as illuminating as analyzing positive achievements."[1] If the state's oppression of women actually generated their resistance, as Michel Foucault's theory on the reciprocity of power suggests (see the Introduction), then it is meaningful to explore how women both incorporated and resisted the modern state's discourses on Japanese women.

How did some female activists and artists act in response to the dominant state discourses on the bodies of women? What were the possibilities and limits women faced in transgressing the borders of female bodies, as drawn by state officials? What is the significance of women writers' descriptions of female migrant bodies in relation to the expanding body of the Japanese empire? By tackling these questions, I explore how some prominent leaders of women constructed themselves as subjects of knowledge and agents of action instead of as passive and silenced subjects of the empire. This chapter primes the reader for some Japanese women's discourses against and within the state discourse on the bodies and borders of women. Through my exploration of the importance of migrant bodies in discourse, the reader will be prepared to enter the literary worlds of Yosano Akiko, Tamura Toshiko, and Hayashi Fumiko in the following chapters.

Women's Resistance

When commentators and critics examine how women construct their agency instead of succumbing to a state of passivity, they often focus on the resistance of women as rebels against men, family, and/or the state. As pointed out in the Introduction, studies of Japanese women's history as late as the 1970s and analyses of Japanese women's literature even today often adopt schemas that analyze women as (1) rebels, (2) transgressors who transcend the boundaries that confine them, (3) resilient strugglers at the fringes of society, (4) victims, or (5) protectors and nurturers of peace. The following discussions look at how some female Japanese intellectuals, activists, and artists actively challenged the hegemony over definitions of women and their bodies in modern Japan, and also analyze some of the seminal academic writings on them.

Bodies of Mothers and Wives

In the political context in which the concept of family empire emerged out of *yūkitai kokka ron* (the organ theory of the nation-state) and *kokutai ron* (the theory of the national body), women in modern Japan were expected to function as the body parts of *kokutai* (chapters 1 and 2). Against the state discourse that situated women as the reproductive physical resource for the empire, some female intellectuals and artists celebrated the reproductive/procreational body as the source of women's creative production.[2] The female writers and artists who contributed to the journal *Seitō* (Bluestocking, 1911–16), and who came to be called "New Women," require some attention here, since both Tamura Toshiko's and Yosano Akiko's writings appeared, among other places, in *Seitō*. In the inaugural issue of the journal, founding editor Hiratsuka Raichō began "The Seitō Manifesto: 'In the Beginning, Woman Was the Sun'" (1911) as follows:

> In the beginning, Woman was truly the Sun. An authentic person.
>   Now, Woman is the Moon. Living off another, reflecting another's brilliance, she is the moon whose face is sickly and wan.
>   And now, it is here that *Seitō* has been born.
>   Created by the brains and hands of today's Japanese women, *Seitō* has been born.[3]

Here women in the historical context of the 1910s emerge as faces that mark sickness and weakness, reflecting the light of others rather than emitting their own. By exhorting woman's rebirth as the sun, "The Seitō Manifesto" celebrates women as the source of radiance and, implicitly, health and strength. It also presents the female body as "the brains and hands" that create an artistic work, rather than as the womb bearing a child for the empire. In this way, the manifesto challenges the state discourse on man/patriarch as the brain/mind (chapter 1). "The Seitō Manifesto" continues:

> As women of today, we have done everything we could here. We have given our all in giving birth to this child, Seitō. All right—even though she may be a retarded, deformed, or premature infant—nothing more can be done. For the time being, we must be satisfied with her as she is.[4]

This passage celebrates the birth of a child (the journal Seitō) even though its body is imperfect. The importance of accepting the mentally challenged and physically irregular and weak child is threefold. First, it challenges the discourse initiated by the Ministry of Education on women as "good wives, wise mothers"—namely, as the reproductive source of children who must grow up to become educated, healthy, and strong subjects of the empire. Second, "The Seitō Manifesto" equates a child with the journal Seitō, a product of artistic creation, and thus reinvents the female reproductive body as a source of production. Finally, in Jan Bardsley's words, "The maternal imagery . . . enjoined them [the bluestockings] to become the mothers of their own rebirth"[5] rather than mothers of the empire.

Hiratsuka also voiced the possibility of having no children and of refusing to enter the family system before her marriage to Okumura Hiroshi. She posed the following questions to Okumura publicly in "To My Parents on Becoming Independent" (1914):

> If I hate the relationship between man and woman under the existing marriage system, and do not wish to have a legal marriage, what attitude will you adopt to this? . . . What kind of view do you have of children? If I love you and have a sexual appetite but have no procreative desire, how will you respond?[6]

Hiratsuka's "sexual appetite" countered the dominant discourse of the time, which drew a sharp distinction between the procreational desire of "good wives, wise mothers" and the "carnal" desire of prostitutes. Moreover, her hypothetical rejection of the family system headed by a patriarch questions the idealization of that system as a microcosm of the family empire under *zokufu* (the emperor as patriarch).

"The Seitō Manifesto" also challenges the state discourse on women as patriotic and thrifty wives who engage in reproductive and productive duties at home for the economic prosperity of the empire:

> So long ordered to tend to housework, women have had their powers of spiritual focus completely blunted. Housework can be done amidst distractions and with no sense of purpose. Because it is such an unsuitable environment for spiritual focus and the realization of dormant Genius, I loathe all the irritations that go with housework.[7]

By defining housework as something that "can be done amidst distractions," Hiratsuka subverts the ideology of the "good wife" created by the Ministry of Education, which defined household duties as women's main focus. Moreover, contesting the chain of "natural" loyalty that women as wives should display toward the patriarch of the family empire, the manifesto finds "no sense of purpose" in women's reproductive domestic(ated) duties. Rather than domestic(ated) women being empowered as the subjects of empire, and their female bodies functioning to instill the spirit of ancestors in Japanese children (chapter 2), women's spiritual powers are weakened ("blunted"). Furthermore, home is an "unsuitable" place for women, Hiratsuka wrote, contradicting the Civil Code of 1897, which specified home as women's proper place. Finally, she contends, the duties the state prescribes for women at home prevent them from cultivating their talent ("dormant Genius") for creative, productive work.

As we have seen, Hiratsuka's "Seitō Manifesto" begins with the use of a metaphor of nature/sun (women as mothers giving birth to the child *Seitō*) that politicized the state discourse on women in modern Japan. Her subsequent denaturalization of women as "good wives, wise mothers," and of their proper place as the home, can be understood as a direct or indirect response to a speech given a decade earlier by a male socialist leader, Kōtoku Shūsui. Addressing the Socialist Women's Seminar (Shakai

Shugi Fujin Kōen, 1904), Kōtoku said, "There must be a relationship between politics and the kitchen, therefore women also have a connection with politics."[8] He raised awareness of the politics (rather than the nature) of woman as mother and wife, and denaturalized woman's proper place as being the home. A decade later, Hiratsuka politicized the concept and reality of a devoted mother and wife who nurtures both her children and her husband as *sekishi* (babies) of the emperor.

Under Hiratsuka's leadership, "The Seitō Manifesto" called for women to be empowered by new laws, and thus to cultivate a realm beyond the legal boundaries laid down for them by the empire in the 1910s:

> With the bright virtue of a sun that renews itself each day, the New
> Woman is trying to build a new realm of the spirit, a realm
> endowed with a new religion, new morality, and new laws. Indeed,
> the mission of the New Woman lies in creating this new sphere.
> If this is so, where is this new realm? What is the new religion?
> The new morality? The new laws? The New Woman herself does
> not know.[9]

Although she did not know how to create the new realm and its laws, the New Woman knew how to cross the conventional borders delineated for her. As a graduate of Japan Women's College and the daughter of a German-language scholar who was a high-ranking civil servant in the national accounting offices, Hiratsuka crossed the boundaries drawn for women from the educated and privileged class. As Jan Bardsley points out, two scandals in particular marked Hiratsuka as a woman opposed to public mores. The first was her and her fellow middle-class bluestockings' visit to the Yoshiwara pleasure quarters in 1912 to assess the conditions of women sold into prostitution. Crossing the boundaries drawn for sexual laborers from the lower class meant physically violating the borders of the proper place of home as a site of procreative desire, and was therefore perceived as an outrageous act. As Bardsley mentions, a cartoon appeared shortly thereafter in *Tokyo pakku* (Tokyo Puck) that satirized Hiratsuka and a bluestocking companion by depicting them with facial hair on their chins, and critics attacked the visit to the pleasure quarter as "women acting like men."[10] The second scandal was Hiratsuka's "same-sex love" with Ōtake Kōkichi, a flamboyant young artist who had joined *Seitō;* their relationship also threatened the purported heterosexual, reproductive desire of "good wives, wise mothers" of the family empire. Thus even if New Women did not know how to create a new sphere, they certainly transgressed the existing boundaries of gender, sexuality, and class drawn by state officials and cultural critics.[11]

Against the state's ideology of women's sexuality as either (a) mothers' heterosexual procreational desire or (b) prostitutes' carnal desire, different sorts of discourse on sexuality began appearing in women's journals, including *Seitō*. On the Modern Girl sensation that followed the New Woman phenomenon in the media, Miriam Silverberg argues that although the Modern Girl was not organized, and makes only a brief appearance in the histories of prewar Japan, she was a political and militant activist who protested through sensuality and mobility the ideology of the "good wife, wise mother" from the late 1920s to the 1930s. Silverberg presents a case in which women transgressed the gender, sexuality, and class boundaries by refusing to accept the division of labor that confined middle-class mothers and wives at home, by playing and working outside the home alongside men, and by presenting their sexuality outside the "good wife, wise mother" ideology. The Modern Girl was thereby liberated from the fetters of class, gender, and sexuality both by casting aside the assumption that women belonged to the home and by publicly expressing her private desires for work, play, and sex. Thus the Modern Girl embodied the dual images of a working woman and a middle-class adolescent at play, and despite the state's censorship, women found different forms of sexuality outside of the confines of the ideology of "good wives, wise mothers" versus whores.[12]

Bodies of Workers

Some female intellectuals, artists, and activists who were associated with socialism described the bodies of female workers as the site of resistance against the state discourses of the Home Ministry and the factory laws. Vera Mackie's study explores the depiction of female workers' bodies in contrast to male ones. Citing *Ude* (Arm, 1929), a painting created by Ishigaki Eitarō, Mackie points out that male workers are shown as having muscular bodies; the clenched fists and kicking boots of the proletarian class represent their power to confront the capitalists with violence.[13] In addition, Ishigaki's painting is an example of the discourse on the body of male worker as arm/hand. White-collar workers, intellectuals, or policy makers use the brain, whereas it is the arm/hand that male workers use to carry out their manual and physical labor at factories. Furthermore, *the painting's title* metaphorically refers to the skills *(ude)* of workers.[14] In contrast, Mackie contends that women's strength is expressed through solidarity. Arms that link with others and legs that march through the streets on the cover of the journal *Rōdō fujin* (Working women) mark the female workers' demonstrations and strikes against the exploitation of female bodies.[15] Within the contexts of limbs as parts of the body of empire (chapter 1), female artists and intellectuals who contributed to *Rōdō fujin* described arms and legs in opposition to how these limbs were (ab)used by the state-led capitalism of the empire.

Some socialist women also depicted female workers' maternal bodies as the site of ambiguity and difficulty. Within the state discourse of the 1911 Factory Law that constructed female workers as future mothers (chapter 2), bodies of lower-class women, as both mothers and workers, were important to some socialist women. For example, *Rōdō fujin* depicts a breast-feeding maternal body against a background of factory chimneys, thus repeating the dilemma of state officials who used lower-class women to engage in both reproductive work at home and productive work outside the home.[16] A maternal body against the backdrop of factory also re-creates the image of Japan as an empire empowered by industrialization and embraced by the nurturing mothers of workers.

As examined in chapter 2, some female workers in the textile industry compared themselves to prostitutes because of factory owners' physical and economic exploitation of their bodies. Prostitution was not spared censure by some female activists. For instance, the Japanese Women's Christian Temperance Union (Nihon Kirisutokyō Fujin Kyōfukai, WCTU), with reportedly 155 chapters throughout *naichi* and *gaichi* in 1926, vigorously opposed the state's system of licensed prostitution.[17]

In the face of repressive effects of discourses and practices of the state institutions, Socialists and anarchists negotiated with the statist solutions to women's problems. As an anarchist, Takamure Itsue's point of contestation with Socialists was their focus on women's productive labor and neglect of their reproductive labor of bearing and rearing children. Countering the Socialists' advocacy of publicly supported child-care facilities, Takamure argued that children belonged to mothers rather than public institutions. Opposing artificial state-run institutions and communities, she envisioned women in the natural sphere of a village community, a

utopian society that would replace the state. She believed she could identify an anarchist tradition (i.e., autonomous, nonhierarchical communities, *museifu kyōsan shakai*) in Japanese village communities.[18]

Other anarchist women in modern Japan have caught the attention of
scholars as agents of action as they challenged the state discourse in radical ways and were punished by violent state measures. The list of these
anarchists includes Kanno Suga, Itō Noe, and Kaneko Fumiko. Kanno
was sentenced to death for alleged involvement in an attempt to assassi-
nate the emperor (the Great Treason Incident, 1910). Itō Noe, who for a
time edited *Seitō*, was beaten to death by the police, who used the opportunity of the chaos following the Great Kantō Earthquake of 1923 to mur-
der anarchist and socialist militants.[19] Kaneko was also arrested in the
aftermath of the earthquake for conspiring against the emperor; she took
her own life in prison.[20] Scholars have often characterized these women as
victims or brave martyrs.[21] By analyzing the diaries written by Kanno and
Kaneko in prison, Hélène Bowen Raddeker offers another perspective—
namely, that their writing functioned as a discursive strategy to construct
agents of action for empowerment against the state.[22]

After the Kantō earthquake, the Japanese government purged not only
Socialists and anarchists but residents of Korean descent. Yamakawa Kikue
recognized the uneven effects of "bourgeois principles" and exposed in-
equalities in class, gender, and race in *naichi* (the inner territory). During
the debates with members of the Political Research Association and the
Hyōgikai union federation in the 1920s, Yamakawa wrote in "Racial Prejudice, Sexual Prejudice and Class Prejudice":

> Even in a proletarian country, it is necessary to make explicit [the
> principle of equality regardless of sex, "race," or religion], because,
> in a society with deep-rooted customs of discrimination, if we
> simply say "the people" *(minshū)*, there is a danger that this will
> be taken to mean only people of the ruling race *(shihaitekina
> minzoku)*, and people of the ruling sex *(shihaitekina sei)*.[23]

Yamakawa exposed the politics of "the people"—a term synonymous
with Japanese men—who excluded "non-Japanese" and women from
their political rights and economic privilege. As Mackie recognizes, Yamakawa's treatise was especially important in the context of the Immigration Act passed by the U.S. Congress in 1924. Yamakawa problematized

Japanese critics' emphasis on the unfair restrictions against Japanese immigrants in the United States and their simultaneous neglect of exclusive provisions against women and the colonized population of the Japanese empire.[24]

Yamakawa's points on gender, sex, class, and race are important to this book. In *naichi*, Yosano Akiko's and Tamura Toshiko's texts from the 1900s problematized the limited status and rights of women in modern Japan. The material written in the 1920s and used for Hayashi Fumiko's *Hōrōki* (Diary of a vagabond, 1928) exposes the problems of the lower socioeconomic class of women and the marginalized race and ethnicities in Japan. In *gaichi*, Yosano tackled the problems of coexistence and conflict between diverse cultures and nations in Manchuria in 1928. Tamura Toshiko's texts on the Japanese female immigrants in Canada and the United States from the late 1910s to the late 1930s negotiated with the discursive forces generated by the empires of the United States, the United Kingdom, and Japan. Hayashi's writings on China and French Indochina also raise questions about the relationship between the colonizer and the colonized races and ethnicities within the boundaries of the nations and empires.

Many female activists voiced their opposition to the authoritarian regime, which restricted the space for women's activities by drawing certain boundaries. Women were prohibited from entering the political arena—attending or sponsoring political discussion meetings or joining political associations—first by the Law on Assembly and Political Association (Shūkai Oyobi Seishahō) in 1890 and then by the Police Law (Chian Keisatsuhō) of 1900. Women who attempted to participate in political movements were deemed to have violated "the laws of nature" "physiologically," according to Baron Fujimura Yoshiro in 1921.[25] This statement was made in response to numerous attempts by women, from the 1890s on, to repeal provisions of these laws. Deliberately ignoring the admonitions of officials, who defined women's duties as belonging in the home, women stepped out of the house and into the political arena by engaging in political movements. For example, the WCTU protested the government's decision in 1890 to prohibit women from observing the Diet.[26] Fukuda Hideko, from a socialist group called Heiminsha (Commoners Society), led the socialist movement from 1904 until 1909 to modify article 5 of the Public Peace Police Law. Hiratsuka, Ichikawa Fusae, and Oku Mumeo organized the New Woman's Association (Shin Fujin Kyōkai) and petitioned the Diet for revision of the same law. In 1919 they tried to gain women's suffrage.[27]

From the 1890s on, some individualist, maternalist, liberal, social, communist, and anarchist women challenged how their bodily functions were defined and how women's opportunities were limited by Japan's state-driven nationalism. As already mentioned, studies of Japanese women's history and analyses of Japanese women's literature have often celebrated women as rebels who fought against men and the state. I next explore how some women's resistance nevertheless contained within itself a measure of conformity with the state discourse.

Women's Conformity

In negotiation with the state's education policies targeted at creating "good wives, wise mothers" since the late 1890s—and with the Civil Code (1897), which defined the home as a public sphere in which women were to carry out their duties for the empire—"The Seitō Manifesto" was not entirely independent of the state discourses. In the scholastic community inside and outside Japan, its author, Hiratsuka Raichō, is defined as one of the representative figures of maternalist women's movements of the Taishō period (1912–26).[28] Relying on the "mother's rights" (boken) theory of Swedish feminist Ellen Key, Hiratsuka exalted motherhood and asserted the necessity for the state to protect mothers during the motherhood protection debate (bosei hogo ronsō, 1916–19).[29] By doing so, she did not so much resist as rely on, and therefore reinforce, the concept of Japanese women as mothers controlled and protected by the state. Although Hiratsuka aspired to cultivate a "new realm," her discourse submitted to the state's definition of the biological and social functions of the female body as the maternal body, thereby enhancing the nation's international power and status.

Nor was the relationship of socialist feminists with the state subversive on every count. For example, the former Heiminsha member Nishikawa Fumiko stressed the link between socialist philosophy and feminine values, and identified socialism as a compassionate philosophy that was particularly amenable to women. In her estimation, because of their essentially maternal and caring nature, women were fit to build a compassionate society. Nishikawa's vision of socialism as a maternal and therefore compassionate philosophy was linked with pacifism, in contrast to the state's masculine, aggressive values of capitalism and militarism.[30] In this sense she celebrated feminine values in contrast to masculine ones. Yet by affirming the maternal and caring instincts as woman's essential nature, Nishikawa repeated the state's definition of women as mothers. Among male Socialists, as already seen, Kōtoku Shūsui politicized women's domesticated and unpaid duties and denaturalized woman's place in the home, especially in the kitchen, where women had the duty to prepare nutritious food for the children of the family empire.[31] It has been pointed out, however, that female sympathizers of the socialist and communist movements had to succumb to their male comrades' demands that they engage in unpaid domestic and sexual labor to serve their needs.[32]

The anarchist Takamure did not question the sexual division of labor, in which women held the primary responsibilities for child care in the private sphere.[33] Takamure shared maternalist feminists' tendency to identify motherhood with nature, to essentialize motherhood, and to idolize mothers' power and compassion. As nature's representatives, Takamure averred, it should be women who control reproduction and child care.

Women's affinity with the state discourse is most evident in the Patriotic Women's Association (Aikoku Fujinkai), the largest women's organization in the Meiji period, founded in 1901 by Okumura Ioko. With the publication of its own journal, *Aikoku fujin* (Patriotic woman, 1902–), the organization's membership had expanded to 807,000 by 1911.[34] Although founded as a private women's association, it operated within the official discourse on women as "good wives, wise mothers" due to having been founded with the financial assistance of Konoe Atsumaro, the president of the House of Peers, the Home Ministry, and Army Ministry. Excluded from conscription, women affiliated with Aikoku Fujinkai carried out their patriotic activities by sending packages to soldiers, joining the war front as nurses in *gaichi*, and consoling people who had lost family members on the battlefield. Aikoku Fujinkai grew by incorporating other women's organizations and also by establishing branch offices in Taiwan and Korea in 1937.[35] Thus women's organizations and associations led by Aikoku Fujinkai supported the nation-state's expansionist ideals and activities in both *naichi* and *gaichi*. Members of the WCTU also actively cooperated with bureaucrats during the Sino-Japanese (1894–95) and Russo-Japanese (1904–5) wars.[36]

It is true that many women became more supportive of the state-driven nationalism that contributed to the expansion of empire in the 1930s and

1940s, when the government redoubled its war efforts in China, Southeast Asia, and the Pacific.[37] Numerous critics have argued that this was merely an aberration during all-out war.[38] Many women shared the bureaucrats' values, however, and had worked, consciously or unconsciously, for the progress and prestige of the empire from the 1890s on. For example, in agreement with the official discourse that increasingly linked the maternal body with the expansion of the body of empire (discussed in chapter 2), many women associated their reproductive capacity with the power and growth of empire.

This was most evident in Aikoku Fujinkai, which helped create women's agency by acting on the ideas of women as mothers and as the nurturers of soldiers who would fight and die for the Japanese empire. Aikoku Fujinkai is the most obvious example of how women's discourses were shaped by nationalist/imperialist values of essentialized women as mothers and wives. Female activists and artists of modern Japan who came to be categorized as individualist, maternalist, socialist, and/or anarchist feminists in the 1970s had also written within the nationalist and expansionist discourse of the state rather than outside it.

When Hiratsuka Raichō wrote that "in the beginning, Woman was the Sun," her point of reference was the Sun goddess Amaterasu, who was re-created in the state-led Shinto ideology in the Meiji era as the deity from whom the present emperor had descended. Thus the discourse of maternalist feminists such as Hiratsuka Raichō and Yamada Waka, who supported Hiratsuka's call for the state to protect motherhood during the motherhood protection debate in the 1910s, was not unrelated to the state discourse on women as essentially mothers who are the reproductive source of the nation's military and economic power. Takamure Itsue, known as an anarchist during one of the phases in her writing career, maintained her feminist position throughout her life. As Sonia Ryang shows, Takamure's essentialization and celebration of motherhood as a superior virtue and her positivistic stance on the matrilocal customs of Japanese matrimony led her to embrace Japan's imperialism.[39] As I show in chapter 4, the writings of Yosano Akiko, who is often defined as an individualist or liberal feminist, were quick to shift from resistance against to affinity with the state discourse on women as maternal and procreational bodies. The ideologies of Tamura Toshiko and Hayashi Fumiko— often discussed in recent scholarship as women writers who transcended the borders of the nation—also find affinity with the state discourse on race and ethnicity, as I examine in chapters 5 and 6. As my analysis of these three writers will show, not only were women's movements reinvigorated as a trope for nationalist and imperialist ends by the state, but some women actively sought to gain power within the dominant political system. They found extensions of their own freedom, strength, advancement, and status by identifying with the state agenda for the liberation, power, progress, and prestige of the Japanese empire. In this sense, the state-driven nationalism was the context—and the text—within and against which women in Japan engaged in individual and collective political actions to force into movement the idea of the empire and women as its body parts. Nationalism thus gave both possibilities and limits to Japanese women's movements against the authoritarian regime.

Migrants: Bodies in Motion

In analyzing the paradox of women's resistance to and conformity with the nationalist and expansionist agendas of the state in modern Japan, the concepts and practices of migrants, and of their bodies in motion, are particularly important. On the one hand, in prewar Japanese nationalism, consumed as it was by the political contest to expand the borders of empire, crossing national/imperial borders apparently gave female writers an alternative place. As I examine in detail in chapters 5 and 6, Noriko Mizuta and some other critics contend that both Tamura Toshiko and Hayashi Fumiko and their fictional characters aspired to move beyond the borders of family, gender, and the nation of Japan when they physically left for North America and French Indochina, respectively. Did crossing the border into the realm of "others" give writers and intellectuals new discursive tools to use in articulating their positions and constructing their subjectivities? When they were expected to subject themselves to the discursive forces that united the organic body of Japan, how did they position themselves and perform their roles as writers? As social and cultural critics, they faced the dilemma of simultaneously critiquing the empire's society and culture and carrying out the duties of the subjects of empire.

The idea of the "migrant" in Edward Said's *Representations of the Intellectual* presents points of departure for tackling this problem. Said states that the modern intellectual is by definition a "migrant in exile." In the sense that migrants in exile are disruptive minorities who question the majority and the norm, they reside at the periphery but move in and out of the central discourse. In the modern period, when the nation-state overwhelmingly exerts the central, dominant, and normalizing force in determining one's identity, the intellectual or artist can function as a migrant who disrupts the effectiveness of the nationalist discourse and liberates herself from it. Following this logic, I contend that migrants in exile, as the travelers or immigrants/emigrants in literature, enable author or reader to envision and reenact movements that make it possible to transcend the borders of the empire and liberate herself from nationalist and imperialist confines.

Said writes:

> Liberation as an intellectual mission . . . has now shifted from
> the settled, established, and domesticated dynamics of culture to
> its unhoused, decentered, and exilic energies, energies whose
> incarnation today is the migrant, and whose consciousness is that
> of the intellectual and artist in exile, the political figure between
> domains, between forms, between homes, and between
> languages.[40]

This concept of the migrant—whose consciousness is that of the artist in exile, or who embodies liberation as a political mission—is a dominant theme in the fiction of Yosano, Hayashi, and Tamura. The characters in their stories exert the exilic energies of migrants who free themselves from the purportedly settled and domesticated dynamics of culture established by the Japanese nation-state and attempt to empower themselves as the decentered and unhoused. Along with these three authors' and characters' movements in *naichi* and *gaichi,* their discourse seems to traverse the boundaries of national/imperial domains, literary forms, and languages.

As Japan expanded as an empire, some female writers, including Yosano, Tamura, and Hayashi, had the opportunity to travel and reside overseas. With their movement to foreign soil, the three writers and their characters negotiated with the state's discourse on women, and proceeded to describe (and epitomize) migrant bodies in their texts. Yosano traveled extensively in *naichi* and *gaichi* to Manchuria and Mongolia, as well as to France, Britain, Belgium, Germany, Australia, and Holland.[41] Tamura identified herself as a migrant in self-imposed exile, moving from Tokyo to Vancouver, Los Angeles, and Shanghai. Hayashi and her characters were vagabonds at the peripheries of empire. Hayashi's overseas travels extended to what are now called the Republic of Indonesia, the Socialist Republic of Viet Nam, the People's Republic of China, Taiwan, and the Republic of Korea, as well as the French Republic and the United Kingdom of Great Britain. These authors and their characters thus moved between homes and domains by transcending provincial and national limits.

They also moved between forms and languages. Yosano cultivates a wide range of genres, such as poems, short stories, children's stories, and essays. Tamura's discursive cultivation assumes form in the Japanese and Chinese languages. As Seiji M. Lippit points out, Hayashi's writings exemplify the theme of movement across "a fluid cultural and social landscape."[42] Moreover, their texts present "the possibility of freedom by prescribing a form of expression whose opacity, obscurity, and deviousness—the absence of 'the full transparency of its logical genesis'—move away from the dominant system, enacting in [their] 'inadequacy' a measure of liberation."[43] The female migrants in Yosano's, Tamura's, and Hayashi's writings also present a form of liberation by moving away from the dominant system of Japanese women as domesticated servants to the state. By acting inadequately as the subjects of the empire, they deviate from the logical movements that unite the organic body of Japan and enter a field that is opaque as the subject of empire.

The narratives of Yosano, Hayashi, and Tamura and their characters as migrants acquire even more meaning when we contemplate Said's definitions of exile, which in my study are encompassed by the various possible states of a migrant: "Exile is predicated on the existence of, love for, and a real bond with one's native place; the universal truth of exile is not that one has lost that love for home, but that inherent in each is an unexpected, unwelcome loss."[44] As the following chapters show, these three authors and their characters feel love for their native land. But they have experienced losses of relationship with their families and friends living on the nation's and empire's home soil. They and their characters have experienced the suffocation of living a domestic(ated) and fixated life, and have physically moved away from the spaces of confinement. Furthermore, Tamura's and Hayashi's status as wandering migrants made it impossible to capture the sweetness of home. Thus they lived and wrote about the transient nature of their relationship with their native land.

Yosano, Tamura, and Hayashi acted in modern Japan by becoming and describing female bodies in motion. On the premise that it is the body of the female migrant, as the surface of inscription and enactment, that constructs the subjectivity of authors and readers (discussed in the Intro-duction), I examine how these three writers' works of literature negoti-ated with the state-driven nationalist discourses on women in the empire of Japan. On the one hand, the migrants in these works move from what is considered to be the ideal, conventional, and domesticated to what is provisional and undomesticated, at the social margins. Thus they seem to pose the possibility of transgressing the discursive borders and body of empire. Migrant bodies in these works of literature violate the bound-aries imposed on women and deviate from the norms of a united, organic body of Japan. More specifically, the activity of these three female writers and their characters ideologically moves away from the central discourse of the state on gender, sexuality, and class in *naichi*.

However, even as (or because) the three authors and their characters physically distanced themselves from the Japanese homeland, their writ-ings on race and ethnicity strengthened the state discourse on the empire of Japan. In other words, the female migrant bodies of their characters act as integral parts of empire in modern Japan. In the end, the migrants and their bodies in motion in the discourses of Yosano, Tamura, and Hayashi did not transcend but, rather, redrew the imperial borders.

The earlier discussion in this chapter explored how some female in-tellectuals, activists, and artists in modern Japan both resisted and con-formed to the nationalist and expansionist endeavors of the nation-state. With its examination of the concept and practice of the migrant, this chap-ter has also prepared the reader to explore the paradox in the discourse of Yosano, Tamura, and Hayashi. As the following chapters show, it is specifically the concepts, depictions, and practices of (1) mobility, (2) bodies in motion, and (3) maternal and procreational bodies in their writ-ings that contain the contradiction of resistance to and affinity with the empire of Japan. The texts by these three writers question the relationship between (a) women's "personal" advancement, freedom, and strength, and (b) the political progress, emancipation, and empowerment of the empire. An analysis of the bodies in their works of literature will give us insight into both the discontinuities and the continuities in the discourse on the body of empire that expands and the bodies of women that move in modern Japan.

CHAPTER 4

Behind the Guns:
Yosano Akiko

B Y QUESTIONING THE CONCEPTS OF ORIGINALITY and independence that have often been associated with Yosano Akiko (1878–1942) and her texts, we can gain insight into the political paradox in her literary world that both disconnects and reconnects women with the Japanese empire. It is Yosano's metaphorical use both of the procreational female body and of mobility in her poems and prose that at once challenges the state-driven nationalist discourse on women in *naichi* (the inner territory of Japan) and celebrates war, reaffirming the expansion of the empire of Japan in *gaichi* (the outer territory). Yosano's writings explicitly enforce the discourse of aggression of the empire when she mobilizes the bodies of women as active agents that reproduce the Japanese empire and even the world itself, rather than as passive recipients of state stewardship and protection. Before offering my analysis of Yosano's discourse on the bodies of women and empire, I first explore how the meanings of her texts have usually been formulated.

Narratives on Yosano Akiko

According to Hasegawa Kei, coeditor of an anthology of modern Japanese women's literature, Yosano is among the three most important writers of modern Japanese women's literature, along with Higuchi Ichiyō and Hayashi Fumiko.[1] Watanabe Sumiko emphasizes Yosano's colossal capacity to produce and reproduce: "Yosano Akiko is an extraordinary woman. Her extraordinariness marks her as a first-class Japanese poet. . . . no one could have produced as many poems in one lifetime as Yosano."[2] Yosano's accomplishments include more than fifty thousand poems; modern translations of *Genji monogatari* (The tale of Genji), *Eiga monogatari* (A tale of flowering fortunes), *Murasaki shikibu nikki* (The Murasaki Shikibu diary),

Izumi shikibu nikki (The diary of Izumi), and *Tsurezure gusa* (Essays in idleness); biographies; novellas; children's literature; and essays and lectures—in addition to bearing thirteen children and raising the eleven that survived infancy.[3] Her massive body of work has engendered a substantial corpus of studies on her life and writings, as is evident in the holdings of the National Diet Library in Japan.

Despite the prestige and growing academic and popular attention given to Yosano, critical approaches to her life and work remain somewhat limited in scope. The great majority appear to cast Yosano as (1) a poet who reformed the Japanese tradition of poetry with her innovative use of language to freely express the truth and beauty of the modern self, (2) a rebel who challenged militarism and protected peace, and (3) an individualist or liberal feminist who fought for women's rights, liberation, and empowerment against state-driven nationalist ideas. Absent from these approaches is any view of Yosano as a political writer, especially with respect to her affinities with nationalism and empire. Pioneering contributions to the study of women and the empire include Steve Rabson's essay "Yosano Akiko on War," which correlates the changes in her writing with the chronology of her life and the history of modern Japan. Rabson dates her support of the empire to the trip she and her husband, Tekkan, took to Manchuria and Mongolia in 1928.[4]

The dominant approach is to view Yosano as a pioneer of modern Japanese poetry *(shi* verse and *shintai shi)* who freed the conventional style of Japanese poetry *(waka)* from rhythm and association. Her contribution to the reform in poetry was part of larger movements in the Meiji era (1868–1912) to modernize not only poetry but also novels, plays, and paintings. To discuss Yosano's poetry, which is understood to be distinctly modern, it is important to examine its relationship with romanticism. Romantic movements began in Western Europe in the 1750s, but made inroads in Japan from the late nineteenth century to the early twentieth century. Mori Ōgai, Shimazaki Tōson (especially his poetry), Higuchi Ichiyō, and Yosano Akiko are often included in reference to romantic movements in Japan. Unlike Enlightenment rationalism, romanticism finds the source of aesthetic experience in intuition and strong emotion—passion, love. It also emphasizes the strong individualist's achievements and seeks freedom from classical artistic forms. All these aspects of romanticism apply to Yosano's poems. *Midaregami* (Tangled hair, 1901), Yosano's first short book of *tanka* poetry, is understood to be a major contribution to the romantic movements in Japan. Aesthetic romanticism can also be seen in her autobiography, in which she wrote, "I was able, by summoning up an almost death-defying courage, to win the freedom to love and at the same time, to escape from the prison of the old-fashioned household in which my own individuality had been pent up for so long."[5]

The key words used by many critics in explaining Yosano's life and art are "expression of the self" and "freedom, beauty, and truth of the self." Janine Beichman's *Embracing the Firebird: Yosano Akiko and the Birth of the Female Voice in Modern Japanese Poetry* is a major contribution to the scholarship on Yosano up to the age of twenty-two, and on her poetry in the early part of her career. Beichman explains that Yosano's poetry is "the direct, transparent, unmediated expression of the inner life" and that "poetry writing for Akiko was a form of release through which she was able to express her own most intense feelings."[6] The poet and critic Matsudaira Meiko concurs, noting that *"Midaregami* is a collection of songs that epitomized and defined the release and exhibition of the self of a modern person."[7]

As the scholar Nakagawa Yatsuhiro sees it, "Pursuit of beauty and freedom was the core of Akiko's poetic tradition."[8] Hence the free and candid expression of female sexuality in *Tangled Hair* has also been understood as a means of revelation of the modern self.[9] From the free expression of the inner self, the truth comes forth. Yosano herself wrote: "I don't know how to write poetry other than to sing my true mind / heart with a true voice."[10]

These views have often discouraged examination of the politics in Yosano's poetry, especially her affinities for or opposition to the state discourse. For example, Nakagawa maintains that "Akiko's poetry sings passions of a certain time. We must not extract from her poetry political ideas at our own whimsy."[11] And in reference to Yosano's "Kimi shini tamōkoto nakare" (Brother, do not offer your life, 1904), discussed later, Noda Utarō feels that "Akiko is passionate but can never be called an anti-war thinker."[12] According to these critics, the free flow of emotions should never be equated with ideology or political thought.

Yosano's own statements about her works complemented, and perhaps influenced, contemporary interpretations of her writing as apolitical. When "Brother, Do Not Offer Your Life" was criticized as antiwar and antistate, Yosano and her defenders argued that the poem was personal and therefore apolitical. According to the poet Kennan, the poem expressed Yosano's wish for her brother's safe return from the battlefield, which hardly constituted "dangerous thoughts."[13] Yosano herself dismissed any political meaning by writing "are wa uta ni sōrō" (that is a poem).[14] Her poetry, she averred, had nothing to do with politics, especially war or nationalism. Moreover, it is her femininity that disconnects her poems from the politics of war: "As a woman, why should I sing a song like the present war song?"[15] Thus Yosano's self-representation has also served to dissuade readers from exploring the politics of her poems.

When critics do consider her politics, they often emphasize Yosano's resistance to the state, its militarism, and war. Her opposition to the status quo is reflected, so it is understood, in the poem "Brother, Do Not Offer Your Life." Contemporaneous male critics, including Ōmachi Keigetsu, called her *ranshin* (unpatriotic) and a *zokushi* (traitor) who should be punished as a criminal. Itō Nobuyoshi understood Yosano's "poem as in line with the antiwar rhetoric of Kōtoku Shūsui and others."[16] The poem proceeds as follows:

Dearest Brother,
I weep for you.
Do not offer your life.
Did your mother and father,
whose love for you, the last born,
surpassed all others,
teach you to wield the sword?
To kill?
Did they rear you these twenty-four years
saying,
"Kill and die"?

You,
who shall inherit the name of our father—
a master proud of his ancient name
in the commerce of this town of Sakai—
do not offer your life.
Whether Port Arthur falls or not
is no matter.

Do not offer your life.
The Emperor himself does not go

to battle.
The Imperial Heart is deep:
how could he ever wish
that men shed their blood,
that men die like beasts,
that man's glory be in death?

Dearest Brother,
do not offer your life
in battle.
Mother, whom Father left behind
this past autumn,
suffered when
in the midst of her grief
her son was called away.
Even under this imperial reign,
when it is heard
that the home is safe and secure,
Mother's hair has grown whiter. . . .[17]

In interpreting this poem, some contemporary critics have acknowledged
Yosano's resistance against the doctrine that demands subjects (soldiers)
to sacrifice their lives for the emperor as the central and paternal figure-
head of the family empire. A contemporary scholar, Vera Mackie, explains
that Yosano placed the individual family *above* the family empire to which
the Japanese owed their greatest allegiance during the Russo-Japanese
War.[18] Mackie therefore argues that Yosano's insistence on independence,
rather than passive support, marks resistance to state-driven nationalism
and militarism. Critics also point out that the poem denounces armed
conflict and challenges the state discourse on the sacredness and purity of
empire by defining soldiers' bloodshed and death as the way of "beasts."
Indeed, in continuation with this line of argument, Yosano condemned
militarism in Japan in 1918 as "barbarian thinking."[19] Moreover, she claimed
that militarism "is the responsibility of us women to eradicate."[20]

    With the focus on this poem, Yosano's many postwar critics have re-
imagined her stance against war as one that stressed peace. Steve Rabson
makes this point in his examination of the first biography of Yosano, written by Yūri Kaoru after World War II. Rabson points out Yūri's chapter

about "Do Not Offer Your Life," subtitled "A Heart That Loved Peace" ("Heiwa o ai suru kokoro"), in which Yūri writes: "With the new Japan embarking as a peaceful nation, we Japanese can be proud that in our past we had a woman who so loved peace and advocated it so courageously."[21] Yūri also contends that "the antiwar philosophy expressed in this poem and her hatred of military men and bureaucrats permeated her whole life."[22]

The idea that Yosano was a rebel who challenged militarism and protected peace throughout her life is based almost entirely on "Brother, Do Not Offer Your Life," which is the poem most often quoted in reference to her views on war. In exploring the relationship between Yosano's texts and the empire of Japan, it is important to cast a critical eye on this exclusive focus. My argument that Yosano was a contradictory participant in the nationalist discourses is, in contrast, based on numerous poems and essays, and also on her 1928 travelogue *Manmō yūki* (*Travels in Manchuria and Mongolia*). I demonstrate later in this chapter that these works implemented, sustained, and strengthened the colonial empire.

Mobility and Body

The examination and celebration of Yosano's originality, independence, and freedom are significant in themselves. However, they have also suppressed and silenced her other voices. By adding another angle to the notion of originality and freedom in her writing, I explore how her work in fact negotiated with the state discourse on the expanding empire. Based on the position that Yosano's discourse was enmeshed in prewar power relationships, I look at the paradox that her writing challenges the state-driven nationalism regarding women yet simultaneously celebrates war and reaffirms the expansion of the empire. This is nowhere more evident than in her depiction of mobility and female bodies.

In investigating the concept of mobility that Yosano uses in challenging the dominant discourse on women, it is important to pay attention to her essay "'Onnarashisa' to wa nanika" ("What Is 'Womanliness'?" 1921), which emphasizes flux and impermanence as the crucial concepts in promoting women's movements:

Buddhism taught the Japanese "the swift impermanence of this world" from early times, and we also learned very early the

Confucian teaching "Make yourself new from day to day."
However, these ideas were interpreted only through the
pessimistic lens (the view that this world is one of suffering) of
Hinayana Buddhism, and Japanese were unable to accept the
optimistic Mahayana Buddhism, in which the teaching "All
dharmas are in constant flux" is precisely what is constant about
human beings. In modern times, thanks to imported art and
scholarship, we've come into contact with the ideas of
unceasing changes and evolution, but we see people who are
inclined to curse modern life and who try to maintain moldy old
conventions and customs. These people only look backwards and
are reluctant to face up to contemporary reality; furthermore,
they are cowardly about considering the future. I think such
people are found both among the conservatives and among the
false progressives.

   What disgusts me is that these people frequently include in
their denunciations of "women's androgynization" attacks on the
movement for the liberation of women, which is one of the critical
women's concerns of modern times.[23]

By citing Buddhist, Confucian, and Western ideas and practices, Yosano
emphasizes the importance and inevitability of change. With her under-
scoring of the teleological movement of time, she promotes women's
progress and denounces the forces that work to keep them in a state of
stagnation. Yosano uses the ideas of change and evolution to mobilize
women's energies for renewal of their role and place in society, and for
activism as well.

   Her strong call for women's movements is also evident in her poem
"The Day the Mountains Move" (1911):

   The day the mountains move has come.
   I speak, but no one believes me.
   For a time the mountains have been asleep.
   But long ago they all danced with fire.
   It doesn't matter if you believe this,
   my friends, as long as you believe:
   All the sleeping women
   are now awake and moving.[24]

With the choice of mountains as a metaphor, this poem emphasizes the enormity of women's presence and the potential magnitude of women's movement. By invoking the explosive activity of volcanoes in the past, the "I" in the poem declares that women are in actuality awake and moving for a massive change. In this poem, the subject "I" speaks and represents herself as a woman, instead of being spoken and represented by the state discourse.

Yosano's writing also challenges the dominant state discourse on Japanese women through its concept of impermanence. In "What Is 'Womanliness'?," the locus of power and the authority of the state's definition of femininity are not essential, absolute, or eternal but, rather, historical:

Among human activities, are there biologically determined things men do or women do that therefore must be imposed on them? I cannot find a division of labor that should be imposed on human beings with finality because of the sexual difference between men and women. . . . Femininity, which is specific to women . . . does not exist in the end. . . . A certain kind of "femininity" discussed by some critics is regional and changes according to time. Therefore, femininity can never be the source of the state's authority to control our lives.[25]

Yosano's writing repudiates the sexually differentiated biological body as the determinant of femininity. It also points out the regionalism of "femininity" and questions the absolutist nation-state's derivation of authority from its definition of femininity. Denaturalizing the state's construction of women's roles and position leads Yosano to challenge both the connection between the state and women and the existence of "Japanese woman":

Conventional writings have been unable to accommodate wide views and compare [women in Japan with] women of the world. What they [male critics] consider to be the merits of Japanese women turn out to be the common characteristics of women in any country, and therefore neither characteristics nor merits of [Japanese women].[26]

In the sense that "Japanese femininity" is indeed based on the common characteristics found in women of any nationality, "Japan" does not define a woman. Yosano's writing creates a split between "Japan" and "woman," and thus fractures the identity of "Japanese woman."

In disconnecting women from the nation-state, Yosano's writing cuts the umbilical cord of the maternal body from the body of empire. Her writing urges women to achieve independence from the state discourse by rejecting the definition of women as mothers: "Let me be clear in first of all stating that 'femininity' should not be explained exclusively through motherhood."[27] In the print debate in the 1912 *Seitō* issues on the "New Woman," Yosano wrote against Hiratsuka Raichō's position on the desirability of state protection for the maternal body:

> I cannot agree with the demand of the European women's movements for the state's special economic protection of women during pregnancy and childbirth. I, who feel that it is slave morality for women to be dependent on men because of their procreational role, must refuse dependency on the state for the very same reason.[28]

In this context of the *bosei hogo ronsō* (motherhood protection debate), Yosano's writing addresses the problem of the relationship between the state and mothers: "The wise women of the future, who will forge themselves, will always be conscious of human independence and will never think of giving up their pride and looking to the government for help or the protection of motherhood."[29] This abhorrence of the state's protective policies regarding motherhood and belief in independence from the state earned Yosano the label of "individualist feminist." According to Yosano, it is not women's maternal bodies per se but women's dependence on men and the state's protection of women's procreational function that degrade women to the status of slaves.

Yosano also challenges the male-dominated discourse on women that advocates that they in essence degenerate into a state of submission and lethargy as convenient kitchen appliances or sexual toys for men's pleasure.[30] When attacking the objectification of women's bodies—and the education policies designed to produce the dichotomy of "good wives and wise mothers" versus whores—Yosano states forthrightly that "women are human beings just as men are":[31]

> When women have been liberated from the word "womanliness," they will have been awakened to their humanity and will no longer

be reproductive or cooking puppets. They will be humans and no longer dolls.[32]

By questioning state-defined gendered inequality, Yosano thus advocates humanist and universal values. According to Yosano, a woman becomes a human being by demanding and attaining what men already possess—namely, equal rights and freedom in education, occupation, distribution of property, and political decision making. Her aspirations for women in these fields earned her the label of "liberal feminist" (or "humanist," "bourgeois," or "women's suffragist" feminist, which are often used synonymously).[33] She was labeled a liberal or bourgeois feminist because she paid scant attention to the dominant economic system, which was congenial to the middle class and above.[34]

Thus we have seen that, in fact, Yosano's writing (1) questions the state-driven "nationalization" of women and asserts that Japan does not determine, or define, women; (2) cautions against the disproportionate glorification of motherhood, and against rendering the procreational functions of the female body dependent on the state's protective measures; and (3) urges women to liberate themselves from servitude to the state and empower themselves as independent human beings. In her writings, the body emerges as the strategic site where women can move from a condition of stagnation to one of progress, emancipation, and empowerment. It is, however, also the body in Yosano's texts—especially the female procreational body—that enforces the state discourse on the expansion of the empire. Thus, although Yosano uses the concept of mobility to *disconnect* the bodies of women from the state's definitions of them within the space of *naichi,* she also uses corporeality to *reconnect* women with the empire, as explored in the following section.

Paradox in Politics and Poetry

In *Embracing the Firebird,* Janine Beichman directs our attention to the multiple voices—and shifts from one voice to another—within even a single piece of Yosano's poetry.[35] My analysis of Yosano's poems and prose recognizes voices and positions that shift from disconnection to affinity with the nationalist discourse that supports the expansion of the empire. As already seen, Yosano is acknowledged as a pioneer who negotiated with the conventions of *waka* (Japanese poetry) and broke free of associations. Karatani Kōjin argues that *shintaishi* (new form poetry) has been freed from both association and rhythm.[36] Beichman, however, demonstrates that association is in fact the organizing principle of the poems in Yosano's *Tangled Hair*.[37] As for rhythm, Yosano herself wrote in "Uta no tsukuriyō" (How to compose poems):

> The rhythm of five and seven syllables corresponds with the circulation of the blood and with the breathing of us Japanese, and has over several thousand years. It constitutes the rhythm that has performed life since the time of our ancestors. That is why we can easily get accustomed to the rhythm and resonate with it. When our true feelings reach the point of burning, they dance out in language with the rhythm of poem.[38]

According to this statement, the unbroken lineage of blood and breathing since the time of ancient ancestors determines the unchanged rhythm of Japanese poems and lives on in the present. Yosano's description of this unbroken lineage of the blood of Japanese bodies resonates with the state discourse on the continued lineage and purity of the Japanese people.

Moreover, the "true" and passionate feelings inside the poet material-ize when they dance out with a rhythm that has been determined by the body of Japanese for "several thousand years." This is the flesh that creates the self whose passion dances out as the language of her poems. In "Jimon jitō" (Self-Reflection, 1904), Yosano wrote:

> Especially now, I can calmly
> look at myself clearly.
> What is "I"?
> Even though [I] don't answer,
> it is truly interesting that,
> even though it is mute,
> the flesh knows how to dance.[39]

In this poem, the flesh creates the self that moves with the rhythm. Through an intertextual analysis of this poem and the prose piece "How to Com-pose Poems," it becomes clear that the self/flesh in Yosano's poem dances to a rhythm that is determined by the unbroken lineage of Japanese bod-ies. This poem is also reminiscent of "The Day the Mountains Move," in which mountains that used to dance with fire have been sleeping but are "now awake and moving."[40] The blood, air, and fire that continue to circulate seem to formulate the body/flesh of the poet, women, and "we Japanese" in these poems and prose.

What bursts forth from the self is not only "passion" or sexual desire but productive and reproductive energy. The productive site of poems that create "the only truth" is found in woman's procreational body that endures the pain of labor. "The First Labor Pain" was written in 1905, at the end of the Russo-Japanese War:

> Giving birth is in reality
> the creation of the only truth
> that bursts out from inside me.
> There is no right or wrong.[41]

This poem affirms the female body as the site of reproduction of the truth. Furthermore, the female body is constructed as capable of engaging simultaneously in both creational and procreational activities. "I can work my best just before giving birth."[42] Yosano states that giving birth to children and works of literature assist each other.

"Tales of the Delivery Room" also elevates the value of giving birth to a supreme level: "There won't be anything superior to the great role women play in giving birth to human beings."[43] The potency of the procreational body proves women's strength and, furthermore, their superiority to men: "It is strange that among those men who debate women's issues, there are those who view women as being physically weak. What I want to ask these people is whether a man's body could bear childbirth."[44] With its assertion of the superiority of woman's procreational body, Yosano's writing challenges the state discourse claiming that women's bodies are weak and in need of protection (see chapter 2).

According to Yosano's statements, it is the strength of women's bodies that enhances their power to reproduce and produce and makes them superior to men. Thus she reverses the binary opposition between man/woman as the strong/weak and protector/protected. Furthermore, with her strong and superior body, woman is empowered to protect man rather than being protected by him. In response to the criticism that her enormous reproductive and productive activities amount to subjugation to her husband, Yosano claims that the distinction between subjugation and empowerment lies in choice: "I have always felt that I don't want to force [my husband] to work for his existence the way I work."[45] This statement emphasizes the agency of the female subject who chooses and acts to protect men.

Although Yosano is known as an individualist or liberal feminist who stands in opposition to a maternalist feminist, her texts share maternalist and radical feminist ideas by accepting the dichotomies of male versus female, by stressing the essential characteristics of the female, and by reversing the gender hierarchy by giving superior values to the female. Furthermore, in her writings "giving birth" refers to the (re)creation not only of children and art but also of nation and empire. Women's empowerment derives from their reproduction of the empire, as shown later here.

In Yosano's writing, women's empowerment is even more pronounced when it generates force for (instead of receiving protection from) the state and its expansionist agenda. For example, the poem "Sensō" (War, 1914) describes the female procreational body as follows:

> Now is the time to fight.
> Even I who dislike wars
> raise my spirit nowadays.
>
> The time has come for the spirit, flesh, and bone of the world
> to groan once and for all.
>
> The time for major labor pains has come.
> The time for the worries of birth has come.
> The world will even give birth to new life yet unknown
> by the baptism of rough bloodshed.
>
> What is it, if not the spirit
> that brings true peace to all humankind?
> Now is the time to fight by making any sacrifices.

At the outbreak of World War I in 1914, when the Japanese state was redoubling its efforts to participate in the battles of the Western imperial powers, Yosano's poem places value on fighting and making sacrifices to a great cause. In continuation with her other poems and essays already cited, words such as "flesh," "blood," "labor pains," "giving birth," and "truth" play an important role in creating the self, poems, and the world.

What is notable in this poem is the grandiosity of the nation-state's war effort, in its ability to give birth to peace as a new life, and as the truth of humankind and the world. To create this meaning, the poem constructs the world as the battlefield of World War I, and furthermore identifies the world as the body, which encompasses "the spirit, flesh, and bone." Moreover, the body of the world as the site of military power struggles is equated with the female, procreational body. It is precisely the female body as the world that sheds blood in pain to give birth to a new life—that is, peace to the world.

If the world is the female body and the battleground, those who are shedding blood are the soldiers who die for the great causes of the state's war efforts. In this sense, the female body is neither the one that needs protection from the state nor the one that supports the state's war efforts but the site of the battleground of imperial powers and the agent that encompasses soldiers, uses them as women's body parts, and brings about peace to the world. Thus Yosano's writing celebrates the female reproductive body when it attains agency that becomes the major force of the war effort of the Japanese empire encompassing *gaichi*, instead of being relegated to a state of passivity and weakness that must be protected in *naichi*. Yosano's writing on the reproductive capacity of female body reconnects woman with the Japanese empire on the world stage.

Yosano's description of the female body as the site of reproduction of the empire on the scale of the world foreshadows the text *Kokutai no hongi* (The essence of national polity) issued by the Ministry of Education in 1937:

> Force of arms bears harmony at its root, it breeds discord, but this promises generation and development, and gives life to things through conflicts. In this sense, war is not intended to destroy, oppress, and conquer others, but to create by following the way and to realize Yamato, that is peace.[46]

According to *Kokutai no hongi*, war efforts engender peace for the world. The ideology of the war effort of the Japanese empire as a means to bring peace to the world and to reach a higher level of universalism in 1937 was already present in Yosano's 1914 poem, "War."

In "Hirakibumi" (Open letter), Yosano dismisses the state's definition of women's ability to bear children as the determinant of femininity. However, Yosano's "War" celebrates the agency of women's procreational body that determines humanity and the world. The elevation of femininity to humanity is also evident when she writes, "It is clear that femininity is human nature itself and is consistent with the whole human being and not specific to woman."[47] In her equation of femininity with humanity, humanity is defined by femininity rather than masculinity. Furthermore, Yosano reaffirms Japanese women as the bodies that bear children when they become the source of reproduction of the empire and gain importance on the human, world, and even the universal scale.

The connection between Yosano's nationalism that supports the expansion of the empire on the premise of the ability of the female body to formulate humanity and the world may also find its source in the romanticism of her writing. Her romantic vision of the vitality of body is evident in the poem "The Universe and I" ("Uchū to watashi," 1923).

> The universe is born out of me
> I who exist within the universe
> for some reason
> am distant from the universe.
> I am lonely even when I am with you.
>
> And
>
> But, again, from time to time
> I return to the universe
>
> I do not know whether I am the universe
> Or the universe is me.
> At certain times, my heart is the heart of the universe;
> At certain times, my eyes are the eyes of the universe.[48]

In this poem, the universe and the self are indistinguishable. The universe is the source of the birth of the self. The self is the source of the universe. Yosano's text not only depicts the body on the level of the world but also elevates it to the level of the universe.

Yosano's re-creation of the body in the scale of the universe, and also of women's bodies on the world stage, is evident in the poems examined above. Her writing further claims that Japanese women's bodies are world class because of their fertility. In 1917, three years after the outbreak of

World War I and the publication of "War," Yosano claims, "The core characteristic of Japanese women, a source of pride for the world, lies in the high birth rate despite their weak bodies."[49] As explored earlier, Yosano's "Open Letter" dismisses the glorification of women as mothers as well as the connection between Japan and women. However, Yosano reconnects Japan and women when the female reproductive body attains agency through war and the empire engages in a power struggle on the world stage. Hence Yosano exhorts Japanese women to use their fertile bodies to bear more children for the empire. Within the context of the expanding body of Japan and the institutionalized social imperialism of the prefectures and government (chapter 2), Yosano also states that overpopulation inside Japan will cause no problem as long as some people leave the country: "It is good as long as we can find places for children to emigrate."[50] It is important to her that the high birth rate among Japanese women proves their strength and supports the reproduction of the empire.

In Yosano's discourse on the world of the battlefield as a female body in labor giving birth to peace, the blood that emerges is that of soldiers dying. The celebration of the "sacrifices" of soldiers and of the women behind the guns (*jūgo*) becomes clearer in her poem "Citizens of Japan, a Morning Song" ("Nihon kokumin asa no uta"), written in 1932, a year after the Japanese colonization of Manchuria in 1931:

Ah, the augustness of His Majesty's Reign
That inspires people's hearts!
It is a time that ignites our sense of duty.

It is a time to cease empty arguments,
And smash sissified dreams of compromise.
Knowing their course to be just,
Our forces attack through sufferings a hundredfold.

Though his is the body of one soldier,
Carrying the canister of destruction,
He dances through the barbed wire,
And transforms that body into powder.

Though his is the body of one major,
He expects no mercy from the enemy,

And scatters that body, purer than a flower,
Giving life to a samurai's honor.

And these men are not alone.
Patriotic heroes with hearts like theirs
Rise to the challenge whenever the Emperor's forces go,
To the north and to the south.

And they are but one example.
For we, too, the people behind the guns,
Redouble our own courage many times over
And rally everyone to the cause.

Blood also courses in the eager hearts
Of our countrymen who are not soldiers.
They dedicate their lives day by day
To serve on the nation's behalf

An example is this poem of mine
That springs from the devotion of those men
Who, grasping the canisters of destruction,
Ran to hurl themselves through barbed wire,

Even I, a powerless woman,
Am thus committed to our cause,
As are those people, superior among us,
Who carry out the esteemed ways of our peerless ancestors.

Ah, the augustness of His Majesty's Reign
That inspires people's hearts!
It is a time that ignites our sense of duty,
A time to unify in loyalty.[51]

"Citizens of Japan, a Morning Song" urges Japanese women to rally to the cause behind the guns. Nonwarriors become one with the warriors in their patriotism and willingness to sacrifice their bodies for the empire. Thus Yosano's writing validates war, bloodshed, and the dismemberment of bodies for the sake of empire. With this validation, Yosano embraces and further reinforces the state-driven nationalism that helps mobilize the bodies of people/subjects to fight and die for Japan.

Her celebration of soldiers' martyrdom is also evident in her *tanka* on the Pacific War in the early 1940s:

> Raised with the teachings
> of 3,000 years of the gods—
> the mighty people
> of the Eight Great Islands
> in the east.[52]

Employing the discourse of the imperial line, sacred and unbroken for "3,000 years," Yosano's poem exhorts the strong army of Japan to fight in battle.

In another war poem, "Daitōa sensō kashū Tenri Jihōsha" (Poetry of the Greater East Asia War), published in 1943, the year after her death, Yosano re-creates the subject as an ailing mother at home who wishes for the safety of her son on a battleship in *gaichi:*

> Though I await news
> from the battleship
> with my son aboard,
> it does not come.
> Ah, may the fortunes of war
> be with him!
> My son's ship
> crossed the Black Current and
> the battle has lasted for days.
> "Is there still no outcome?"
> his sick mother asks.[53]

As the life of the "I" withers, it is the son as a soldier and his state of being that helps re-create the self as a mother in Yosano's poem.

As we have seen, Yosano has often been celebrated as a modern poet who reformed the poetic tradition with her expression of freedom, who challenged the state's war efforts, and who repudiated the maternalist feminists' support of the state protection of motherhood. The change in her writing from resistance to support of the state discourse on war and empire has been understood to take place in the 1930s and 1940s, as Japan engaged in all-out war. My assessment, however, argues that Yosano's expansionist stance on the empire derived from her paradoxical discourse on the potency of the female body and mobility. When it is a question of women in *naichi,* Yosano's writing urges them to refuse the subjugation that state protection brings and to move away from the central discourse of the state. But when her writing concerns the war efforts of the empire that expand its territories in *gaichi* in contest with Western imperial powers, the female procreational body is re-created as a site that attains agency to reproduce the empire. As a result, her discourse moves toward the focus of the state discourse and a procreational faculty that reconnects the bodies of women, Japan, and the world on the universal scale. The poems and prose examined in this chapter, and my assessment of them, may not be the determinant of Yosano's stance on nationalism and empire. However, my analysis here at least reveals aspects of her writing that explain the relationship between women's bodies and mobility and the expansion of the Japanese empire.

Migrant in Manchuria and Mongolia

In further examining Yosano's re-creation of the empire of Japan, I here turn to her depictions of the bodies and spaces in *gaichi* (the outer territory) in her travelogue *Manmō yūki* (*Travels in Manchuria and Mongolia,* 1928), which has been translated into English by Joshua Fogel. The following discussion concerns how Yosano moved through Manchuria and Mongolia in 1928, and how her discourse in and about *gaichi* re-created the relationship between the Japanese empire and its peripheries.

At the historical juncture when Yosano traveled, Manchuria had become an increasingly dangerous site of imperial and territorial conflicts among the Western and Japanese empires, the space of multinational and multiethnic groups, and the discursive field of contest and construct among the Japanese and Western imperial powers. Although it was not official until 1931, the Japanese empire had achieved "informal" or de facto colonization of Manchuria by the time of Yosano's trip there.[54] Yosano Akiko and her husband Yosano Tekkan traveled to Manchuria and Mongolia from May to June 1928; they spent forty days sightseeing along the line of the Japanese-owned South Manchuria Railway Company (SMRC), in places such as Autung, Harbin, Liaotung, and Port Arthur.

During the trip, they found themselves among the tourists and "continental drifters" *(tairiku rōnin)* who made up most Japanese residents in Manchuria before 1931. In *Travels in Manchuria and Mongolia,* Yosano re-creates imperial agents who entertain themselves in the landscapes, lifestyles, and spectacles of the Japanese empire and who celebrate the power of the state that dominates ordinary Chinese people. Her writing simultaneously constructs and consumes the hybridity of the extended parts of the empire and re-creates the dichotomy between Japan and China, both of which contribute to the discourse of aggression against the Chinese. Yosano participated in the discursive field that re-creates the empire of Japan; spaces, bodies, experiences, and sentiments described in her writing are connected to the history of expansion and dominance of the Japanese empire.

Travels in Manchuria and Mongolia was also a response to the readership in Japan that entertained images of Manchuria through the literary and visual media. Reports and advertisements contributed to the initial Japanese group tours to Manchuria in 1906; Manchuria as a travel destination became enormously popular after 1931. In today's context, Yosano's travelogue may belong to "the memory industry," a topic Mariko Asano Tamanoi studies in her *Memory Maps: The State and Manchuria in Postwar Japan.* Tamanoi's focus is on sets of images that have been passed down to readers "through the media of memory—through paintings, architecture, monuments, ritual, storytelling, poetry, music, photos, and film,"[55] and that function as "the memory industry, which has replaced the Japanese state" and "has been playing the major role in assisting the Japanese people to forget the power of their own state."[56] The analysis of Yosano's travelogue that follows examines how her writing on Manchuria asserts the power of the Japanese state that dominates ordinary people in a place in which she stands and that she attempts to re-create.

By 1928, about 240,000 Japanese had moved to the cities in southern Manchuria, the region opened by the SMRC. They had done so in response to the Japanese state's encouraging emigration to Manchuria and Korea as a result of the worsening relationship between Japan and the United States over Japanese immigration to California. Tamanoi explains: "Except for Japanese state employees, including soldiers, most Japanese residents in Manchuria before 1931 were so-called 'continental drifters' *(tairiku rōnin),* not settlers in the strict sense of the term."[57]

Hybridity of population in Manchuria and the ideology of harmonious coexistence are well documented in Tamanoi's recent study. Manchuria in the age of empire was the land of diverse populations—multinational, multiethnic, and multiracial groups.[58] The census according to Dai Harubin Annaisha included thirty groups—among them Japanese, Taiwanese, Korean, Chinese, Soviet, Russian, American, British, French, German, Italian, Polish, Jewish, Greek, Dutch, Turkish, Austrian, Hungarian, Danish, Latvian, Portuguese, Czech, Armenian, Belgian, Serb, Swedish, Romanian, Swiss, and Indian.[59] The concept of multinational and multiethnic Manchuria as an extension of Japan is evident in the Japanese government's keeping track of the number of its subject-citizens who settled in Manchuria precisely because it was considered a part of Japan proper.[60]

In this melting pot of imperial powers, the official slogan of the Manchukuo state claimed by the Japanese government was "ethnic harmony" (*minzoku kyōwa*). The declaration of independence of Manchukuo states:

> The will of 30 million people declares the establishment of
> Manchukuo and its separation from China. . . . There should be
> no differences among all the people who reside within this new
> land. In addition to the Han, Manchu, Mongol, Japanese, and
> Korean people who have already lived here, people of any other
> nationality will be treated equally, as long as they wish to live
> permanently in Manchukuo.[61]

Behind the idea of Manchukuo as a racial and ethnic melting pot was the Manchurian Youth League (Manshū Seinen Renmei), which was formed in 1928, the year Yosano traveled to Manchuria. According to the league, "Japan and China" (Nik-Ka) coexist as equals in harmony, and develop culture and the economy of China together. At the same time, however, the league emphasized the importance of the Japanese as a superior race in leading and enlightening other ethnic groups (*minzoku shidō*).[62]

The ideas of multiethnic and multiracial Manchuria, the harmonious coexistence of nations, and the heightened beauty of nature and growth of the economy of China under the leadership of the Japanese empire all found ways into Yosano's discourse on Manchuria. The ideals and ideologies of hybridity, coexistence, and harmony in her writing broke down, however, as tension between the Japanese and Western imperial powers and Chinese resistance to Japan quickly led to the creation of a strict dichotomy between superior Japan and inferior China.

By the time Yosano traveled to Manchuria in 1928, most Japanese women had withdrawn from the area. Yosano was aware of the tension and the physical danger of being there: "As a precaution against every eventuality, though, all Japanese women residents there had been evacuated, and only the male personnel from the South Manchuria Railway office remained."[63] She reflects on the rarity of her presence and movement in the occupied area of the Japanese empire.

From the onset of the trip, Yosano remarks on the space where she finds herself: "The grounds form the shape of a rocky human belly, divided into left and right" (35). The "human belly" is the site at which Yosano stands before stepping into the interior of Mongolia and Manchuria. "As I stared out at this desolate and lonely world of sand, I felt as though I was taking my first step into the interior of Mongolia" (61). Her use of the metaphor of a belly *(hara)* to connect a nation under Japanese military control and a human body part is important in interpreting the relationship between Japan and its periphery in Yosano's writing.

It is the engineering of the SMRC that penetrates the inner depths of nature and enables Japanese to travel to Manchuria. Manchuria allows the penetration of the Japanese engineering and, even more, embraces it:

> We were told that, scattered in the ravines of the mountains, were
> a number of ancient temples and Buddhist and Daoist houses of
> prayer, that there were as well the remains of cities dating to the
> Koguryo period, and that the area was rich in scenery as the
> mountains hugged the rail line. (48)

Using the technology of the South Manchuria Railway Company, Yosano travels into the depths of Chinese nature, which welcomes Japanese engineering. "Beautiful scenery" that encompasses the ancient Chinese culture gently and quietly embraces Japanese "advancement" and development, according to Yosano's texts (29).

Despite (or perhaps because of) the heightened tension, Yosano attempts to Japanize Manchuria and re-create it as calm and gentle. As she travels from Mongolia to Manchuria, their body and nature in her writing morph into a Japanese garden, an extension of the Japanese empire:

> Nearby were paddy fields maintained, oddly enough, by the
> hot springs hotel, with frogs croaking and a thicket of trees
> reflected on the surface—the whole scene had a Japanese flavor
> to it. (54)

The "paddy fields" were indeed maintained by Chinese and Korean farmers, who were asked to increase the quota of various crops to be delivered to Japanese authorities.[64] Yosano's writing anesthetizes this power relationship between the Japanese empire and the people under its control, making it look natural and peaceful.

The nature of Manchuria is grandiose, but it appears to be quiet and gentle, a reflection of the fact that it can be tamed for economic development by the military conquest and geopolitical expansion of Japan. "I imagined," Yosano writes, "that in the future, northern Manchuria would probably become enormously valuable economically. At nightfall the moon appeared, and the view from our window grew even more spectacularly gentle."[65] Nature in China is overpowering to Yosano, but nonetheless tamable by Japanese engineering. The contrast between the nature/body of China and the advanced technology of Japan is evident in her writings.

The unofficial colony of the Japanese empire "under the control of the South Manchuria Railway Company" (41) thus enables the Japanese, including Yosano, to enjoy

> a landscape replete with majestic rock caves and overpowering
> beauty. The hot springs was discovered by chance by a
> company commander in the communications division who was
> stationed here at the time of the Sino-Japanese War. It is now
> indirectly managed by the South Manchuria Railway Company,
> and the bathing guests are primarily Japanese from Andong, as
> it has become a site frequented by Japanese traveling the
> An-Feng rail line. . . . We love hot springs and were wearing
> ourselves out traveling around to all the hot springs of
> Manchuria. (54)

By immersing herself in the "belly" of the empire, Yosano consumes the nature and culture of the Japanese empire in *gaichi*. At the intersection of Japan, China, Korea, Russia, and other nations, the technology of the SMRC enables diverse bodies to interact with one another:

Because it was so convenient to travel along the trunk line of the
railway, the Japanese living in Manchuria frequently came from
north and south to enjoy the baths here. It was particularly
bustling in the early summer when Russian and Chinese bathers
stopped in as well. (23)

By bathing their bodies among peoples of other nations and consuming
their food, the Japanese travelers, including Yosano, rejoice at the multiethnic empire of Japan in *gaichi:* "We had a taste of the Chinese-style
beauty of willow trees and water" (103). "The few dishes of Russian food
we ordered for dinner were thoroughly satisfying. The beer that the men
were drinking was German" (89).

Yosano's discourse on the harmonious coexistence of various nations
must be situated within the Manchukuo state's official slogan of "ethnic
harmony" among the diverse populations. During her journey, Yosano
re-creates the multiethnic body of a Japanese empire that consumes the
beauty of the land of Manchuria and Mongolia, classical Chinese art and
literature, and the cosmopolitanism of the area invaded by the Japanese
imperial enterprise.

As much as she makes reference to the nature and culture of Manchuria, Yosano is aware of the site as an economic and political construction and contest among the nations:

It is divided into the northeast, known as the old city—namely,
the Chinese city—and the southwest, known as the new city—the
Japanese city. The Chinese city began to thrive significantly after
the Russo-Japanese War. . . . The Japanese city survived the Russo-
Japanese War intact and was rebuilt because it served as a link
between the Korean and Manchurian railways. On the opposite
shore lies Korea, a large railroad bridge linking the Korean city of
Sinuiju with Andong. (50–51)

According to this statement, the Japanese victory in the Russo-Japanese
War (1905) contributed to the economic growth of China and the link
between Manchuria and Korea. At the heart of the thriving economy is
the Japanese empire. She further declares: "Politically, economically, and
ethnically this international city had to be the center of the Manchurian
and Mongolian enterprise, especially for Japanese" (100).

Although she appreciates moving through multiethnic Manchuria and immersing her body in its nature and culture, Yosano is aware of the potential physical danger caused by the Chinese resistance: "We learned from Mr. Nishimura that the local anti-Japanese climate had in fact grown tense to the point of danger" (66). In the eyes of the Chinese, Yosano was part of the imperial power because of her physical presence. Yosano comes to know that she is identified by the Chinese as the "lady warlord" (86) of imperial Japan: "A corps of troops suddenly saluted us under their officer's orders" (86). And it is her Western clothes that particularly alarm the Chinese:

> While we were waiting, a crowd of people gathered around us. Their eyes were fastened particularly on me, with the Western clothes I was wearing, and because I associated this with anti-Japanese stories that had circulated since the Jinan incident, I had a bit of an ominous sense. (17)

Jennifer Robertson defines the Japanese empire as an "anti-colonial colonizer"[66] that resisted the Western imperial encroachment on Asia and yet became an imperial power dominating neighboring nations; the Western clothes that wrap Yosano as the "lady warlord" thus appeared in the eyes of the Chinese to signify one of the imperial powers that invaded and dominated Manchuria.

The reader can see the shift from celebration of harmonious coexistence of multiethnic and multicultural nations in Manchuria to condemnation of Chinese resistance to Japanese control in Yosano's writing. Tamanoi explains:

> The ideology of the harmonious coexistence of Japan and China rose in response to a rising Chinese nationalism contesting Japanese and Western imperialism. Here we should not ignore the political environment in which the association [the Manchurian Youth League] was formed—a rising Chinese nationalism opposing Japanese and Western imperialism.[67]

In facing Chinese nationalism and overwhelming resistance against the Japanese endeavors, Yosano's gaze on the Chinese warlords hardly cloaks her animosity toward them: "When I consider the Sino-Japanese issue from the perspective of a Japanese . . . these despicable bloodcurdling faces press in before my eyes"(56). "As for men like Zhang Huanxiang, the little spoiled brat of the Chinese warlords, their bald-faced, illegal, anti-foreign actions" (95) resist the endeavors of the Japanese empire. In her writing, Chinese nationalist efforts are "despicable" and "illegal." Yosano's depiction of the Chinese stands in contrast to the benevolent and "sagacious" acts of the Japanese:

> Who knows the extent of the good fortune he [a Japanese officer of the South Manchurian Railway Company] has contributed in over twenty years to the relations between Japan and Manchuria-Mongolia? In the back of my mind, I was happy to see the sagacious manner in which the South Manchuria Railway Company assigned the right man to the right place. (46)

While the SMRC opens a path to Japanese and Manchurian coexistence and co-prosperity, Chinese warlords, according to Yosano's discourse, put up an illegal and antiforeign resistance. Yosano's writing celebrates the Chinese only when they embrace Japanese "advancement." By defining Chinese resistance as unwise and unlawful, Yosano displaces Japanese aggression and atrocities.

Led by wise leaders, "good" Japanese soldiers offer up their bodies for the advancement of the empire. In contrast, the bodies of Chinese soldiers, misled by the "foolish" Chinese leaders, die like beasts, according to Yosano in her poem "Kōgan no shi" ("Rosy-Cheeked Death," 1932):

> To the west of the river
> we see something in the trenches.
> Approaching, we find enemy corpses—
> enemy corpses, lying one upon another.
>
> The saddest among them
> are the 200 student soldiers.
> Youthful at 17 or 18,
> None have faces over 20.
>
> How could their gentle mothers
> bear to see this?

Some even have pretty fiancées,
chosen for them in the old Chinese custom.
. . .
Who prayed for the peace of their nation.

Who is it that deceives them,
with their youthful naïve hearts,
teaching them to hate
their good neighbor, Japan?

Who is it that entices them
to turn in their pens for swords,
and scatters their young lives to the winds
before the plum flowers bloom in spring?

It is the foolish Ts'ai T'ing-k'ai,
commander of the 19th Route Army.
He does not know that, before the day is out,
his regiments must fall.

To the west of the river
we see something in the trenches;
200 rosy-cheeked youths
lie mired in blood and dirt.[68]

According to this poem, it is the Chinese leaders' folly and deception, rather than Japanese aggression, invasion, and atrocities, that have led Chinese soldiers to resist and end up as corpses mired in blood and mud. Before the morally and intellectually superior leaders of the Japanese army, the Chinese regiments must inevitably "fall" in Yosano's poem. And in her *Travels in Manchuria and Mongolia,* celebration of hybridity of the Japanese empire quickly changes into re-creation of the dichotomies of Japan/China as new/old, wise/silly, sagacious/deceptive, and superior/inferior.

Conclusion

Yosano's poems and prose both question the state's nationalist definition of its subjects and participate in the expansionist discourse of the modern

Japanese empire. Central to the paradoxical politics of resistance against and support for the empire is Yosano's description of bodies that give birth to, occupy, and move through the spaces of empire of Japan. In her writings examined here, Yosano's romantic vision of the individualist achievements and passion proves to be not so much personal as political. Furthermore, the universal values of humanity and the world in her writing were determined by particularism of the female body and Japanese nationalism. The discourse on hybridity of the Japanese empire encompassed the dualism of Japan as the superior self and China as the inferior "other," thus justifying Japanese imperial endeavors.

As examined earlier, Yosano's poems and essays call for women's independence and refuse to accept the state's protection of female bodies, deeming it a sign of enslavement. However, when her writing constructs the world as the procreational body through which Japan participates in the conflicts of imperial powers, Japanese female bodies become a powerful source that can give birth to new soldiers for the militarist expansion of Japan. Yosano thus re-inscribes and redefines the faculty of reproductive/productive women's bodies as the source of empowerment for both women and the empire.

Universalism in Yosano's writings was connected with the particularism of the nationalism of modern Japan. Her writing celebrates humanity and the world, but it is the particularity of the female procreational body that is the determinant of these universal values. Yosano reaffirms the potency of fecund bodies when she confers a human and universal quality on them, and also agency for the imperial expansion that contributes to world peace. Thus Yosano's aspirations for woman's freedom, movement, and empowerment were not unrelated to the power of the empire of Japan.

Moreover, Yosano's celebration of the poet's ability to give birth to the truth and to describe the beauty of space enforces the state discourse that operates as a political tool to create and expand the empire. In the extended part of the Japanese empire, Yosano's *Travels in Manchuria and Mongolia* re-creates China as "beautiful," if only insofar as its nature and culture embrace the Japanese imperial enterprise (since Chinese soldiers become entrenched in mud and blood when they resist the conscientious and wise leadership of the Japanese). Although her discourse celebrates hybridity and diversity of nations and cultures, it quickly changes into the re-creation of intellectually and morally superior Japanese in contrast to inferior Chinese when the Chinese resist the Japanese attempt at "co-prosperity." By serving and strengthening the discourse of hierarchy that justifies Japan's colonization of Manchuria, her writing actively reproduces the empire. Thus Yosano's poems, essays, and travelogue examined here clearly participate in the discourse of Japanese aggression.

By the time Yosano Akiko moved through Manchuria in the late 1920s, Tamura Toshiko, the focus of the next chapter, had left Japan and moved to North America. Just as Yosano's writing re-created the female body in the spaces of Japan, its occupied territories, and "the world," so Tamura's writings on the world (i.e., the United States and Europe) re-created the Japanese empire and its relationship with the Western imperial powers from the late 1910s until the late 1930s. The crossroads between Manchuria, which Yosano moved through, and North America, to which Tamura migrated, are found in the fact that, as already mentioned, "the Japanese state encouraged its people to emigrate to Manchuria and Korea, partly in response to the worsening relationship between Japan and the United States over the Japanese emigration to California."[69] Tamura's writings on migrants who move between the two empires of Japan and the United States are part of the analysis in the next chapter.

· CHAPTER 5 ·

Self-Imposed Exile:
Tamura Toshiko

Tamura Toshiko (1884–1945) and her texts written in Japan, North America, and China invoke the imagination of a female migrant in self-exile whose body moves in the historical context of the body of the Japanese empire. Tamura lived in Tokyo from 1908 to 1918, in Vancouver from 1918 to 1935, in Los Angeles from 1935 to 1936, in Tokyo from 1936 to 1938, and in Shanghai from 1938 to 1945. As she migrated from place to place, so did her characters' bodies. These movements both parallel the expansion of the Japanese empire and demarcate women's shifting relationships with different phases of the empire. As Japan expanded its borders, which collided with the empires of Britain and the United States, Tamura inscribed the female migrant bodies as parts of the body of the Japanese empire. This chapter explores the discursive forces of the empire present in Tamura's descriptions of women's transnational bodies that move both between homes and between the empires.

Tamura chose the life of a wanderer in self-imposed exile. Her decision is striking, given that she made it at a time when the nation-state was creating a family empire that demanded that a woman marry, bear and rear children, and depend on father, husband, and the state for her financial security and social standing. Instead of being domesticated in the household and within the homeland of Japan, Tamura led an unconventional, nomadic life. She was separated from her father at an early age; did not register her marriage to Tamura Shōgyo in 1909; chose not to have children; began living with a married man, Suzuki Etsu, in 1916; and broke ties with her parents and relatives.[1] She spent eighteen years in North America and almost seven in China. She described herself as "an impoverished wanderer" in March 1936, during her two-year stay in Japan between North America and China:[2]

· 81 ·

A sorrow surges up that resembles the feeling experienced while
on a trip. A vague sorrow that occurs on trips when I don't know
where I am. I am no longer traveling, and yet somehow I feel like
I still am. . . . I will leave here again sometime. . . . It's the kind of
sorrow when you are on the verge of drifting far away.[3]

With no sense of a firm ground in space, Tamura found herself ever in
motion. In December 1938, after two years and ten months in Tokyo,
Tamura left for China as a correspondent for the news organization Chūō
Kōronsha. Although her initial intention was to work there for a month or
two, she founded a forum for writing in Shanghai, published the journal
Josei (Women's voice), and never returned to Japan. She died in Shanghai
in 1945.

Stories about Tamura Toshiko

To set the stage for the analysis later in this chapter, I first explore the texts
and contexts that have heretofore determined the meanings of Tamura's
life and writing. Tamura established her place in the field of modern Japanese literature in Tokyo in the late 1900s. After the premature death of
Higuchi Ichiyō, who died of tuberculosis after a year of trying to make a
living as a professional writer,[4] Tamura rose to stardom as the first successful, professional female Japanese novelist and journalist. She was also one
of the first generation of Japan's literary feminists. According to Hasegawa
Kei, Tamura's achievement in the genre of fiction is equal in importance
to Yosano's accomplishment in *tanka*.[5]

Most scholarship to date has focused on Tamura's writings in Tokyo,
despite her living outside Japan for almost twenty-five years. Scholastic perceptions of her life and texts in the 1910s cast her as (1) a "woman writer"
who was able to express the truth of the ontological, essential woman,
(2) a New Woman who ultimately failed, and (3) a person who showed a
"loss of artistic talent" after her departure for North America in 1918.
Recent scholarship has given her a resurrected importance as a critic of the
Japanese government's imperialism. In 2005, *The U.S.–Japan Women's
Journal* and *Kokubungaku kaishaku to kenkyū* published special issues
on Tamura's writings after 1918, broadening the scope of scholarship and
exploring complex allegiances and themes of her work in the shifting international context.[6] Earlier approaches had mostly seen Tamura as someone

who resisted and went beyond the dominant discourse of the nation-state on women, family, and family empire. I explore the contributions of these approaches here, before offering my contrasting analysis of Tamura's description of the female body in relation to the body of the empire.

Female Bodies in Tokyo in the 1910s

Tamura's literary career is sometimes said to have coincided with the rise and fall of the print debate in the journal *Seitō* (Bluestocking, 1911–16). Even before her contributions to *Seitō*, however, Tamura led a life of vibrant literary activity. She began as a disciple of Kōda Rohan, a leading romantic novelist of the Meiji literature. Tamura wrote the novel *Tsuyuwake goromo* (The robe to share tears with, 1903) before she received recognition for *Akirama* (Resignation, 1911), which won the Osaka Asahi Shinbun literary prize. With *Miira no kuchibeni* (Lip rouge on a mummy, 1913) and *Onna sakusha* (Woman writer, 1913), Tamura became a bestselling author, and she contributed many pieces to such mainstream literary journals as *Chūō kōron* and *Shinchō*.

The emergence of *Seitō*, led by Hiratsuka Raichō, gave Tamura a new venue for her work and situated her among other women defined as New Women. Tamura associated herself with the journal by becoming a supporting member and also by publishing her novella *Ikichi* (Lifeblood) in its first issue in September 1911. When the newspaper *Yomiuri shinbun* serialized a section called "New Woman" from May 5 to June 13, 1912, Tamura was chosen as the second of the twenty-six "New Women" it profiled, eleven of whom were associated with *Seitō*. Tamura's writings in the 1910s emerged in accord with the following remark by Hiratsuka:

> The New Woman does not find fulfillment in the life of a woman who is made ignorant, a slave, and a lump of flesh by man's egoism. . . . The New Woman hopes to destroy the old morality and law that were made for men's convenience.[7]

In agreement with Hiratsuka's definition, Tamura was perceived as a New Woman who wanted to attain mental and physical awakening, independence, and freedom from male oppression. The vogue for the New Woman affected reception of Tamura's work; she and Hiratsuka were responding to the same intellectual and social climate.

The literary texts and also the contexts of the 1910s contributed to Tamura's writing being understood as "a naked picture of her inner truth as a woman writer" in her battle against male domination.[8] After publication of Shimazaki Tōson's *Hakai* (The broken commandment, 1906) and Tayama Katai's *Futon* (The quilt, 1907), which received critical acclaim from the *bundan* (literary establishment), naturalism became the dominant style of writing in Tokyo. This literary trend among the male writers/readers in the *bundan* situated Tamura as a writer who was able to express the truth of women. For example, the critic known as XYZ encouraged Tamura to confess the innermost truth of a woman: "Isn't it good for a woman to expose frankly the psychology of woman, as man anatomizes boldly his psychology and writes without scruples?"[9] Of course, a critical statement of this sort presupposes an essential existence of "true womanhood" that only women can express. As Mitsuishi Ayumi has explained: "For the *bundan* and the world of critics, the productions of *jyoryū sakka* (women writers) were met with the expectation that they would describe women's internal psychology, which was a mystery to male writers."[10] Rebecca Copeland's 2006 edited volume, *Woman Critiqued: Translated Essays on Japanese Women's Writing,* expands the picture I am painting and guides the English-speaking community to additional, highly relevant reading about the evaluative systems under which Japanese women produced their writings.

Tamura was also deemed successful in revealing the inner self of a true woman because of how she described female bodies. Citing her descriptions of the senses—smells, the touch of the skin, the perception of colors—male critics argued that Tamura was expressing "sensuality" specific to "the real woman." Tamura's descriptions of women's bodies and the critics' reading of them fed each other at a time when *inshō (teki) byōsha* (impressionistic description) and *kannō (kankaku teki) byōsha* (sensual description) were becoming new modes of writing. Although naturalism was still a dominant trend, descriptions of "impressions" and "senses" were introduced as new literary skills capable of overcoming the "objective" description of naturalism. The distinction between the impressionistic and the sensual was understood as follows: "Sensual description should be understood as the description that incorporated so-called second senses, such as smell, touch, and taste, which have not been valued in conventional literature," whereas impressionistic description concerned the visual, such as colors.[11] Masamune Hakuchō wrote at the time that "women should be much more sensual than men,"[12] while Aozukin contended that "as

sensual art, there is no art that is as excellent as [Tamura Toshiko's] art. . . .
I think Toshiko is making progress as a woman writer should."[13]

The naturalistic (descriptive), impressionistic, and sensual, however, are
interrelated. The critic Kobayashi Aio noted at the time that in Tamura's
writing, "so-called sensual description is a sort of impressionistic description," and "the descriptive, sensual, and impressionistic cannot be considered separately."[14] Indeed, Tamura describes objects exactly as she per-
ceives them through her senses and impressions. By writing about and
with the bodily perceptions of reality, in the literary contexts of naturalism, impressionism, and sensualism, she therefore fulfilled the desire of
male readers of the *bundan* that she express the so-called truth of womanhood. Jan Bardsley explains the effects of essentializing women writers for
some of the male writers:

> Choosing to frame their argument in essentialist terms allows
> them to conflate women's creativity with their female bodies while
> leaving the mind—and all its potential to soar past the body—to
> men.[15]

> Indeed, it is women who are gendered, women who must be
> *women* writers, and women who must create from their sexed
> bodies, while men . . . are ultimately allowed to soar in the
> transcendent space of the intellect as writers.[16]

In these statements, Bardsley rightly points out the desire of some male
critics to essentialize women's bodies so that they can essentialize the
mind as their own property. Some feminist critics contend that "Tamura
emphasizes sensuality as an expression of the pleasures of the flesh and as
a means of self-expression, and expression of the fulfillment of sexuality in
becoming herself."[17]

In another dominant trend among critics to view her novels and her life
in parallel, Tamura's works of literature are understood to be naturalistic,
impressionistic, and sensual expressions of her struggles with her husband, Tamura Shōgyo. In reading Tamura's novels as her autobiography,
critics such as Enomoto posit that her struggle with her husband gave birth
to such representative works as *Onna sakusha* (The woman writer) and
Miira no kuchibeni (Lip rouge on a mummy). Enomoto notes, "Tamura
Toshiko repeatedly described . . . intense conflicts between men and

women as centered on the problems she had with her husband Shōgyo."[18] This sort of critique fits in with the one directed at the "woman writers" who "could narrate 'realistic depictions' of 'family experiences'; and perhaps, above all, possessed 'abundant physical sensibilities.'"[19] Tamura and her characters neglect wifehood and motherhood, recklessly pursuing pleasure against the backdrop of the world of entertainment in downtown Tokyo. Adherents of this approach even trace the source to Tamura's mother, who was never satisfied with being a mother and wife but pursued actors and material possessions, which led to her early demise.

Some of the key terms critics use in analyzing Tamura's writing before 1918 seem to come down to "disillusion about men and husband," feelings about the confinement of home, and hope for self-expression and freedom. It has been emphasized that Tamura's fiction challenged and went beyond the state discourse on women, family, and family empire.[20] When the Civil Code (in effect from 1897) defined home as women's proper place, Tamura wrote about domesticity but defined it as a battleground rather than a safe haven. Home is depicted as a confining space where women have to fight constantly with husbands for their freedom and self-expression. Instead of promoting the "good wife and wise mother" who serves the family, Tamura wrote of women who challenge men in domestic spheres. Instead of celebrating women's reproductive desire, which reproduces healthy bodies for the empire, Tamura wrote about the self and its sensual pleasure, which was considered to be morally corrupt.

When the state discourse defined the subjugated bodies of women as part of the body of empire, Tamura wrote about a woman whose body was the conscious agent of her decisions and actions. In *Hōraku no kei* (Burning at the stake), Tamura wrote:

> My body is now entirely mine. . . . she couldn't resist rejoicing in the feeling of freedom. . . . it was all right to think anything, to do anything, to abandon anyone, to oppose anyone. . . . Ryūko's heart soared with the feeling that her life from now on would move as she wished it to.[21]

This passage occurs in the context of the heroine Ryūko's enjoying illicit affairs outside marriage. Her assertion of freedom challenges the morality of the "good wife, wise mother" who must reproduce the subjects of the empire and obey the law written by men that prohibits adultery. The heroine claims that it is her free will, rather than men's moral standards and laws, that determines her actions. It is her body that is awakened, independent, and free to act and move as she wishes.

However, Tamura's writings in the 1910s have also led some critics to conclude that she was a failure as a New Woman because of her dependence on a man. Yukiko Tanaka points out that although Tamura's female characters yearn for autonomy and liberation, they are unable to separate themselves from men for fear of losing sexual satisfaction and financial stability.[22] Izu Toshihiko finds that women in Tamura's novels such as *Kanojo no seikatsu, Akirame,* and *Onna sakusha* struggle for independence and liberation from men but fail. Mitsuishi Ayumi explains: "She was a failure [in the eyes of the male readers of the *bundan* (literary establishment)] when asked for her ideas and awareness as a 'new woman' and 'woman writer.'"[23]

This sort of remark is often made about the end of the novel *Miira no kuchibeni* (Lip rouge on a mummy):

> The male mummy and female mummy . . . fell on top of each other. Their color was gray. And the eyes of woman, who was all eyes like a wooden doll, were looking up. The color of her lips was a vivid red. It was a dream in which Minoru stood by a large glass box and looked at what was in it.[24]

The red lips in contrast to the gray color of the rest of the body invoke the sexual desire of a woman and her attachment to a man even after death. On this ending of Tamura's novella, Izu notes: "In *Miira no kuchibeni,* [Tamura] writes sadly of the unalterable destiny of man and woman, who after all are fated to be tied to each other with bones, although the woman insists on the independent self that is separate from man."[25] Izu further posits the limits of Tamura and her characters' independence:

> Her claim of self is intense only when compared to men's arrogance and violence. . . . While maintaining that she would live for herself, . . . her view couldn't avoid being narrow and small. While confronting men intensely and while laying claim to the self, she could live only by clinging to and relying on men. She was neither able to pursue the problem of self as a single human being who lives in an open world, nor grasp the problems of men and women in such an expanse.[26]

Izu contends that Tamura's battleground was limited to the "narrow and small" domestic space where women suffer from men's violence. Although she did tackle the questions of "the world" and "the problems of men and women in such an expanse" in North America after 1918, Tamura seems to agree with Izu's assessment when she reflects on her own writings in Tokyo in the 1910s. She wrote in 1937:

> The group New Woman was the liberator of women in the home. It was a time when [New Woman] stayed within an extremely narrow concept of woman's self-awakening that measures freedom, strength, and the progress of an individual life only with respect to men's control.[27]

In the late 1930s, upon her return from North America and before departing for China, Tamura declared that she had abandoned her past novels that "described the struggle that is filled with lust and attachment to self."[28]

After she became a critically acclaimed "woman writer" in the 1910s in Japan, Tamura left for North America and produced different sorts of writings. But curiously, most critics have neglected what she wrote after she left Tokyo.[29] Tamura departed for Vancouver, Canada, to join her then lover, Suzuki Etsu (1886–1933), who had left *Asahi shinbun* (Asahi newspaper) and taken a position at Vancouver's Japanese newspaper *Tairiku nippō* (Continental daily) in 1918. Before returning to Tokyo in 1936, Tamura lived in Vancouver from 1918 until 1935, and in Los Angeles from 1935 until 1936. During her eighteen years in North America, many people thought that she stopped writing because she produced no novels and only one short story.[30] This critical neglect also derives from the idea that her writing in North America, which was mainly journalistic, lacked aesthetic quality. Most of the recent scholarship reevaluating Tamura's writing from 1918 on has emphasized her search for freedom by leaving the Japanese system, which enshrined not only gender and family but the nation-state. Noriko Mizuta contends that Tamura's appeal derives from her self-realization as a writer and her desire to go "outside the system that regulates women's way of life such as marriage and home, outside the community called Japan, and outside the cultural system of sexual differences."[31] Critics who emphasize Tamura's crossing of borders thus find importance in the transnationalism of her writings after 1918.

When she returned to Japan in 1936, Tamura found a readership that anticipated her writing based on her literary reputation in the 1910s. Prominent journals in Japan, such as *Chūō kōron,* gave her a forum in which to write. Tamura wrote nine novels and fifty-six essays, critiques, and translations from October 1936 to December 1938. But they received little critical attention. According to critics such as Setouchi, Izu, and Kurosawa, Tamura had lost her will and ability to write and failed to reclaim her fame in the Japanese literary establishment after her migration to Vancouver in 1918 and marriage to Suzuki Etsu.[32] Kudō Miyoko, who explores Tamura's activities after 1918 in her book *Bankūbâ no ai* (Love in Vancouver), dismisses Tamura's ability to write after she left Tokyo in the late 1910s.[33]

After eighteen years in North America and a two-year stay in Japan, Tamura left for China in 1938 and ended her writing career as the titular editor of *Josei* (Women's voice), a Chinese-language periodical under the auspices of the Japanese authorities in occupied Shanghai. According to Tamura Hisashi, who assisted Tamura in Beijing, she became friendly with people at the headquarters of the Japanese military in various regions and received financial support for her daily expenses. *Josei* received financial assistance from the Japanese consulate and military.[34] With Watanabe Sumiko's recent translation of *Josei* from Chinese to Japanese, more critical analyses are expected to emerge.[35]

I have explored the texts and contexts that have heretofore determined the meanings of Tamura and her writings. I depart from these aspects of traditional Tamura criticism: (1) viewing Tamura's texts of literature as the autobiographical informant of the author's life; (2) acceptance of her ability to express the truth of the ontological, essential woman; (3) assessment of her as a failed New Woman; (4) critical dismissal of her works after her departure for North America in 1918; and finally, (5) definition of Tamura as a wanderer who went beyond the boundaries of gender, family, and family empire. Next I explore the forces of her discourses that embody the empire in the bodies that cross the imperial borders.

Female Bodies of the Japanese Empire in Vancouver, Canada

In what follows, I investigate how the migrant bodies of female characters move from *naichi* (the inner territory of Japan) to North America in Tamura's writings. Against the backdrop of the expanding body of the

Japanese empire, I particularly examine how Tamura depicts the female bodies that moved from the center of Japan to the West, and that were pushed to the margin in Canada. In the restricted circumstances of pre-war North America, Tamura's descriptions of Japanese women's physicality functioned as a discursive strategy through which the writer and her readers might survive, empower themselves, and make "progress." More specifically, in the face of anti-Japanese sentiments, movements, and measures in Canada, Tamura described the bodies of female migrant workers who carried out specific roles and missions for "Japan" as it empowered itself and expanded as an empire. By examining Tamura's writings on Japanese women's bodies, I expose how gender, migrant labor, and empire intersect in her texts. My analysis (1) puts aesthetics in a bracket, (2) understands the author as part of the social constitution rather than as the sole source of textual meaning, and (3) concentrates on the politics of Tamura's writing. In the following section, I investigate the poetry and essays she wrote for *Tairiku nippō* from 1918 to 1924. (Due to the limited availability of source material Tamura produced in Vancouver, I must concentrate on writings during these years.)[36]

The Social and Political Contexts of Vancouver

To examine Tamura's writing in Vancouver, it is instructive to explore the social, political, and historical contexts in which she wrote.[37] Until 1918, Tamura wrote predominantly of the world of literati and the downtown culture of entertainers in Tokyo. After 1918, she wrote about the community of Japanese immigrants in a newly founded city, Vancouver. Most Japanese immigrants in Canada belonged to the working class, and almost all lived in British Columbia, with a heavy concentration in Vancouver. They established their own recreational, religious, and regional groups (*kenjinkai,* or associations of individuals from the same prefectures in Japan), Japanese newspapers, and the Canadian Japanese Association (Kanada Nihonjinkai).[38] Although the Japanese newspapers and the association served immigrants from Japan, "Japan" was not an exclusive determinant of their identities in their early years in Canada. As the existence and activities of numerous *kenjinkai* suggest, Japanese immigrants in Canada shared a strong sense of community based on the origin of their *kuni*—that is, the prefecture or village where they had been born. Those who identified themselves ethnically with *ken* (prefecture) and *mura* (village) were called *kuni-mono* (people of nations). Many also constructed their identities based on occupations, hobbies, and/or religions.[39] Thus the immigrants shared multiple identities with one another.

Discourse on what it meant to be "Japanese," created by the government in Japan, was now distant from the reality of the lives of the Japanese immigrants in Vancouver. Whereas the architects of the Japanese nation-state targeted health, wealth, and national identity as the foundation of Japan as a militarily strong and materially wealthy nation, Japanese immigrants in Canada lived with illness, poverty, and ambiguous identity. Tamura's second husband, Suzuki Etsu, observed of the community of Japanese immigrants in Vancouver in 1922:

> On the windows, there hangs a diaper or some unidentifiable cloth that makes you sick to your stomach just looking at it. Windows seem like they have been painted with grime. And in front of the window stands a woman who wears clothing that looks like either pajamas or a sack all covered with stains, over which she puts a grotesque, dirty apron. . . . Walking by them, I am struck by their disgusting smell, like that of excrement. They lead lives that are as low as we can possibly imagine. This is not a story about other unknown countries. This is about matters here in Vancouver. This is a scene that can be found in any place where a few Japanese gather.[40]

Newspaper articles also depict the Japanese immigrant community as one afflicted by ignorance and illness. For example, two years before Suzuki's description, *Tairiku nippō* had reported the following "white" physician's assessment of the Japanese immigrants' living conditions:

> Surprisingly, the stupidity of the situation just persists. The airflow in their rooms is poor, sunlight is insufficient, water gathers, pathogens erupt endlessly. The Japanese way of feeding children is poor and irregular, and Japanese ignore time. Japanese children's teeth are worse than those of other nationalities.[41]

Examples of intellectuals, policy makers, and writers who treated "pathogens" of the body of Japan literally and metaphorically can be found in the Meiji period, when the government made concerted efforts to eliminate disease and poverty with the theories of bacteriology and hygiene. Thus the Japanese state claimed to have been concerned with purging the impure ever since the time of the Meiji Restoration.[42]

While the architects of the nation-state of Japan promoted the discourse of the Japanese as the central and leading race in Asia, however, Japanese immigrants in Canada experienced discrimination as one of the "Oriental" racial/ethnic groups at the periphery.[43] The Anti-Oriental Act of 1924, for example, legally justified discrimination against Japanese immigrants in Canada, and pushed them to the social and political margins. Moreover, in contrast to the ideology of the "good wife, wise mother" who rears children to become healthy and diligent, women from Japan in Vancouver reproduced ill nourishment, illness, and irregularity. Thus the physical and social conditions under which Japanese in the center purportedly lived were different from the conditions of those on the periphery. This may help explain why critics in Japan (and those attuned to conditions there) proved unable to evaluate the quality and aesthetic force of Tamura's writing during her self-imposed exile in Vancouver.

As an "inferior" race on the periphery, Japanese immigrants in Vancouver experienced anti-Japanese sentiments, movements, and measures from the 1890s to the 1940s. In 1907 a rioting crowd used racial slurs and physical violence to emphasize its will to exclude Japanese immigrants and protect "White Canada."[44] Without suffrage, Japanese were deprived of full citizenship in Canada. Repeated implementation of anti-Japanese measures restricted entry to Canada and limited immigrants' employment opportunities and compensation.[45] After the 1907 riot, the Canadian government reduced the number of visas for male laborers from Japan to 400 a year in 1908, and further reduced it until just 150 visas were issued in 1923. Women were not included in these numbers, however, so they came to Canada as picture brides and married Issei (first-generation) husbands. Women's migration contributed to the formation of families and to the birth of Nisei (second-generation immigrants) in the 1920s. These migrant women worked mainly as washerwomen, temporary strawberry and bean pickers, waitresses, hair stylists, and dressmakers.[46]

The Migrants' Formation of Japanese Identities

The intensity of Canadians' discriminatory and exclusionary measures threatened the livelihoods of immigrants and made them increasingly and keenly aware of their identity as "Japanese." Thus, although the early immigrants had dismissed their connection with the Japanese government, the 1907 Vancouver riot inspired them to unite: "The Japanese in Canada were deeply distressed at the movement that impaired the dignity of the Japanese race."[47] Although immigrants had found diverse sources of identity in various *kenjinkai,* occupations, athletic clubs, and religions, they came to perceive themselves as a united Japanese race in the eyes of "white" Canadians.

One strategy to counter discrimination was for the immigrants to identify themselves as subjects of the Japanese empire living in Canada. Japanese immigrants in Canada could appeal to the Japanese government and its diplomatic ties with the United Kingdom because Canada was a member of the British Commonwealth of Nations. The obligations of the Anglo-Japanese Alliance Agreement (1902–20) resulted in abolishing numerous anti-Japanese acts that had been passed by the parliament of British Columbia. The obligations of the allied relationship between Canada and Japan during World War I resulted in the Japanese being exempted from the Anti-Oriental Act. In "Canada and the Japanese: In Commemoration of the 2600th Anniversary of the Japanese Imperial Calendar," prepared by the Kanada Nihonjinkai (Canadian Japanese Association), this approach is described as follows:

> [After the riot in 1907,] they resolved the solidarity of the Japanese and the maintaining of the dignity of the Empire of Japan. The Japanese called the problem *hainichi undō,* the anti-Japanese movement, and they thought that the only possible solution to it would be through diplomatic channels. Accordingly, they reported the riot situation in Vancouver to both foreign ministers of Japan and Canada and appealed for any assistance and solutions the two governments could provide. The federal government of Canada wired the city of Vancouver expressing her regret on learning of the indignities and cruelties which were inflicted on certain subjects of the Emperor of Japan, a friend and an ally of His Majesty the King, and we hope that peace will be promptly restored and all offenders punished.[48]

In negotiating with the Canadian authorities to avert violence against the immigrants, the Japanese government made explicit the presence and power of the Japanese empire in Canada. Japanese consuls played an active role in enforcing Canada's observation of the international alliance treaty and abolition of the anti-Japanese measures. They also clearly identified Japanese immigrants in Canada as subjects of the Japanese empire. For example, in March 1906, the consul, Morikawa Shirō, had asked the Foreign Ministry in Japan about the education policy for immigrants in Canada and received the following response:

> In regard to educating the subjects of the empire living in foreign countries, it is our policy to not let them lose the spirit of the Japanese people and also to intensify the development of their Japanese character.[49]

This perception of an explicit presence of the spiritual Japanese empire within Canada was epitomized in 1926 by the claims of the Japanese consul, Kawai Tatsuo:

> The Japan Association exists as an autonomous association only within the limits of the consul's oversight. The Japanese Association must be interpreted as an autonomous group under the large umbrella called the [Japanese] consulate.[50]

Thus Consul Kawai granted autonomy to the immigrants in Canada only as subjects of imperial Japan.

To counter Canadian discrimination, Japanese associations in Vancouver adopted various strategies as well. One strategy, advocated by Suzuki Etsu, was to erase their Japaneseness, form labor unions with the Canadians, and raise their living standard to that of Canadians. In promoting this idea, Suzuki opposed the notion of uniting ethnically as *kenjin* (people of prefecture) or *nihonjin* (Japanese), and called instead for the solidarity of workers,[51] assuming that by elevating Japanese migrants' working and living conditions, the problem of racism would be resolved. Therefore, his approach to the problem of class was inseparable from the issue of Japanese immigrants' racial status as a whole. The Japanese Association also encouraged the immigrants to volunteer to fight in the European theater during World War I (1914–18), thus displaying their loyalty to Canada.[52] The immigrants' allegiance to Canada was quite pronounced when Tamura moved to Vancouver in 1918.

The immigrants' relationships with the Japanese consulate, the Japanese government, the Canadian people, and the Canadian government shed light on the conflicting and discontinuous ways they constructed their identities. On the one hand, some Japanese immigrants came to rely on the Japanese consulate in Canada and on the government in Japan as the source of their security and identity. By asserting their presence and identity as subjects of the Japanese emperor residing in Canada, these immigrants constructed an extension of Japanese empire in Canada.[53] The treatment of Japanese residents in Canada as subjects of the Japanese empire can be seen in the fact that the first census conducted in Japan, in 1920, included Japanese in Canada. On the other hand, Suzuki, as a representative of the Japanese Association, claimed that "the Japanese Association is autonomous under the Canadian government, but not under the Japanese government."[54]

The Japanese Association's self-identification helps us further understand the competing and discontinuous ways in which the immigrants constructed their identities. "Canada and the Japanese" summarizes the history of the association through three transitional periods. First, in the 1890s, the association was formed to unite Japanese laborers and to protect their rights and profits while promoting friendship with Canadian "Caucasians." Second, in 1908, a year after the Vancouver riot, "Japanese" was dropped from the name of the association to erase the Japaneseness of the immigrants and assimilate with Canadians. Third, in 1936, the year Tamura returned to Japan, the organization restored the word "Japanese" to its name to emphasize its members' Japanese origins.[55] Thus the conflicting and changing political conditions and identities of the immigrants residing in Canada were experienced in temporal dynamics—that is, diachronically over time—even though the wider changes described earlier also occurred as phenomena limited to the time in which Tamura wrote. As a result, when we note different voices and activities within Japanese communities in the same period, it becomes clear that they appeared synchronically in the immigrants' claim of independence, in their efforts at assimilation, in their exclusion from the Canadian community, and in their dependence on the Japanese national empire.

Tamura as a Migrant

Tamura was a migrant herself—both in the context of the expanding body of the Japanese empire and in terms of the Japanese immigrants' experience of being pushed to the margins of society in Canada. In the face of emotional, physical, and legal discrimination against the Japanese, Tamura tackled the problems of the identity of "Japan" and "Japanese." Moreover, she reconfigured the bodies of the female migrant workers who had moved from the empire of Japan to a territory of the British Empire to carry out specific roles and missions for Japan. Tamura's descriptions of these workers' corporeality provides a site of analysis for examining the politics of gender, work, and the Japanese empire.

Tamura's move from Japan to North America is symbolized by her newspaper pen name, Tori no ko ("Baby Bird"), which shows that she identified with migrants who had flown from Japan to Canada and who "are in the [state of] traveling and drifting and are distant from their home country."[56] As a traveler in a distant land, the narrator of Tamura's journalistic pieces written in Canada feels estranged from her surroundings:

> This traveling bird has begun to feel even more sorrowful these
> days. It is because things around me will not at all . . . become
> familiar to me. . . . Even when I look at the stars at night, . . .
> unlike the ones I see in my home country, they will not pour
> into my inner heart the sentiments that melt at the bottom of
> consciousness with the meetings of my eyebrows and the twinkle
> of those stars. . . . The shades of foreigners who walk here and
> there disappear in the middle of the night. But, . . . there is no
> poetry. I cannot know their feelings. And of course, they, too,
> don't even try to incorporate the sound of my heart into them.
> The sorrow of the sound of my footsteps on the soil of this
> country! You . . . who tread only on Japanese soil will probably
> not be able to imagine this sorrowful feeling.[57]

With such "impressionistic" and "sensual" descriptions, Baby Bird depicts the disconnect both between her heart and those of "foreigners," and between her footsteps and those of readers who still tread Japanese soil. Thus she inscribes a sense of displacement from both her adopted land and her homeland.

Tamura's writing also uses a narrator who claims that the unfamiliar surroundings in Vancouver make her body ill, thereby disabling her as an artist:

I . . . have already lost the nerve to struggle to attain poetry. Furthermore, I no longer possess even the nerve to be disappointed by surroundings with no art to appreciate. I feel like seeing my body as that of a disabled person who has just been made an idiot by the Spanish flu. All of my aesthetic senses, appreciation, and passion for pleasure have become dim.[58]

With the loss of the senses, the ill body of the narrator no longer has the intellectual and aesthetic capacity to appreciate and produce pleasurable art. While engaging in the dialectic struggle between the foreign and home, however, the narrator regains the ability to tell stories by imposing the familiar on the foreign. The poem "Totsukuni no haru" (Spring in a foreign country) appeared on April 19, 1919:

After having lived in a foreign country,
the spring has arrived here, too. . . .
Walking through a field, visiting the sounds,
. . . the familiar lurks there.
Ah, I have not forgotten
the song of the water! . . .
Ah, I have not forgotten
the sound of the song. . . .
Why, with the same resonance,
do you waters flow gently?
In the shade, this foreigner stands.
Do the sounds of the river know the mind that thinks of home,
. . . the roar of the harmonious flow,
the sound of the song that resembles home?

The pleasurable sounds of the water that flows "with the same resonance" between the "foreign country" and "home" reactivates the narrator's senses and re-creates the harmony between the "foreign" and "home" for her. By resolving the discord between them, the narrator's ill and disabled body regains the ability to walk and to write poetry. On January 1, 1919, Tamura had written:

Wide roads shine
in the foreign country in the early spring

I think of my happiness
I will walk alone.[59]

Although she regained the power to proceed and to produce art, Tamura remained alone in Canada, in that she was distant from the *bundan,* whose recognition had established her status as a writer in Japan, and from the debates printed in *Seitō,* in which she had participated from 1911 until 1912.

However, Tamura soon found readers for whom she narrated her stories:

> With regard to this new column [in *Tairiku nippō*], I would like to continue as much as possible to be a good companion of the women who reside in this town, inform them of what has come to my heart and mind, and talk to them. And this is one of those first stories.[60]

The titles of the articles Tamura wrote for the serialized "Saturday Women's Column" in *Tairiku nippō*—"Kono machi ni sumu fujintachi ni" (For the women who reside in this town) and "Mizukara hatarakeru fujintachi ni" (For women who work on their own)—identify her targeted readers as the migrant Japanese women in Vancouver. By addressing them, Tamura continued to tell her stories during her stay in Canada.

From the outset, Tamura as "Baby Bird" distinguished between her status as a temporarily uprooted urban intellectual and her readers' status as permanently settled rural immigrants:

> I already don't intend to stay in this place for a long time. . . . Therefore, I don't have profound empathy with this Japanese society in Vancouver. To say it flatly, the life of this Japanese society . . . will in the near future disappear from me as a mere phenomenon of my trip. . . . I am indifferent to this Japanese society. While being indifferent, however, the one thing I constantly paid attention to and was concerned about was the lives of women in this land and of their children.[61]

Thus the narrator known as "Baby Bird" set herself apart even while she wrote for the female Japanese migrants and their children, aware that their experience in Canada would disappear if it were not for her descriptions. Yet the narrator also identified with her readers as migrants who were belittled and powerless. Tamura's "Tabigarasu no onshin" (Correspondence of a traveling crow) appeared in 1918:

> I am in the sorrowful state of having my soul become atrophied by the threat of the massive, enormous, great material civilization, and of feeling keenly with my body the pathos of a traveling bird that has flown from a small island.

The immensity and materiality of Canada's "civilization" are contrasted with the smallness and soulfulness of nature. The threat posed by this civilization is felt physically, as if by a small bird that has flown from a small island, Japan. The narrator goes on to contrast "our women" (the Japanese migrants) with "foreign women" (Caucasian Canadians): "How weak and depressed our women who reside in this town are in comparison to the foreign women, whose air and attitudes are all filled with lively and articulate power!" Thus she identified Canadian women as strong, lively, and clearly represented, and Japanese women as weak, ill, and ambiguously represented. By internalizing "Orientalism," the narrator thus recreates the dichotomy between the West and Japan as the "Orient."

In Tamura's writing in Vancouver, the world of "Europe and America" is materially and culturally superior. Due to the inferior position of Japan, female Japanese migrants are deprived of power and health:

> The material civilization of Europe and America is far superior to that of present-day Japan. There is no comparison between them. It [their superiority] is even [evident] in their power of (material) wealth. . . . Foreign women live and exist in this sort of society, and even more, they live within its customs and manners.[62]

The "foreign" is also constructed as an oppressive race:

> When one takes a step outside, there is only occupation by the foreign race. Whether playing in the park or at the beach, our women just cannot taste . . . freedom as joyfully as one would like when playing within one's own yard. Or, even when we women go to a merchant . . . we cannot be at ease picking up and examining

homemade products like other foreign women, who calmly appreciate and choose. Thus there are only hateful, trying constrictions and uneasiness in our lives.[63]

The narrator evokes displacement with the metaphors of home, yard, park, and store. The world in which she engages in daily activities of play and consumption of material goods is divided into "them" and "us," the foreign and the familiar, occupation and freedom, and constriction and choice. As the occupier of the physical and material world, the "foreign race" constricts the bodily movements of the female Japanese migrants.

In negotiating with the occupying race, Tamura wrote in 1919 of the futility of the immigrants' attempts to assimilate with the Canadians by naturalizing the differences between Japanese and Canadian bodies:

[An attempt to imitate] will ... become nothing but [the object] of contempt ... by foreigners. ... They are different from us and wear unfamiliar hats and shoes. Even if we turn ourselves upside down, Japanese women cannot attain their taste for luxury or their natural manner. When all is said and done, we will end in imitation and disharmony.[64]

Not only is the physicality of the "foreigners" strange to the narrator, but they are naturally "different from us." In opposing the immigrants' efforts of assimilation, Tamura naturalizes the difference between the foreign body and the Japanese body: hence the dissonance results from disturbing what is "natural." As noted earlier, the narrator Baby Bird imposes the familiar on the foreign in order to dissolve the discord between the foreign and home. However, she also admonishes Japanese female immigrants not to imitate the body of Americans and Europeans, thus refusing to re-create the West as the original that initiates and Japan as a mimic that follows the West.

Japanese Women in "the World"

To tackle the problem of the constriction of Japanese women's bodies by the "foreign race," Tamura's writing encourages the migrants to "work." But to work, the migrants must first know Japanese women's place in "the world" (Europe and America). Tamura's narrator Tori no ko ("Baby Bird") continues, "You must know . . . the degree to which women in the world have made progress, and . . . have been 'working' with rich knowledge . . . and the degree to which women born in our country are inferior."[65] Tamura urges women to achieve gender equality with men by becoming aware of Japanese women's inferior position to men and making their own progress in Europe and America a goal. She contends that knowledge and awakening will arise from living and working as female immigrants in Vancouver, and that women's progress must be achieved by acting in the public sphere and on the world stage. Her sense of women's independence, freedom, and power is directly connected to her wish for Japan to rise above its second-rate status as a second-rate empire. As discussed in chapter 2, in the late 1880s, the leading architect of Meiji education, Mori Arinori, had contended that women's education was the foundation of the nation's advancement. But whereas Mori had emphasized formal education, Tamura was operating within the context of Japanese immigrants' labor and efforts to be seen on a par with the Western imperial powers.

In continuing her earlier argument, the narrator Baby Bird creates the spaces of the foreign country and of home, occupied by the Europeans and Americans and by the Japanese, respectively. The narrator also situates women as moving forward or lagging behind along the linear development of time. In the hierarchy she re-creates, Japanese female immigrants occupy an earlier time and inferior position. According to the earlier statement, it is the knowledge of the work achieved by the "women in the world" that should inspire "women of our country" to make "progress."

Furthermore, Baby Bird contends that it is Japanese women's inferior status compared to men that contributes to the Canadians' racial discrimination against Japanese nationals:

Isn't it unavoidable that the nation where women's position is lower than men's, and women's independent thought is not prevalent, will be rejected because it is considered second-rate?[66]

This statement, written by Tamura in 1921, is reminiscent of the position from which Fukuzawa Yukichi wrote in the 1880s about the status of women and the nation of Japan. As the leading proponent of the Westernization of Japan, Fukuzawa's idea of men's and women's independence and freedom was connected to the idea of Japan's independence and freedom in the Western, "civilized" world. He lamented women's lack of social awareness and was a major contributor to the narratives addressing the awakening of women, based on his observations during his trips to the United States and Europe. Tamura, in contrast, observed Japanese immigrant women in Vancouver and wrote directly to them:

> It is no wonder that Japanese are disdained as the nationality *(minzoku)* most behind the times, if Japanese women who have immigrated to the home of European and American women . . . do not . . . engage in activities in the public sphere with a level of knowledge and power that is at least not inferior to that of European and American women.[67]

According to Tamura, it was vital for the female migrants to understand the specific national space they occupied and to work to achieve gender equality with men so that Japan could elevate itself from the status of a second-rate nation.

Female Immigrants and Women in *Naichi*

Although they were inferior in status to Canadian women, Tamura asserted that Japanese women in Canada enjoyed a higher status than middle- and working-class women in *naichi* (the inner territory of Japan), whom she understood as follows:

> At the beginning of the Meiji Restoration, when Japan opened to the West, enormous changes occurred in the living situation of the nation. Among women who had humbly bowed to the authority of "women's three lessons of obedience [of Confucianism]," there were those wonderful women at the time who . . . became the pioneers of oversea studies. . . . The unique thing they gave their less privileged countrywomen was the exploration of "knowledge based on education" and the liberation of the women who have customarily been confined to their home.[68]

In this statement, the reader can see Tamura shift from how the "home" of American and European women restricts the bodies of Japanese immigrant women to how the "home" of Japan confines women who live there. What remains consistent is her emphasis on knowledge as a means to liberate women. It was the privileged women in Japan who could liberate themselves by studying overseas. However, despite their achievements, Tamura claims, modern Japanese women's "awakening" was so sudden that they have since been like "drunkards." In her writing, these Japanese women appear awakened but still unsure of their ideas, positions, directions, and aims.[69]

In her assessment, Japanese women seem to have made more progress as Modern Girls (discussed later) than as New Women. In their material and aesthetic pursuits, Tamura writes, Japanese women from the homeland have made as much progress as foreign women have. When middle- and upper-class Japanese women visit Canada, they enjoy material wealth and display manners comparable to those of Canadians:

> When I went shopping at a certain Japanese store, I heard the
> following: These days, women who come from Japan have
> become flamboyant, and use nothing but expensive and superior
> products. . . . Young women who go abroad from Japan at the
> present time have grown up in the midst of the flowering material
> improvement of the homeland, which has become more civilized
> and more . . . luxurious every day, and therefore their aesthetic
> knowledge is far more advanced than that of the women who have
> traditionally gone abroad. . . . It's natural that [women from Japan]
> try to realize their own knowledge and taste even more by
> comparing it with the clothing of the civilized foreign women. . . .
> This might . . . mean Japanese women's progress in civilization.[70]

Tamura made this statement in 1919, in the post–World War I era. The culture of materialism and consumerism of women from the "homeland" was not unrelated to the appearance of the "Modern Girl" in Japan. Although Miriam Silverberg contends that the Modern Girl emerged after the Kantō earthquake (1923), some historians argue that the phenomenon coincided with the end of World War I, which gave rise to economic growth, materialism, and consumerism in Japan. In Tamura's writing, we can see the mobility of the economically privileged Japanese women, who could travel to North America and consume its "superior," "civilized" goods. In this sense they certainly occupied a more advanced position than the impoverished Japanese female migrants to Canada, who struggled with material and physical restrictions there.

However, what makes the migrant women superior both to privileged middle-class women and to lower-class women in Japan is, Tamura claims,

their bodily strength to engage in work, and to endure hardship unimag-
inable to the women in Japan. Tamura wrote in 1919:

> In comparison to the women who are usually in Japan and who
> have an occupation, . . . I find especially in the will of [the female
> Japanese migrants] something stronger and more self-conscious.
> I sense the appearance of the specific power of will that glows as
> the result of certain unavoidable stimuli from their surroundings.
> Those who can have this sort of stimulus in their lives, and who
> can live with such readiness, are living beings of great power. . . .
> At the moment she understands the spirit and readiness there, and
> awakens, that person's power of living fills her whole body. . . .
> This is a precious stimulus of life and also a good living experience
> that can never be possessed genuinely by women who sleep, sit,
> and eat inside the country of Japan. . . . [The female Japanese
> migrants] are a few levels higher in their spirit, and also in real life
> [experience], in comparison to the women who are sleeping with
> laziness and ease in Japan.[71]

Due to the specific conditions and stimuli in the Canadian "settlement of
migrants," Tamura maintains, female Japanese migrants' bodies are awakened and empowered. The elevated level of their self-consciousness, will,
and spirit thus sets them apart from working- and middle-class Japanese
women, who indulge in leisure at home or abroad.

On the same occasion, Tamura wrote, "Women who have some sort
of occupation master directly with their bodies *(taitoku)* all the stimuli
and readiness that men can feel, experience them, and also make a living."[72] Female migrants have been working with their bodies alongside
men, motivated by the same stimuli, in the setting of Vancouver. They are
higher in the social hierarchy, Tamura contends, not only because of their
bodily strength but also because of their power to achieve equality with
men. Gender equality among Japanese immigrants will, in turn, help Japan
elevate itself to the status of a first-rate nation.

Although she separates Japanese women in Canada from those in *naichi*,
Tamura stresses that the migrants' work in the "foreign country" is predicated on their attachment to the "home country" of Japan:

> Upon the soil of the country of Japan, they [immigrants] can
> feel the love and sentiments for the blood tie that cannot be

severed. At the same time, they spur themselves on with the readiness, will, and discipline that they must take back to the home country that they created, so to speak. This is the tremendous stimulus that those who once left the home country, regardless of whether or not they are educated, feel about their own lives.[73]

In this statement, although they occupy a space outside "the country of Japan," Japanese female immigrants are connected to the soil and blood of Japan. Creative work in Tamura's writing thus becomes essentialized—and transcends class differences—in its capacity to connect all the migrants to the nation of Japan in blood.

The Mission of Female Japanese Migrants

According to Tamura, it is through creative work that female Japanese migrants can make the same progress achieved by women in America and Europe. As pointed out earlier, Tamura's encouragement of migrant women to make progress for themselves derived from her wish for Japan to move forward in the linear development of time. Indeed, she was convinced that the female migrants' work would enlighten women in Japan by liberating them from the ideology of the "good wife, wise mother":

> The cry of we who are abroad [must] awaken the women who sleep inside the country of Japan, and must awaken them to change the thought of women who are buried at home by being obstructed by the trite idea [of the] "good wife, wise mother."[74]

This statement recalls the discourse about New Women, led by Hiratsuka Raichō, in the 1910s in Japan. As Yosano Akiko's poem "The Day the Mountains Move" states, "All the sleeping women are now awake and moving." In Tamura's writing, however, it is Japanese female immigrants working in "the world" who carry a specific status, rather than the educated and privileged women in Japan. Tamura envisioned a particular purpose for Japanese women in the world, and for the Japanese empire.

Tamura's poem "Fujin yo" (Attention, women), which appeared in 1924, criticizes enshrined female virtue as it affects women's bodies and calls for women's actions for change:

Attention, women:
Make broader strides
and walk with assurance. . . .
The world no longer will praise
women who are chaste, timid, and reserved.

Women:
Open your eyes wide
from under the crown of chastity and virtue
and look around you. . . .
    Your modest smiles make truly ridiculous shadows
around your eyes.

Women:
Please look at your reflection
in the mirror . . .
and you will notice that
modest smiles are the expressions of sorrow.

Women:
Please laugh.
Please open your mouth widely and laugh.
Please laugh from your heart.

For the sake of women's happiness,
for the sake of women's lives,
for the sake of women's rights,
please laugh more merrily.

In order to laugh
you must take off from your head
the weighty crown of chaste virtue.

You cannot laugh with your mouth open
because of the weight of your heavy crown,
and you will spend life
smiling bitterly.

When the crown leaves your head
your heart will lightly leap to life;
your face that has tended to droop
due to the weight of the crown
will look up radiantly at this great sky. . . .

Women:
You will soon feel the weight of the crown.

In this poem, the heavy crown is the sign of dominance that deprives women of health, power, and progress. The shadows around their eyes indicate their illness; the tilted face suggests women under oppression; and their short strides signify the limited progress they have made. Rather than endorsing the morality that confounds women, the narrator asserts, they should lift the crown of feminine virtues from their heads, compose themselves, observe "the world," make their voices heard, and progress in the contest for power and prestige. The use of perceptions—seeing and touching—in this poem is embedded in the discourse on the immigrants' contests against constraints imposed on them because of their gender, race, ethnicity, and nationality. Note the changes here from Tamura's texts before 1918, when sensual perceptions were used as the expression or description of sexual desire within the discourse of gender politics in Japan.

On women's movements, Tamura wrote in "Jiko no kenri" (The rights of the self), which appeared on August 30, 1919, in *Tairiku nippō*:

Personal consciousness has risen among the class of the weak who exist by being always oppressed. . . . Even in the class struggle, which is about to cause the beginning of the revolution in this world, what makes us feel appropriate and grabs our attention are these women's movements.

In her writing targeted to working-class women among Japanese immigrants in Vancouver, class and gender struggles are situated within the power politics of the Western and Japanese imperial nations.

In Tamura's texts, the standard against which Japan measures its upward mobility in the world is either Canada or "America and Europe." Her earlier texts posited Japanese women's bodies and their manners as naturally different from those of Canadian women. By 1921, however, Tamura contended that this difference could be erased by the political function of the migrant women, as mothers who could transform their children into "true Canadians":

> There is almost no one, except a woman who is a mother, who has the power to demand suffrage from the present government so that Japanese can become true Canadians. . . . Only these mothers can understand all the demands and rights of women's real lives. . . . All women's activities find their motivating power here.[75]

In modifying her earlier statement that female migrants in Canada carry a specific role as workers (rather than being like the "good wives, wise mothers" in Japan), Tamura here confers on working women as mothers the exclusive power to represent migrant women.

Tamura stresses that working mothers attain more meaning when they are migrants in a "foreign country": "Those of the same nationality must not forget that women's power—that is, mothers' power—must necessarily be greater in this settlement of migrants than in the home country."[76] Tamura emphasizes that migrant women as "mothers with children . . . have all the authority, . . . the duty and huge responsibility, for the life of the immigration settlement."[77] Note the difference between this statement and her writing in Tokyo before 1918, in which she envisioned women who were neither good wives nor wise mothers (leading to her being construed to have transcended gender, family, and the nation). In Vancouver, in her call for mothers to work to elevate Japan's status, her discourse shifts to focus on women as mothers advancing Japan's status in a time of economic and military competition with the Western imperial powers.[78]

It is also significant that Tamura discusses migrant mothers as "public figures" who must engage in "social work":

> For women, as mothers and as public figures, to gain the opportunity to attend . . . the council [of representatives hosted by the present Japanese Association] with men does not mean only that a path has been opened for women's progress. It also means that a path will soon be opened for the next generation to attain rights that will make them true Canadians. . . . The newly established association, with mothers at its center, will be responsible for all the social work.[79]

Once female migrant workers and their "fellow countrymen" attain the political right to vote in Canada, their children will become "true Canadians." Thus "public" and "social" work intersects with Japanese immigrants' "political" advance in Canada and their identification with Canadians. More specifically, Tamura's view of "public" and "social" work is embedded in the political forces generated by the hierarchy of nations and empires in which Japan was struggling to elevate itself.

Paradoxically, Tamura's call for migrant women to work to become true Canadians is tied to her wish for Japan to attain a higher status in the "superior civilization of America and Europe." Moreover, her prescription of the public and social duties of mothers for the political advancement of Japan echoes the discourse in Japan that defined women's activities that were in conformity with the state discourse as "public" and "social" and those which were against it as "political."[80] According to the ideology of the "good wife, wise mother," women in modern Japan were expected to conduct public and social services at home. The Japanese constitutional system made it explicit that a woman's place was the home, and the Civil Code of 1897 defined the family and home as a public sphere rather than a private haven. The home became women's proper place for their public, social, and therefore "apolitical" duties, both for the individual family and for the larger family of the nation-state.

Tamura's writing on gender and "work" in Canada is inseparable from the discourse on Japan as a nation and empire that empowered and expanded itself in the economic and territorial contest of the prewar era. Tamura's writing operated in the political contexts in which Japanese migrants struggled to construct their identity, secure their position, and survive in the face of anti-Japanese sentiments, movements, and laws in Canada. Tamura thus addressed and re-created Japanese migrants in terms of the dichotomies of home country/foreign country and Japanese women/ Canadian women (or Japanese women/European and American women).

In her negotiation with the "oppressive race" in North America, Tamura—as one of the female migrants herself—engaged in creative activities to rebuild the bodies of female Japanese migrant workers and mothers who saw Japan's inferior position in "the world" and therefore redoubled their efforts to elevate it. Yet she also once wrote to her migrant readership, "Let's put aside for a while the pride of Japanese women in the world, the duty of Japanese women for Japan, or, in sum, the whole life of a progressive Japanese woman."[81]

Whether or not she was conscious of it, Tamura's writing from 1918 to 1924 in Vancouver advocates Japan's higher status in "the world"—and female Japanese migrants' specific duty and responsibility to help accomplish it. The restrictions that migrants experienced as subjects of the Japanese empire living in Canada determined her sense of women's and Japan's liberation, power, and progress in America and Europe. Against the backdrop of the competition for power and prestige in Japan, in Japan's occupied territories, and in the West in the prewar period, Tamura moved in 1918 out of the center of culture in Japan and crossed the imperial borders to the social margin of the Japanese immigrant settlement in Vancouver. There she actively participated in the discourse that delineated the female bodies of the Japanese empire.

Bodies in Los Angeles: The 1930s

In the modern period of the Japanese empire's eastward expansionism, which collided with the "westward manifest destiny of white America," Tamura herself moved from Tokyo, the metropolitan center of the Japanese empire, to Vancouver, Canada, a part of the United Kingdom of Britain, and on to Los Angeles in 1935.[82] After the death of her husband, Suzuki Etsu, Tamura moved to Los Angeles and resumed writing for *Rafu shinpō* (Los Angeles news), a Japanese immigrant newspaper. Under the pen name Yukari, she produced 104 submissions to a column called "Kariforunia no hitosumi kara: Hito ni au" (From the corner of California: Meeting with people). This column featured Tamura's thoughts on her interviews with members of the Japanese immigrant communities in Los Angeles during her two-year stay. Her subject matter was the Japanese immigrants situated within the competing discourses of the state-driven nationalism of the Japanese empire and of the United States; the Japanese and American governments' surveillance over the lives of immigrants; and Japanese immigrants' conflicting patriotism for Japan and for the United States in the mid-1930s. The idea of "the potency of the national in transnationalism," as Eiichiro Azuma characterizes the Japanese immigrant history in the United States before the Pacific War, is instructive for my analysis of Tamura's texts in Los Angeles.[83] Here I expose the discursive force of the Japanese empire in the bodies that cross imperial borders in Tamura's writings in and after Los Angeles.

Upon her arrival in Los Angeles, Tamura described "America" and its nationalism in her column as follows:

> This is the country of Roosevelt. I who live in King George's country, called Canada, which is the territory of Britain . . . came to America, and find it a wonder. . . . A whiff of the smell of nationalism is naturally different. . . . It is the same nationalism, but here the smell of commercial imperialism that is specific to America is dense, and the whiff smells everywhere. . . . To this [commercial imperialism], an incantation is attached: "We do our part." For the recovery of American economy, all the people chant, "We do our part."[84]

According to Tamura's discourse, American nationalism has an over-whelming odor that intoxicates everyone in the United States. In a state of intoxication/indoctrination, people chant the slogan "We do our part," celebrating themselves as part of the American empire built on the capi-talist economy. Thus Tamura uses a sensual description of smell to make a statement about the effective dissemination of nationalism in the United States. She also touches on the sensual nature of the "commercial imperi-alism" that captivates Americans in every corner of the social landscape: "When observing this talisman [i.e., the incantation "We do our part"] everywhere that may reach even ants' eyes, I am impressed by how the advertisement of American nationalism quite reaches out."[85]

Within this all-pervasive American nationalism, Tamura also recognizes the expanding Japanese empire and its surveillance of Japanese immi-grants living on the West Coast of the United States. From her interview with the owner of a bookstore called Taishūsha (Company of the masses), Tamura learns that the Foreign Ministry of Japan has put the store on its blacklist because its name indicates that it is a venue for Communist Party publications.[86] Thus the dictates of the nationalist and capitalist discourse that supports the expansion of the Japanese empire extended both to Japanese immigrants in America (Issei) and to foreign-born Japanese (Nisei).[87] Moreover, the Japanese government's surveillance of Issei coin-cided with their exclusion from the mainstream of American life. Tamura explores this problem in one of her columns.[88] She realizes the colliding forces of the Japanese empire and the American empire that permeate the lives of Japanese immigrants in Los Angeles. Migrant women's bodies serve as the site of her political and historical analysis.

The bodies of Issei and Nisei in Los Angeles are situated at the intersection of the Japanese and the American empires. Tamura writes about an Issei immigrant who learns ballroom dancing on behalf of the Japanese empire:

> There is an honor and liveliness *(menmoku yakujo)* in
> Mr. Kiyohara, who compromised his customary principles,
> swallowed his tears, and began taking dance lessons for the
> enormous purpose of international friendship, not for fun or as a
> pastime. . . . According to Mr. Kiyohara, he did it with sweat all
> over him. . . . In 1915, when the consulate office was first
> established, Consul Oyama hosted a party to which white people
> of distinction were invited. Thanks to these [lessons], Mr.
> Kiyohara danced with them triumphantly and with skillful steps.
> He won the great honor for his fellow countrymen instead of
> being embarrassed.[89]

Mr. Kiyohara's efforts can be seen as a continuation of those of the Japanese government officials and diplomats who had danced with Western dignitaries for the sake of the nation at the Rokumeikan in the Meiji era (as mentioned in chapter 1). In Tamura's column, however, the host is the Japanese consulate as an agent of the Japanese empire; the Japanese diplomat is an Issei immigrant; and the dancing takes place on American soil. In this setting, an Issei man dances with "white people of distinction" to elevate the status of his ancestral land of Japan in his adopted land of the United States. In contrast, Tamura contends, Nisei move their bodies merely for pleasure:

> The reason Nisei dance is that they seek the outlet for the pulse
> of their young lives. It is very natural and pleasurable to feel the
> flow of the rhythm of life in each other's limbs [as they] dance
> together in pairs of young men and women. The story that once
> upon a time Issei sacrificed their time and money and practiced
> [dancing] diligently for a purpose, rather than [dancing for] mere
> enjoyment, probably looks ridiculous to Nisei.[90]

Realizing the competing ideas and practices among different generations of Japanese immigrants, Tamura promoted tourism, or exchange of people, between Japan and the United States. After meeting with a civil officer named Yokota from the Japanese government, Tamura saw tourism as one of the "national endeavors" that could disseminate knowledge about Japan's position and military activities in East Asia:

> Civil Officer Yokota is the sponsor of the international tourist bureau, which is the organization of the tourist work of the Japanese government that was established in Los Angeles this time. . . . In Japan, too, tourist work has increasingly flourished recently, and it was 1930 when the tourist bureau, the organization of the government, was born.[91]

> The number of tourists [to Japan] was small because there was a lack of recognition [of tourism] as a national endeavor, and the advertisement [for tourism] did not reflect [this nationalist endeavor]. But, finally, the opinion prevailed of those who had had an eye on this aspect since earlier times. Since the endeavor was finally in concrete shape and the international tourist bureau was established, the organizational activities continued, and gradually the [number of] tourists increased.[92]

> The desire of foreigners to know Japan has become especially notable. This is after the Manchurian Incident, and there are a lot of foreigners who come to Japan for the purpose of seeing Manchuria. . . . In the face of these national endeavors, Japanese who reside in the Pacific, too, should have interest in this endeavor from the mission to connect the east and west oceans, even if they do not seem to be the immediate problem as they do to the Japanese [in Japan].[93]

Against the backdrop of Japan's official colonization of Manchuria in 1931, Tamura advocates tourism not only for Issei but for Nisei, so as to engage them in the aspirations of the Japanese empire. Tourism as a nationalist endeavor of the Japanese government is clear in her writing.

Tamura's last statement in the preceding quotation also appears in the context of the Issei nationalism that arose in the 1930s. Eiichiro Azuma explains:

> The origin of modern *Issei* nationalism can be traced to the rise of Japanese militarism in Manchuria in the early 1930s. This new geopolitical development in East Asia drastically transformed the hitherto estranged relationship between the empire and the immigrant community after 1924. For policy makers in Japan, Japanese residents in the United States became politically relevant again in the context of the growing tension with Anglo-American powers.[94]

Japanese immigrants in the United States also became relevant to Tamura's discourse on the two empires. To bridge the schism between the Japanese and American empires that split their subjecthood, Tamura's writing prescribes a specific movement, in the form of tourism, for Japanese immigrants in the Pacific. Her writing appears also in the context of immigrant societies that expected the internationalized Nisei to perform a mediating role between two empires.[95] Furthermore, Tamura promotes tourism for Japanese immigrant Nisei and also for North Americans, so that they can get to know Japan in the context of its imperial expansion. Tamura's writing merges with the nationalist endeavors of the Japanese government.

Within the context of competing notions and practices between patriotic Issei and indifferent Nisei, Tamura (writing under the pen name Satō Toshiko) created short stories after her return to Tokyo in 1936. In "Kariforunia monogatarai" (California story, 1938), Tamura presents two contrasting American-born Nisei women in their twenties who are in conflict with their Issei parents. In this story, the Issei wish to counter racism in the United States and establish a connection with the Japanese empire by using the bodies of their Nisei children. Wu Peichen contends: "The story shows Issei's wish for their children to marry Japanese or Japanese Americans so that they can maintain the purity of Japanese blood based on Issei's Japanese nationalism and racism."[96] The resistance of the young Nisei women to their Issei parents in the story, however, manifests itself in the female bodies that transcend national borders. Transcendence is a point emphasized by recent scholarship on Tamura's works in North America. My exploration of "Kariforunia monogatari" recognizes the conflicts between the Issei and Nisei generations and provides readers with an aspect of Tamura's writings that may be recognized as "transnational." However, this is only one aspect—rather than the determinant—of the entire body of Tamura's works produced in and after her stay in Canada and the United States.

In "Kariforunia monogatari," one of the two main female characters, Nana, marries a Nisei at the demand of her Issei father. This is an attempt by her parents to maintain the Japanese "pure" blood lineage. Through the notion of the pure blood running in their bodies, Nana's Issei parents can identify with the expanding empire of Japan and elevate their racial status as Japanese immigrants living in the United States. For Nana's father and the Andō family she marries into, Nana's value depends on her ability to bear a legitimate child who will inherit their pure Japanese blood. When she becomes pregnant, however, Nana loathes her body:

> Nana couldn't believe it was true that the thing that is about to be born anew is breathing inside her flesh. . . . But if there is something that is about to be born, it was Yasutarō's child, because the only person who touched her flesh was the one she married. From that time on, Nana couldn't help but hate her flesh. Going by the day count, the American doctor diagnosed that she had become pregnant after marriage. But Andō's mother's doubt didn't disappear, and she preferred to believe the nurse's diagnosis. Whether Nana's mother-in-law doubted or believed it was irrelevant to Nana.[97]

Both her Issei father's forcing her to marry Yasutarō and her Issei mother-in-law's doubts about the paternity of her child deprive Nana of agency over her own body. Not surprisingly, she resents her impregnated body that carries the Japanese lineage of the Andō family.

Moreover, the household of the Japanese immigrant family that encompasses Nana's body is described as a dark space of confinement: "Every glass window and even the back door were shut black and tight like a prison door."[98] Nana has nowhere to go but must remain in "the Japanese home" as an enclosed space, despite attempts to escape: "Nana has left the house of Andō several times and returned to the native home of Yamaki. And she asserted her desire for divorce to her father every time. But she was accompanied back to Fresno by her father after all."[99] Her father claims that "parents must take care of their daughters."[100] Thus "Kariforunia monogatari" re-creates the patriarchal household as a battle-field—a theme of women's struggles in Tamura's writings in Tokyo in the 1910s—for the Japanese immigrant women in Los Angeles in the 1930s. With the depiction of a patriarchal Japanese immigrant household in the United States, "Kariforunia monogatari" problematizes the extension of the hierarchical structure of families in Japan beyond its borders.[101]

Like Nana's father, the Issei mother of the other main female charac-ter, Rui, wishes to make a bodily connection with the homeland of Japan by using her Nisei daughter. After the death of Rui's father from heart disease,

> Mother sent Rui carrying the bones [of her father] to Japan, to
> bury them in the hometown of Shinano. On this occasion, Mother
> had a plan to lay a natural path from the American national land to
> the Japanese national land (kokudo), where she could send Rui
> into married life.[102]

Here "Mother" contends that the link between Japanese immigrants and the national space of Japan is natural, and is established by the body parts of the imperial subject. By making Rui travel across the ocean to bury her father's bones in Japan, Rui's mother imposes on her a filial obliga-tion to help maintain the Japanese lineage of the family. She also wishes to connect her lineage with the homeland by marrying Rui into a Japanese family in Japan. Azuma explains the political context:

> Japanese immigrants often viewed Japan's ascendancy in Asia in
> such a way as to bolster their own ideology of racial empowerment
> in the American context, which motivated many parents to send
> their children to the racial homeland in the first place.[103]

Japanese immigrants' dependence on the expanding Japanese empire for their sense of racial empowerment is clear in "Kariforunia monogatari." Giving her daughter a mission to travel to Japan, both to bury her father's remains in its soil and to marry a Japanese man there, not only reaffirms the supposedly natural lineage of the Japanese blood of the Issei parent (Rui's mother) but also helps elevate the racial status of Japanese immi-grants in the United States.

The Nisei daughter Rui, however, is indifferent to marriage. For her, it is independence (promised by her production of art) rather than dependence (on a Japanese husband, family, or the expanding family empire) that will make her personal life expand.[104] Unlike her friend Nana, whose body is confined at a Japanese home by her filial and familial obligations, Rui enjoys a sense of freedom and strength. The narrator describes her body: "It was a figure that was as if along a strict line from top to bottom; the softness and weakness of a woman's body were stripped away."[105] Rui tells Nana: "You don't have to worry about anything. Life is vast and immense. . . . As if to show its vastness, Rui extended both her arms with her thin chest open."[106] Her self embodies a vision of life that is free and filled with potential for expansion in the "wider society." For Rui, independence is based on her separation from both the United States and Japan:

> Rui didn't think at all that her work made her superior among the
> Japanese daughters and sons who were born in America. Her work
> was "Rui's" work as far as she was concerned. All parents think
> that their society consists only of Japanese society. Our society is
> wider. So, provided we do our job as a job, it will resonate with a
> wider society immediately.[107]

Thus the young Nisei women's point of view, as declared by Rui, transcends that of their Issei parents, who are solely concerned with the social and racial status of the Japanese immigrant community in the United States (and specifically in Los Angeles).

In "Kariforunia monogatari," Tamura inscribes bodies to show (1) Issei attempts to connect with their ancestral land, and (2) Nisei efforts to transcend the borders of nations and empires. Recent scholarship has emphasized the transcendence of the framework of nations in Tamura's texts.[108] My analysis of her various writings on the Japanese immigrants in North America, however, exposes these migrants as moving targets for the Japanese, Canadian, and American governments, which sought to mold their bodies and minds as they moved both away from and toward the center of the imperial discourses. Wherever she lived outside Japan, and thus found settings for her narratives, Tamura continued to depict the bodies and movements of Japanese immigrants. She told stories that show the Japanese immigrants' shifting, divergent, and sometimes simultaneous affinities with the empires of both the West and Japan.

Bodies in Tokyo: The 1930s

After her return from North America in 1936, Tamura wrote: "I just returned to Japan, and there are a lot of things that I do not understand.
Only the outer fence expands, and I am insecure [not knowing] where the
internal organ *(naizō)* is."[109] Although she has become familiar with
the expanding border of the empire, Tamura claims, she is unfamiliar with
the inner workings of Japan. Visiting a factory in 1937, the year of the outbreak of the Second Sino-Japanese War, Tamura nevertheless problematized the conditions of the female workers as the arms/hands of Japan.
Again using the pen name Satō Toshiko, she wrote in "Futsuka kan":

> At the front of the industry, behind guns, are these female
> workers. . . . Their fingers produce most of the munitions of the
> Japanese military. . . . Even after I left the factory with Mr. A,
> the nerves of the fingertips of female workers press heavily upon
> me. Why are the hands of laborers valued so cheaply to this
> extent?[110]

Tamura laments the ruthless use of women's physical labor after the loss of
the male workforce due to the empire's demand for soldiers on the battlefield. Thus in Tokyo in the 1930s, she repeats the same concern she voiced
in Vancouver more than a decade earlier, for female workers who were
exploited because of their gender and socioeconomic class. Moreover,

> Japanese women do not have political rights as weapons with
> which to protect themselves, as Western and American women
> [do]. . . . The ones who work receive double or triple oppression
> at home and in the workplace, like slaves.[111]

Tamura also re-created the bodies of female laborers as the womb of Japan
and asserted that the government's abuse of them would lead to the
demise of the nation:

> The state's policies for expanding production . . . would rather lead
> Japan to destruction, . . . [even] if those policies result in the
> degradation of female laborers and even more exploitation of their
> already abused position and deprivation of their health. Women
> are the motherly womb *(botai)* of the Japanese people.[112]

Tamura's writing on working women is not unrelated to the state discourse of the time that constructed and protected female workers as the mothers and wombs of the empire (see chapter 2). In her texts, however, the womb is both personal and political, in that it is the source of power for the empire of Japan and also for women's own lives. "Don't forget," Tamura asked female workers, "always to strengthen and enrich your own power of life. . . . Skills and knowledge should be firmly acquired with the body and be used as the womb from which a sort of strong power of life springs."[113]

Again, Tamura repeated the same concern for women's position in Japan in relation to the national status that she had expressed earlier in Canada. She wrote in 1938 in Tokyo:

> Remnants of feudalistic customs affirm and continue to lower
> women's position and culture, and treat them as though it is
> women's nature. . . . Unless they disappear, the cultural and social
> standard of the whole of the nation-state of Japan will never rise.[114]

Thus Tamura reiterated in the late 1930s her position that the status of women determines the standing of Japan.

Tamura's participation in the state discourse on war is evident in her excitement and expectation for the female writers who joined the army as war correspondents. "Jūgun bunjin ni okuru chikara no bungaku o!" (To war correspondents: Power of literature!) proceeds as follows:

> Especially for women writers who have been added as war
> correspondents for the army, it is predicted that from this
> absolutely supreme experience, literature that is epoch making and
> profound with love for fellow countrymen will emerge in Japanese
> women's literature from now on. Even if they cannot serve the
> army [as soldiers], they are equally involved by engaging in
> writing. This attempt is a great joy for Japanese literature. . . .
> [Joining the army] is not only a fortune for these chosen people
> but a fortune for Japanese literature as a whole. . . . The cultural
> duty that rests on the pens of these chosen people of literature is
> equivalent of the national duty that rests on the guns of soldiers. It
> is inevitable that literature of power will be born from . . . people of
> literature who serve the military. They will replace the erstwhile
> weakness of Japanese literature.

In this statement, the power of writing a work of literature is equated with the power of fighting in the army for the nation. Tamura herself never served in the military. Chapter 6 introduces Hayashi Fumiko, who volunteered to accompany soldiers on the battlefield as a war correspondent in the late 1930s in China. In 1938, when Hayashi marched with Japanese soldiers from Beijing to Hankou, Tamura left for China as a correspondent for the news organization Chūō Kōronsha. In Shanghai, she published the journal *Josei* (Women's voice) in Chinese and worked with the editor Kanro, now known to have been a spy working for the Communist Party.[115] Tamura also had a close link with the Japanese government in Shanghai. Her funeral there in 1945 took place with support from the Japanese government.

As already explored in chapter 4, Yosano Akiko's discourse re-created Japanese female bodies as a powerful source for resisting and rebuilding the empire. There I argued that shifts from resistance to support of the nation-state's war efforts in Yosano's texts can be found in the changing definitions of women's procreational bodies. When Yosano's writing reconstructed the world as the female procreational body where Japan participated in the conflicts of imperial powers, women's bodies changed from being objects of protection by the government to being agents of empire that reproduced soldiers to engage in the military aggression.

The shifts in Tamura's texts from resistance to support of the state's designation of the subjects of Japan can be attributed to the changes in her positions as a woman and a migrant at different times and in different places as the empire of Japan expanded. As we have seen in this chapter, Tamura's focus shifted from the late 1910s to the late 1930s from problems of gender and sexuality to problems of gender, class, ethnicity, and race, as she moved physically from the center of the Japanese empire to the cities of Western imperial powers. Tamura's aspirations for the independence, liberation, and power of women and their bodies found battlegrounds in Tokyo, Vancouver, and Los Angeles, within the context of competing forces of the empires of Japan, the United Kingdom of Great Britain, and the United States.

In Tokyo until 1918, Tamura's writings created the bodies of women within the space of home, as a battleground where they needed to resist the gender politics of the Japanese nation-state.

From the late 1910s until the mid-1920s, Tamura's narratives re-created female immigrant workers and mothers in the space of the "home" of "foreigners," and created their mission to elevate the status of Japan among the American and European imperial powers.

In the late 1930s in Los Angeles, Tamura's texts inscribed the bodies of Japanese immigrants who exert the competing forces of transcending and re-creating the nationalist discourse of the Japanese and American empires.

In Tokyo in the late 1930s, Tamura's texts defined the womb as the source of power for the Japanese female workers and for the empire. Her texts also equated the act of writing with the act of fighting for the military of Japan.

Tamura used the body as a site of political contest and participation in Japan and North America, and she created the discourse on migrants who sought to overcome their marginalized experiences within their homes, workplaces, and empires.

CHAPTER 6

Wandering on the Periphery:
Hayashi Fumiko

THE FEMALE MIGRANT BODIES IN THE WRITINGS of Hayashi Fumiko (1904–51) seem to deviate from the logic that unites the organic body of Japan. With their movements outside the home, the literary characters in Hayashi's texts move away from the dominant institutionalized "good wife, wise mother" ethos as domesticated servants of the state. They exert the exilic energies of migrants who find themselves disconnected from domesticated, established, and settled dynamics of culture. By acting inadequately as the subjects of the empire, they leave the mainstream and move into a discursive field that is opaque. Hayashi's obscure portrayal of female bodies and their logical genesis affords them a measure of liberation. Her female characters attempt to empower themselves as the decentered and "unhoused." Hayashi's texts offer the possibility of transgressing the discursive borders of women's bodies prescribed within the body of empire. However, when Hayashi and her heroines leave the homeland of Japan and set foot on foreign soil, they enter a field that is in some ways identical to the nationalist discourse that supports the expansion of the empire.

Hayashi's primary texts of literature have given birth to secondary analytical texts that continue to create and re-create certain narratives and ideologies about migrant and marginalized women. One weakness of these analytical narratives lies in their exclusive focus on women in *naichi* (the inner territory of Japan) in Hayashi's works as apolitical, or on women's position as being outside the system of the nation-state. By investigating the female bodies in motion in Hayashi's texts in the prewar and immediate postwar periods, I demonstrate the politics of the "personal" female body, and especially the connection between the body of women and *kokutai* (the body of the nation and empire). By exploring the politics of the personal experiences of the migrant women, I analyze how female bodies that move away from the state discourse in *naichi* and move toward it in *gaichi* (the outer territories) disconnect and reconnect the bodies of women and empire in Japan.

Narratives about Hayashi Fumiko: Apolitical Women as Outsiders

Hayashi's popularly and critically acclaimed titles *Hōrōki* (Diary of a vagabond, serialized in the journal *Nyonin geijutsu* from 1928 to 1929) and *Ukigumo* (Floating clouds, serialized in *Bessatsu shōsetsu shinchō* in 1949) suggest that her heroines construct their subjectivity by identifying with the decentralized, unstable, and disjunctive home and native place, rather than the centralized, stable, and united empire of Japan. The narrator in *Hōrōki* declares, "watashi wa furusato o motanai" (I have no native home) and "tabi no furusato e kaerō" (let's return to traveling, my native home). As Janice Brown's biography points out, Hayashi was born as a *shiseiji* (illegitimate child) outside the state system of family registry. This meant that she was unable to be identified by those who investigated the origins of prospective wives, students, and employees before allowing them into the institutions of marriage, school, and workplace.

Hayashi experienced poverty and movement as a way of life. By accompanying her parents, who lived on the road by selling low-quality goods after their failure in operating a used-clothing store in Shimonoseki in 1914, Hayashi floated from one cheap inn to another and attended school only irregularly. While the family continued to move, she enrolled in an elementary school in the town of Onomichi in 1916, wrote poetry, and worked part-time. When she moved to Tokyo in 1922 to await her intended fiancé's graduation from Meiji University, Hayashi took a variety of low-income jobs to survive financially. When the relationship ended in 1923, the year of the Kantō earthquake, Hayashi returned to Onomichi and continued to experience instability and poverty, moving as she did from one job to another as a maid, shop attendant, waitress, and factory worker.[1] With their rootlessness and constant mobility, Hayashi and her heroines lose a sense of stability and travel adrift in *naichi*.

Despite dispossession, displacement, and instability, Hayashi grew up to be one of the most productive, critically acclaimed, and popular writers of the 1930s and 1940s Japan. The 1930 edition of *Diary of a Vagabond* consists of prose and poems written between 1922 and 1928, in the context of the rise of the urban workingwoman and the emergence of

Marxism and anarchism. Brown explains that although the "left-wing" sociopolitical theories attracted large numbers of writers, Hayashi's extreme independence kept her distant from both Marxist and anarchist literary associations and the *bundan* (literary establishment): "Fumiko was not accepted by any literary group, establishment or anti-establishment, male or female."[2] Hayashi lived and wrote as an outsider and vagabond.

In reading Hayashi's writings, critics sometimes label them "proletarian" or "anarchistic," but more often "apolitical." Paradoxically, Hayashi's literature is also often labeled "anarchist" when it is equated with so-called apolitical sentiment (even though anarchism is a political designation) and, less paradoxically, when it is contrasted to her consciously proletarian contemporaries such as Hirabayashi Taiko (1905–71), Miyamoto Yuriko (1899–1951), and Sata Ineko (1904–98). More often, however, Hayashi's literature is deemed to be free of politics; since she demonstrated neither intellectual rigor nor ideological commitment, her writing is considered to be personal and *therefore* apolitical. Joan Ericson explains: "Hayashi's fictional world was 'of the people' *(minshūteki),* but not from a sense of ideological commitment or political correctness. Hayashi painted her portraits small: descriptive depictions of everyday life *(shomin no seikatsu)."[3]*

Although Hayashi's works of literature may lack intellectual and political accomplishment, commentators deem them successful in conveying the resistance of their heroines to seemingly hopeless circumstances. For example, Brown writes:

> An unrestrained poetic manifesto . . . was to appear in Hayashi's poetry, too, yet without the revolutionary platform. Instead, Fumiko directed the scathing anarchist vision towards her own life, demolishing through her poems the prison wall of past personal experience. . . . Thus, the "self-centered" anarchist credo gave impetus to the portrayal of the female vagabond, victim and outcast, struggling to realize her own inner, dynamic potential in spite of the forces arrayed against her.[4]

When Hayashi's struggles against her deprivation are discussed, critics foreground the resilience of the wanderer at the margin of society who triumphs in her "inner struggles." They see these forces as directed toward the confines of her own past and predicaments.

Understanding Hayashi's works as personal and apolitical has prevented many critics from analyzing them in the contexts of history and politics. For example, Komata Yūsuke concludes his critique of Hayashi's *Gyokai* (Seafood) as follows:

> There is no point in investigating Hayashi's attitude toward war, although the historical background of this work is one in which many people who had lost their livelihoods in Japan aimed for the continent, dreaming of success and material riches.[5]

In her investigation of Hayashi's *Ukigumo* (Floating clouds), Noriko Mizuta sees the possibility for women to live outside the system and gain power in the context of prewar Japan. Mizuta says of the heroine Yukiko in *Ukigumo:*

> In Yukiko's case, she has no relationship with the nation and its policies because she leaves Japan by abandoning her place within it and by being disgusted with it. At the national level, she might be understood to be prodded/motivated and carried away by advertising that constructed Southeast Asia as dream and paradise. However, for Yukiko herself, the *gaichi* was a locus for liberation.[6]

This passage suggests that Yukiko's personal life has no correlation with the national imperial policies, and that her freedom in *gaichi* marks her departure for a realm outside the political system of Japan. Most scholarly assessments identify the heroines of Hayashi's works as women on the move, but they gloss over the expanding body politic behind her roaming bodies.

Many critics have also dismissed Hayashi's extensive wartime writing within the dominant political discourse of the 1930s and 1940s, the sheer quantity of which makes it too important to ignore. On assignment for *Tōkyo nichi nichi shinbun* (Tokyo daily news) in 1938, Hayashi became the first Japanese woman to enter Nanjing after it fell to Japanese troops. In the same year, she and Yoshiya Nobuko were the only two women whom the Ministry of Information included in the first "Pen Squadron," a group of writers who toured the war front and wrote for Japanese readers about the soldiers' circumstances and sacrifices. Hayashi was also one of the first Japanese to enter Hankou, on assignment for *Asahi shinbun* (Asahi newspaper). Between 1940 and 1941, she and other Pen Squadron writers gave lectures in Japan, as well as on the military bases and to Japanese communities in Korea, Manchuria, and China. Based on her experiences at the front, Hayashi wrote the war reports *Sensen* (Battlefront, 1939), *Hokugan butai* (Northern bank platoon, 1939), and *Hatō* (Rough seas, 1939). As a war reporter, Hayashi also spent eight months in the Andaman Islands, Singapore, Java, and Borneo in 1942 and 1943.[7] During the intensification of the bombardment in 1945, she withdrew from Tokyo to the countryside in Nagano, writing poetry and children's stories. After the war she returned to Tokyo and wrote vigorously until her death from overwork in 1951. Ericson notes that Hayashi participated in the general enthusiasm for the war effort during the Pacific War, only raising her voice against the death and misery caused by war in the postwar period.[8]

There are two major reasons for the neglect of Hayashi's writings on war as historical and political texts in most of the scholarship on her. First, her wartime reportage is considered poor writing (i.e., mundane and sentimental), and therefore not worth critiquing. Hayashi's articles on war received very little critical notice and are largely dismissed because of her insipid obsession with humdrum experiences. Kawamoto Saburō remarks that Hayashi's emphasis on the minutiae of her own travels and travails is irrelevant to the "larger discussions" (*ōkina giron*) of ideology and politics.[9] Second, critics have disregarded Hayashi's wartime writing on the premise that it is so obviously pro-government that it needs no further exploration. Hayashi had never consciously held any political ideology, had enthusiastically participated in wartime propaganda, and had offered no apologies or explanation for her participation in government-defined roles and in the war effort. In short, her lack of ideological and political consciousness makes her wartime writing unworthy of political and historical inquiry. When commentators discuss the continuity between her prewar and postwar works, it is with respect to her depiction of nihilistic yet resilient vagabonds who engage in their inner struggles at the fringes of society.[10] Thus the personal is disconnected from the political and has prevented critics from exploring the politics of Hayashi's texts. Arai Tomiyo's recent *Chūgoku sensen wa dō egakareta ka: Jugunki o yomu* (How was the Chinese battlefront described? Reading war correspondents) is therefore a rare and important contribution to the studies of women's relationship with war in modern Japan.[11]

Migrants as Political Figures in Hayashi's Writings

With the existent scholarship on Hayashi as a point of departure, my analysis here is guided by the following questions:

> Can women who are uninspiring in their intellectual pursuits and unconscious of their politics, as they are in Hayashi's works of literature, be free from politics?
>
> What are the politics of "personal" experiences?
>
> If Hayashi and her female characters are unconventional, how do her texts operate against the discourse of the nation-state?
>
> How does Hayashi's writing shape the images of subjects as members of an empire?
>
> How is imperialism reproduced, as both geopolitical logic and cultural representation, through women's bodies?

By examining the bodies that move in *naichi* and *gaichi* in Hayashi's writings, this chapter reveals how women's ambiguous and contradictory sentiments, ideas, and actions re-create the modern Japanese empire in the prewar and immediate postwar eras. My goal is to show how Hayashi's heroines, who engage in their "personal" struggles at the margins of society, become relevant and responsible for the seemingly distant and yet dominant power structure of society. To that end, I analyze the female wandering body as a source of metaphor, a locus of structural analogy.

With her novel *Hōrōki* (Diary of a vagabond, serialized from 1928 to 1929 and first published as a book in 1930 by Kaizōsha), Hayashi became an instant success as a writer. The theme of rootless existence and mobility is evident in the title of the novel. Contemplating her body in motion, the heroine in *Hōrōki* thinks, "Alone I walk, just walk."[12] The heroines–narrators in Hayashi's two war reports, *Sensen* (Battlefront, 1939) and *Hokugan butai* (Northern bank platoon, 1939), are also conscious of bodies in motion. A poem in *Hokugan butai* illustrates this point:

> These are the feet that have walked.
> These are the feet that have walked.
> These are the small feet that have walked
> From the plain to the north of the lake. (331)

The theme of bodily movement is also embedded in the sense of transience in time and space. The narrator in *Hōrōki* states, "There are floating clouds in the sky. That is my figure" (84). Clouds that appear and disappear as time passes are a recurring image of impermanence in Hayashi's texts, and *Floating Clouds* is the title of her last complete novel, *Ukigumo* (serialized in 1949 in the journal *Bungakukai* and published in book form in 1953). Focusing on the socially and economically marginalized women who move across the time and space of the empire of Japan, this chapter exposes the changes in women's desires, actions, and memories that re-create the empire in prewar and postwar Japan. The ways women aspire toward liberation and empowerment change as their bodies move in *naichi* and *gaichi* of the Japanese empire. To examine the shifting relationships among women and the empire and its colonies, the next sections analyze the bodies that move (1) within the space of *naichi* in the prewar era in *Hōrōki*, (2) in *gaichi* in *Hokugan butai* during the war, and (3) between *naichi* and *gaichi* in the prewar and postwar eras in *Ukigumo*.

Hōrōki: The Female Body in Motion in *Naichi*

Before I examine the migrant women in *Hōrōki*, an explanation of the choice of this text for the following discussion is necessary. Hayashi revised *Hōrōki* frequently and substantially between 1928 and 1949 to an extent unusual even in comparison to other Japanese writers who turned their serialized work in journals and newspapers into books. Using only one-third of the text that Hayashi wrote for *Nyonin geijutsu* in 1928 and 1929, the first sequel to the book appeared in 1930. Hayashi continued to reorganize the material, revise it in successive sequels, and rewrite the text for each new edition. In different versions of *Hōrōki*, changes in tone, style, and use of language are quite evident. Joan Ericson explains that "discontinuities and unresolved incidents allowed the narrator to revisit specific events—or moments immediately adjacent to those already recounted—and retell the experiences in a new way."[13]

The following discussion is based on the version of *Hōrōki* that became the canonical text in a single volume following the death of Hayashi Fumiko in 1951. This canonical text combines the revisions of 1939 and of the 1949 sequel. One may argue that the challenge *Hōrōki* as a text presents to the state's central nationalist discourse on the empire was possible only as reconstituted memory and from the standpoint in the postwar era.

What is important in my exposition of Hayashi's works is the consistency in her depiction of the migrant women in *naichi* in both the prewar and postwar periods as the ones who live outside the space of home and the institution of the family and the family empire. I emphasize this point to make a contrast between the desires, ideals/ideologies, and actions of the migrant women in *naichi* and *gaichi* in Hayashi's texts.

Hōrōki's heroine, who constantly moves as a loner within *naichi*, declares, "I have neither home nor homeland" (251). Her wandering is predicated on the loss of home and an inability to re-create its sweetness: "The people in my home country have never said anything warm to me" (287). "My feeling deepens that home is not a place where I should return again, even if I become a beggar in a different land *(ido)*" (435). Against the prescription of the Civil Code of 1897, which domesticated women in the space of home, a constant state of movement replaces any fixed space for the heroine. Unable to find residential or financial stability, she floats adrift as a vagabond in *naichi* in the 1920s.

The heroine in *naichi* in *Hōrōki* seems unfit as a member of the family system or household *(ie)*, and also of the family empire. She lives outside the institutionalized womanhood of "good wife, wise mother" and has no desire to get married or bear children: "Why did my poor mom give birth to me?" (329). "I have no intention of becoming a bride. I want to study" (367). "For my entire life, I don't want children" (357). Motherhood and wifehood seem strange rather than natural to her. Thus she deviates from the life course of Japanese women prescribed by the central state discourse. The notion that women's role is to nurture Japan's soldiers as children *(sekishi)* of the emperor carries no significance for her. She recognizes the patriotic women of the Aikoku Fujinkai (Women's Patriotic Society) (77) but gives no further thought to it. Moreover, she clearly challenges the notion of the united family nation/empire of Japan that nurtures its subjects:

> Human beings fight alone;
> There is no need for the force of the crowd.
> Eating meals does not depend on the culture of family or nation.
> (446)

This poem denies the function of the family to nurture the subjects of the nation-state. It is the individual person, rather than the family or nation, who engages in the battle for survival. Therefore, soldiers who fight for the nation and empire of Japan carry no meaning for the heroine of *Hōrōki*. She recognizes that a soldier lies dead in the room in front of her apartment, but her reference to him is minimal: "Probably another soldier died" (68). Neither a nurturing mother nor a wife, she has no function as an integral part of the body of Japan. She says, "I rub the night cream and red water color onto my cheek like a rising sun" (382). The symbol of the Japanese empire inscribed on her body functions not as a confirmation, however, but as a mockery of the nationalism that defines the empire's subjects.

With no home or family, she consciously identifies herself not with the *minzoku* (ethnos, or ethnic group) of the Japanese people but with that of the nomads: "My family *(ichizoku)*, which was like the nomad people, has now settled in a stable land and become a different ethnos *(iminzoku)*, who enjoy what I call semistable life" (292). The heroine uses the notion of ethnos not as a people or nation; rather, she adopts it in her writing to distinguish people whose lives revolve—or are unable to revolve—around the ideas and practice of family and the static space of home.

Boundaries

Although mobile, the heroine of *Hōrōki* is aware of the limited borders of space in which she exists and can move. Against the state discourse on the expanding border of the Japanese empire, she declares that Japan "is a kingdom of confinement" (404). In asserting that "I have come to know different boundaries" (454), she indicates that socioeconomic class determines the space that is allocated to her. By living in the space of a *hinminkutsu* (ghetto) and working in factories, she notes, "I extended my arms and legs within the limit that was allowed to me and closed my eyes" (265). The sense of boundary for the heroine's body is defined in contrast to the presence and movement of the imperial family. Thus she is aware of her difference from, rather than identification with, the body of the imperial family: "I belong to the class that must close *shōji* doors and hold its breath all day just because an imperial family member is going to pass by" (435). As a way of survival, she says, "We sit on our knees and bow, with smiles on our faces even when we are under a burden. That's the only way to live [for us]" (433). Contrary to the modern ideals of freedom of the autonomous individual and the nation, the heroine in *Hōrōki* experiences bodily confinement, weakness, and suffocation in *naichi*.

Class

The state's grand narrative of purity, wealth, and health finds no place in *Hōrōki*. In contrast to the discourse on the purity of Japan, the space of the heroine's residence is described as a ghetto *(hinminkutsu)* immersed in impurity *(yogoremono,* "filthy things") (432). Moreover, unlike the purportedly healthy bodies of the subjects who work and fight for the expansion of the rich and strong empire, *Hōrōki* constructs Tokyo as a space of confinement, filled with the sick and impoverished:

> Myriad people gather in this city,
> Those laid low by hunger,
> Atrophied faces, a whirl of sick bodies;
> The rubbish heap of the lower classes.
> The emperor has apparently gone mad.
> Tokyo—city only of the diseased![14]

Tokyo as the center of the Japanese empire is occupied by the subjects who defy the discourse that gives them the role of loyal and healthy body parts of the empire: "My body is deformed. My mind is deformed, too. The flesh *(nikutai)* has nothing to offer. It is completely burnt out."[15] Her disloyalty to the imperial family is also shown in corporeal terms: "I hate aristocrats. They are the invalids with no elasticity in their skin" (403). The impure, sick, and disabled constitute the empire of Japan in *Hōrōki*.

The heroine's sole concern is the survival of her body, independent of the empire:

> The lower the ideal, the more realistic human beings are, and the
> abyss between the ideal and reality is felt less desperately. But,
> mainly, it [desperation] is related to the tension between the
> amount of power of a human being, the accumulation of energy,
> and . . . the nutrition that the organic body digests. There are two
> paths, of either dying or living. (86–87)

Rather than the spiritual ideal, it is the body of a person, which consumes food, creates energy, and exerts power, that enables her survival. Throughout the novel, the heroine's sense of survival is rooted in physicality: "I only have a sturdy body" (326). "I have no talent, wealth, nor beauty to

live with. The only thing that is left is the body that contains a lot of blood"
(116). Deprived of natural ability, material wealth, and beauty, it is the cir-
culation of blood inside her body that activates her life.

And the body is the source of her writing. Art forms, as the products of
her physical responses, must contain in themselves the flow of blood,
according to the narrator: "It [Dadaism] is . . . word play. There is no blood
flowing. It's unable to say anything honest" (335). Analogously, breathing
is equated with creating poetry: "I feel as though I am merely two bags of
lungs" (301). "I came to loathe myself [as someone] who walks around
carrying a poem called 'My lungs sing' (hai ga utau)" (316). The heroine's
physical response, rather than ideas or ideals, formulates the poems and
prose of Hōrōki. She declares, "Literature isn't about ism!" (377).

> So, I closed my eyes and tried to create poetry. . . . To begin with, a
> memory of smell comes. Then, waterlike tears come to the nose
> and make noise. A voiceless cry comes out, as if I were bit by an
> alligator. My breasts with the weight of a thousand kan press on
> me like a pile of udon powder. (335)

Through the medium of the five senses, she creates poetry. The sexed
body, the animal, and food stimulate the creation of poetry; ideas, ideals,
and ideology seem to play no part in the artistic process for the heroine.

The degraded exchange value of the female body is a continual point
of reference in Hōrōki. "Well, if you need my body, I will give it to you
for free" (239), the heroine says. "Although I am writing my real guts
(harawata) out, I cannot even make a penny (issen)"(380). The heroine
can only create poetry that is immersed in blood and viscera. Thus the
value of her writing is directly connected to the value of her body. Meager
pay, long working hours, and excruciating working conditions lead her to
question the position and conditions of the lower socioeconomic class
throughout the novel: "How long do we have to endure such a stupid way
of living? . . . Like earth insects, our long hours, youth, and health have
been exploited endlessly inside the distorted factory cut off from the sun"
(39). "There are times when I feel hateful, as if I were born to die from
working" (230). Her physical health and livelihood are constantly threatened by poor working conditions in the factory. The hands of female
workers seem to function to repeat the cycle of the lower class: "Various
inferior articles targeted at the lower class flow out like a flood from our

hands to the market everyday" (38). The class at the bottom of the socio-economic stratum seems to produce and consume itself in *Hōrōki*.

The laboring female body is also sexually commodified for the exchange value of the market economy. "My breasts are as heavy as *ikkan*. [My] crazed sensualities. . . . With a glance, I have a facial expression that says 'This girl is for sale'"(319). She recognizes that her body marks her as a prostitute in the eyes of others: "They must be mistaking us for prostitutes" (244). The professions of café waitress, factory worker, and writer are in close proximity to prostitution: "If both peddling and writing are no good, there is nothing that can be done other than selling my body to Tamanoi [a red-light district]" (457). "Prostitution is always women's twilight *(tasogare)* . . . a story that anesthetizes sacrifice" (395). This statement reminds the reader of the lower-class families who sold their daughters to prostitution and anesthetized their sacrifice as a gesture of filial piety (see chapter 2).

Prostitution is also linked to the empire, which sexually abused female bodies not only within *naichi* but also in *gaichi* (chapter 2). The heroine reflects on a coworker who was sold as a sex worker: "The woman called Ohatsu-chan . . . was taken by a man when she was twelve and was kidnapped to Manchuria. . . . She was soon sold to a geisha house" (99). *Geisha* (person of art) is not synonymous with prostitute in its literal sense. However, considering the fact that many prostitutes called themselves *geisha* and also the specific context in which the "geisha house" appears in Hayashi's *Hōrōki*, *geisha* in this text most likely means young women who were forced into prostitution. Belonging to the class that sells their sexualized bodies for economic survival, the heroine also identifies with the ethnically and racially colonized people of the empire of Japan. Her physical proximity to colonials in the factory dormitory in *naichi* links them in adversity: "It was sad to sleep beside the women from Karafuto and Kanazawa with our three pillows next to each other" (88). Association with races and ethnicities other than the Japanese further leads her to equate herself with a slave sold to the "white" race: "When night falls, I sing a useless song with the sorrow of an aborigine *(dojin)* who was bought by the white men's nation" (86–87). The degradation leads her to identify finally with the "nonhuman": "My youth withers and becomes ashes. . . . among the same dust of nonhumans" (330). The heroine declares, "Having reached this stage, there is no room to restore my small honor. What a strange and agonizing way of life!" (380).

In *Hōrōki*, the heroine, who is homeless in her native land and decentered from the nation-state in *naichi,* identifies not with the central discourse on Japanese women but with the sexually, economically, ethnically, and racially exploited female bodies in Japan. Within the boundaries that demarcate the female bodies of the marginalized, she questions the meaning of her movement: "Who on earth am I? What the heck. I wonder why I am alive and moving" (311). "Exhausted, looking as ever for jobs, my youth may wither at twenty years of age. I am really fed up with the life of wandering" (421). Entrenched in the agonizing state of the marginalized, the heroine directs her anger at the mainstream: "There is nothing more hateful than the model people. That is the case of all the people who are walking. They move their two feet in turn and make hasty progress, as if hope hangs in front of their eyes" (422). Against the current of the normal people who make "progress," the heroine explains, "my feet . . . retreat to impossibility" (425).

This sense of impossibility is intertwined with fear, insecurity, and lack of power, which overwhelm her: "The state of fearfulness before execution presses on my chest" (427). "I am as insecure as ever. . . . I don't have any power" (331). With an acute sense of helplessness, the heroine finds no grand narrative in *naichi*: "There is neither beautiful thought nor good thought" (309–10). "I have seen various tricks that make it impossible to know how much is true and how much a lie" (441). Thus, "the natural truth" of the pure and unbroken imperial line and the Japanese people who carry the sacred mission of ensuring peace in the world fails to reach the heroine as a subject of the empire. "Really, there is nothing that is pure" (295). "There isn't peace in this world, is there? . . . There isn't eternity, is there?" (348). She wonders if "there isn't a simpler destiny" (441) for her.

Even after she achieves critical acclaim and popularity as a writer in the narrative, she finds no fulfillment. This is apparent in part three of the novel: "As for my work, it is nothing but various miscellanies. . . . In reality, I have come this far, but it feels as though the road from here has been cut off" (295). With no sense of direction after her success as a writer, the heroine envisions a destiny that may destroy the current state of affairs in *naichi*: "Ah, my life will end as it is. It cannot be helped. Isn't there something that is bright? . . . Isn't there something that is explosive? God . . ." (401). In her desire to destroy the current state of affairs and renew her life, she even invokes war or natural disaster: "I don't think extraordinary things are going to occur in the future. I can't even be given that satisfaction. I want to explode like gunpowder. I wish that an intense and immense earthquake would hit again" (454).

The heroine's desire for destruction of the current state is accompanied by her wish to leave *naichi:* "I thought Tokyo would be filled with many good things, but there is nothing" (322). "I am going to desert Tokyo, which has no truth" (246). "Somehow, I came to want to go to a foreign country. . . . I want to go somewhere far away" (353). The foreign countries she envisions include Korea (327), India (398), France (313), and Russia (327). Although she narrates the destitution of the lower class and race/ethnicity that occupy the fringes of Japan, she also aspires to re-create the periphery as a utopia for the socially marginalized and exploited: "The old newspaper that wrapped *takuan* (pickles) states that there are still tens of thousands of *chōho* of wasteland in Hokkaidō. I think it would be fun if our utopia could be created in such an uncultivated land" (43). The heroine envisions the periphery of Japan as an unexplored place of salvation for her. Envisioning a utopia outside Japan, she wishes for the explosion *(bakuhatsu)* of the society that confines her body.

In the following sections, Hayashi's heroines find happiness in China (in *Hokugan butai*) and French Indochina (in *Ukigumo*). Many of the articulated and unarticulated desires and needs of the body of the heroine that moves within *naichi* in *Hōrōki* assume different physical forms—and correspondingly different fulfillments—in *gaichi* in *Hokugan butai* and *Ukigumo*. In *Hōrōki*, the heroine writes: "I imagine making a direct appeal to the emperor. I have a dream in which he looks at me, likes me so much, and invites me to go with him to a nice place. A dream is a freedom given specially to human beings. . . . Why was I born in Japan?" (334). Through an intertextual analysis of Hayashi's texts, one of the answers to this question is found in *Hokugan butai* and *Ukigumo*. "A nice place" in these texts seems to be the outer territories of the empire. In this space, the heroine's physical movements and actions become part of the expansionist endeavors of the nation-state. It is the female bodies of wanderers who move to *gaichi* that direct them closer to the central state discourses that construct the body of Japan, with the emperor at its center and the subjects as the body parts.

Despite the challenge posed in *Hōrōki* to the discourse on women as bearers, nurturers, and educators of the children within the family system, its heroine does simultaneously voice desire for a family in the future:

"I have nothing but an ambiguous feeling of something like envy for something like a family" (418). "I close my eyes and think of myself aging and withering with a sense of security in this [sort of household and family]" (295). She also notes, "When living becomes suffering, I think of home. People often say that they want to die in their home" (285), and mentions "the so-called warm household with family [that] is ten thousand *ri* away" (315). In a distant China under Japanese occupation in the late 1930s, the sense of family she envisions materializes as the family empire in *Hokugan butai*. As one of the marginalized in society, the heroine in *Hōrōki* lives in a state of suffocation and fear in *naichi*. The heroine in *Hokugan butai*, however, finds security by becoming a family member of the empire and worthy of dying for it. "Japanese songs are primitive and physical *(nikutai teki)*," the heroine in *Hōrōki* asserts (319). In my analysis of *Hokugan butai*, I explore how the body of a woman who moves in *gaichi* and writes a journal/prose/poetry becomes reconnected with the body of Japan.

Hokugan butai: Female Bodies in Motion in *Gaichi*

Female bodies that move in *gaichi* in Hayashi Fumiko's works are found, among other places, in her two war reports, *Hokugan butai* (Northern bank platoon, 1939) and *Sensen* (Battlefront, 1939). After the attack on Bukan began in 1938, the Ministry of Information formed the "Pen Squadron," which sent writers to the war front with the military's financial support and protection. The first Pen Squadron consisted of twenty-two writers; as already mentioned, Hayashi Fumiko and Yoshiya Nobuko were the only two women (working for the army and navy, respectively). Before Tamura Toshiko left for Shanghai as a correspondent for the news organization Chūō Kōronsha in 1938, she had enthused that female war correspondents' writing was as important as fighting in the army. Hayashi and Yoshiya were pioneers for other women writers, such as Sata Ineko, Mikawa Kiyo, and Masugi Shizue. Some wrote about the sacrifices of soldiers at the request of the military, others on assignment as war correspondents, but participation in the Pen Squadron was based on will rather than coercion.[16] As noted earlier, Hayashi had been a war correspondent for *Tōkyo nichi nichi shinbun* in 1938, was the first Japanese woman to enter Nanjing after it fell to Japanese troops, and was also one of the first Japanese to enter Hankou (for *Asahi shinbun*).

Hokugan butai was written as a journal from September 19 to December 28, 1938, with not a day missing. *Sensen* takes the form of correspondence in the same year, depicting life at the battlefront for a week. Both works resemble *Hōrōki* in combining forms of poetry with prose. In the following discussion, I focus on *Hokugan butai* and offer an intertextual comparison with *Hōrōki*.

᪥

The heroine/narrator in *Hōrōki* wanders in *naichi*, whereas the heroine/narrator in *Hokugan butai* finds her physical motion in *gaichi* in the late 1930s: "Even during the day, I . . . walked or rode trucks frequently. Every night, I am in the state of motion. Although I sleep in the same cotton field, I don't encounter the same landscape even for a day."[17] Rather than retreating "into impossibility," as the heroine in *Hōrōki* does, the narrator in *Hokugan butai* moves forward by marching with the Japanese soldiers in China. Unlike the heroine in *Hōrōki*, who denounces the "model people" who use their two feet, each in turn, to move forward in *naichi*, the heroine's body in *gaichi* in *Hokugan butai* marches toward a destination with determination: "I must not be a coward in the face of life, destiny, and way of life. . . . I want to move forward no matter what" (241).

The heroine's physical movement is in unison with the bodies of soldiers: "Morning, afternoon, night, and even in the middle of the night, I heard the voices of the soldiers all the time during this intense attack in the military advance, and I was at all times with the soldiers" (311). Her movement on the battlefield is led and protected by the Japanese soldiers. Moreover, she identifies her body with that of the Japanese soldier in *gaichi*: "Both my home country and parents have receded far away now. . . . My hair is dirty with dust, and with the daily advance of the army I have become completely dark like a boy" (307). "I accompanied Yōsukō Northern Troop. . . . The color of my face is soiled black with dust and grime, and I am no different from the soldiers" (300). Impurity in *naichi* and *gaichi* is the same in its dirtiness and darkness. However, whereas the heroine in *Hōrōki* was indifferent to soldiers in *naichi*, the narrator in *Hokugan butai* becomes one with the soldiers in their bodies. And this is only possible in *gaichi*.

Furthermore, she identifies herself with the soldiers who die for the emperor:

I hear the soldiers say, after being hit by bullets and collapsing, "*Banzai* for the emperor, *banzai* for my mother." I feel that even I

would cry it out from the bottom of my heart, looking at the
heavens and grasping the earth, if I were to collapse on this
battlefield now. (296)

Thus the heroine of *Hokugan butai* celebrates Japanese soldiers as heroes
who cast their lives away in service to the emperor. She also wants to
inscribe their acts onto her body:

I am a noncombatant and, moreover, a woman. But as a Japanese
woman, I want to burn and etch the way of the Japanese soldiers'
battle firmly onto my mind's eye. . . . My eyes are wide open with
utter astonishment at the patriotic passion that has filled my body.
(234)

The heroine in *Hōrōki* was deprived of her youth and health as the lower-
class workingwoman in *naichi*; the heroine in *Hokugan butai* experiences
the fruition of her youth by passionately identifying with the Japanese soldiers in *gaichi*.

The patriotism that overwhelms her body is also shown in her desire to
be part of the family empire:

It seems as though every soldier is always worried about his
homeland *(kokyō)*. Until they achieve heroic and incomparable
deaths magnificently, they always think of their homeland.
They are good husbands, fathers, and older and younger
brothers. (308)

Unlike the men who exploit women's sexualized and commodified bodies
in *naichi* in *Hōrōki*, the men in *gaichi* in *Hokugan butai* are conscientious
family men who are devoted to their homes and homeland. "Soldiers are
all kind and gentle," and also "pure" (256), the heroine writes in *Hokugan
butai*. This representation is striking, given that the Japanese government
was establishing and operating military sexual slavery ("comfort") stations
in occupied and colonized territories, including China (chapter 2).

In contrast to the figure of the prostitute, with whom the heroine identifies in *Hōrōki*, the narrator in *Hokugan butai* wishes to look after the soldiers as a motherly nurse in *gaichi*, in accordance with the ideology of the
Aikoku Fujinkai (Patriotic Women's Society, discussed in chapter 3):

A long time ago, at a small public hospital [in *naichi*], I sometimes
came across lazy nurses. But those who have come here are
absolutely simple and godly people who may become mothers of
the injured and sick soldiers. (215)

In this statement, nurses are equated with sacred mothers of soldiers on
the battlefield. And it is specifically in the space of *gaichi* that the heroine
herself can become a mother: "I want to . . . look after the injured and sick
soldiers," she states (214). Her desire to nurture the soldiers is predicated
on her wish to become a part of the war effort of the empire of Japan: "The
bloodshed of the Japanese soldiers on the Chinese continent must bear
fruit for the people of Japan" (234). Only in *gaichi* is her connection with
nationalism and the empire possible: "I will never forget, for the rest of
my life, the feeling of love for the country. . . . I don't care about my house
in Tokyo" (241). "I want to stay behind" (214).

Whereas the heroine in *Hōrōki* acts through the multiple identities
of the economically, ethnically, and racially marginalized and colonized
peoples of the Japanese empire in *naichi,* the heroine in *Hokugan butai*
reconstructs her identity as a pure and patriotic Japanese in *gaichi.* Her
national identity in *gaichi* is determined by the dichotomy of Japan and
China as clearly separate entities. Earlier in her account, the heroine in
Hokugan butai sees China as an extension of the Japanese countryside: "It
was a landscape that was not at all different from the Japanese garden"
(214). This reminds the reader of Yosano Akiko, who wrote in *Manmō
yūki* that nature in China under the Japanese occupation had a Japanese
feel to it (see chapter 4). Then, just as Yosano did in Manchuria in 1928,
so Hayashi's heroine in *Hokugan butai* makes a clear distinction between
Japan and China: "I was not born in China. I was born in beautiful Japan"
(318). Her description in *Hokugan butai* further re-creates China as the
dirty and stagnant "other," in contrast to Japan as the pure, beautiful, and
advanced self:

[From Shanghai,] I flew on a naval airplane here to Nanjing in
about an hour. Although it was only an hour, the landscape I
viewed from the airplane was boring and made me sick to my
stomach. An area of stagnant lakes and ponds occupied far more
of the earth's surface than the land, and it was a netherworld that
was dark and damp, like parts of rotten fruits. (212)

WANDERING ON THE PERIPHERY

Looking from afar, it felt like a typically decent town with pale colors, but when I entered, it was a town of ruins that were quiet and dirty, like a graveyard. (277)

Chinese who are dirty occupy the space of a devastated battlefield, in stark contrast to the "magnificent" advancing Japanese soldiers, who have "gotten rid of excess" and whose "spirit becomes extremely pure" (281). In this land of dark and stagnant China, what sheds light is the progress of Japanese army: "But I gazed at the monotonous road of red soil and thought that it looked as if a red carpet had been laid for us as far as Hankou" (295).

Furthermore, the heroine in *Hokugan butai* reconstructs her Japanese identity based on physicality. Whereas the Japanese soldiers appear as "magnificent" men (281), the Chinese soldiers are described as children and girls:

Until today, I was tired of seeing the dead bodies of Chinese soldiers *(tsunkopin)*. But the living bodies of Chinese are somehow spooky whenever I see them. They are begging for something with incomprehensible words. . . . Begging facial expressions, crying facial expressions, idle facial expressions, facial expressions speechless from injuries. Each person in the troop of dirty Chinese soldiers is thinking about various things and gazing at me. The majority of them are boy soldiers, and there was an officer who was seventeen or eighteen years old. Their clothes were still new and their eyes were gentle, like the eyes of girls. (306)

It is the heroine who has the power to articulate the weakness of the "incomprehensible," "speechless" Chinese in her clear writing. By describing the Chinese as begging, idle, and dirty, *Hokugan butai* re-creates the Japanese as the ones who provide, make progress, and purify.

Even the corpses of the Chinese soldiers that lie in the "ruins" and "graveyard" of the countryside strike her as being different from those of the Japanese soldiers:

The body of the Chinese soldier looked like nothing but an object to me. While having heart-rending sentiments and admiration for our soldiers who were carried on the stretcher a while ago, I feel like a cold stranger to the dead body of this Chinese soldier. My feeling toward the dead body of that Chinese soldier is completely empty. . . . Moreover, in my consciousness of *minzoku* (ethnos), this is the conflict between enemies that cannot come together. (283)

Thus the sick and dying in the rotten netherworld of China are described as feminine and turn into dead objects.

Although fear, insecurity, and deprivation are recurrent themes for the heroine in *Hōrōki* wandering in *naichi,* marching with the soldiers in China brings the narrator in *Hokugan butai* confidence, security, and fulfillment in *gaichi.* In contrast to the heroine's concern for the survival of her body in *Hōrōki,* the danger of being on the battlefield is transcended by the heroine in *Hokugan butai,* who notes that "the wild bullets make terrible sounds incessantly and rattle my stomach" (271), but also states, "When I was walking the battlefield, I didn't suffer one bit from such insecurity" (320). This is because "everywhere I go, it is full of servicemen from the army and navy. So there is no worry anywhere I go" (322). By marching with the Japanese soldiers, she attains a sense of power: "I wonder about my power that has enabled me to come here with soldiers who have occupied so many forts. . . . The voices and footsteps of the soldiers may have taken me this far" (281). Moreover, her confidence and power derive from a sense of common purpose and destiny with the soldiers:

> I like soldiers.
> One destiny,
> with the speed of a moment,
> flies howling over the army troop on the battlefield
> and smashes and scatters life, way of life, and lifespan.
> There is such a heroic action. (271)

In contrast to *Hōrōki,* which denies any grand narrative of good, beauty, or truth in *naichi, Hokugan butai* creates and affirms those qualities in *gaichi.* The heroine celebrates "good" soldiers and "the beauty and cruelty of this battlefield. . . . It's cruel, and also sublime and lofty" (294). Furthermore, the Japanese soldiers are described as godly: "Every soldier is growing a beard like Christ" (315). The heroine in *Hōrōki* aspired to a "simpler destiny"; the heroine in *Hokugan butai* attains one on the battlefield in *gaichi*: "Things this frank and simple will dissipate [after the war]" (315).

The beautiful and sublime battlefield is where the heroine in *Hokugan butai* achieves the climax of her youth: "As a woman who has come this far with soldiers, I feel the joy of a child and youth" (318). It is in *gaichi*, as part of the occupied area of the expanding Japanese empire, that she spends "truly happy days" and becomes euphoric (318). In contrast, she realizes,

> I wonder what my writing until now was all about. Until now, I continued to grope, and screamed day and night, as though my youth would crumble like dry flowers. When I think about my daily life, which is difficult and sad, I sometimes think, to tell you the truth, that it's all right to die [here] and go home [as the dead]. My life of suffering as a human being will begin painfully after I return home. (296)

As she reaches Hankou, the destination of the Northern Bank Platoon, the heroine begins to contemplate the life she must resume in *naichi*: "Having come this far, I feel that the reality of *naichi* has gradually come closer, and the difficult life and world make me fall into a strange insecurity" (320). "I feel sad that the sense of confidence in walking the battlefield has now begun to shrink gradually" (329). The end of *gaichi* and the beginning of *naichi* mark the loss of security and confidence and a return to uncertainty and fear: "I can't help feeling that something scary is waiting for me if I go back" (321).

As explored earlier, the female bodies in motion in *naichi* and *gaichi* in *Hōrōki* and *Hokugan butai* convey women's paradoxical relationship with the empire of Japan. The interplay between the government's efforts to mobilize women and the refusal and aspiration of women to become integrated into the body politic of the empire manifests itself in the female bodies that move in Hayashi's discourse. The heroine's wartime collaboration in *gaichi* in *Hokugan butai* signifies her quest to gain power within the empire rather than beyond it. As a result, Hayashi's writing becomes part of the forces of aggression and atrocity of Japanese imperial expansion.

In the following section, I analyze how Hayashi's novel *Ukigumo* (Floating clouds) re-creates the relationship between the bodies of women in *naichi* and *gaichi* and the rise and fall of the empire in prewar and immediate postwar Japan.

Ukigumo: Female Bodies in Motion between *Naichi* and *Gaichi*

Hayashi's last complete work of postwar Japanese literature, and allegedly one of the most important, *Ukigumo* (Floating clouds) was serialized in *Bessatsu shōsetsu shinchō* in 1949, and has received critical acclaim and popular attention ever since.[18] Here I show how the depiction of female migrant bodies in Hayashi's fiction in postwar Japan reproduces the body of modern empire as a site of nostalgia and promise. By moving in and out of the geographical center and periphery of modern Japan, Yukiko, the heroine of *Ukigumo*, deviates from acting as a body part of the empire, thereby destabilizing the centralized state's definition of race and its use of women in the expansion of Japan. Most scholarship on Hayashi's works has emphasized women's "personal" experience in Japan's occupied territories as independent of a political movement to colonize the neighboring Asian nations. By tackling the politics of women's personal experiences of freedom within the discourse of the political empowerment of Asia with Japan at its center, I explore both the disconnect and the connection between female bodies in motion and the rise and fall of the modern Japanese empire in Hayashi's postwar masterpiece, *Ukigumo*.

In the very title of the novel, movement is explicitly employed as the theme of the work. *Ukigumo* is notable for depicting the mobility of the body and the malleability of space. Locales in the novel include Tokyo, Ikaho, and Yakushima in Japan, and Dalat in French Indochina (present-day Vietnam). In these spaces, an unmarried woman, Yukiko, enjoys great mobility, and her mobile body disconnects and reconnects the time and space of Japan in the contexts of the rise and fall of the empire. Yukiko's mobility is first highlighted when she leaves her native home after graduating from a women's school in Shizuoka and moves into the house of her brother-in-law, Iba, in Tokyo, where she attends typing classes. In the novel, Yukiko moves from Shizuoka to Tokyo in prewar *naichi;* is posted to Dalat in prewar *gaichi;* returns to Tokyo in the immediate postwar era; travels to Ikaho; and then moves to Yakushima, where she dies and the story ends.

Ukigumo against the State's Discourse

The narrator in *Ukigumo* explains the body of Japan after the war as follows: "Japan had become only a torso, having lost all of Korea, Taiwan, the Ryūkyū Islands, Karafuto, and Manchuria in this defeat."[19] Japan as a headless torso symbolizes the loss of the emperor as the sovereign of the body politic in the postwar era.[20] According to the representations of the national body in the novel, the inner territory of Japan *(naichi)* during the Pacific War is a torso complete with head, and its colonies and territories *(gaichi)* are its arms and legs. Therefore, the subjects of the emperor who moved away from *naichi* to settle in *gaichi* (French Indochina in the early 1940s in *Ukigumo*) were expected to work as the arms and legs of *kokutai*, the body of the Japanese empire. After the war, the empire lost its limbs (i.e., its colonies), so Yukiko's body returns from the periphery of the occupied territory to the center of the Japanese torso (i.e., Tokyo in the postwar era).

As an unmarried woman and typist in Japan before the war, Yukiko struggles economically in the lower and peripheral strata of society. As a migrant on the nation's soil, she is antithetical to the domesticated woman who supports the family and the family empire within her legally prescribed space of home. Yukiko is "unhoused" in prewar *naichi,* and her body fails to function as the womb of the Japanese torso, thus deviating from the prescribed function of women's bodies to populate the Japanese empire. With no stable home or family background, she is not a candidate for the status of sacred wife and mother in either prewar or postwar Japan. Since Yukiko is not respected as a pure woman, she is repeatedly forced to serve her brother-in-law Iba sexually in prewar Tokyo. Raped, sexually repressed, and exploited, the bitter and suffocating conditions she endures on the nation's soil make it impossible for her to recapture or re-create the warmth of home. As the narrator explains, Yukiko "wanted to get away, float adrift, just anywhere."[21] In the sense that Yukiko deviates from the nation-state's prescribed duties for its female subjects, the novel *Ukigumo* contradicts the state-driven national discourse on Japanese women.

Hayashi's *Ukigumo* also challenges the racial hierarchy that served as a discursive tool to thematize and justify Japanese expansion as an empire. For example, in the context of the state discourse on the Yamato (Japanese) race as pure and sacred (see chapter 1), *Ukigumo* depicts the Japanese body in relation to the colonized Annamese in Dalat as follows: "When she placed her hand on the white starched tablecloth, Yukiko felt that her yellowish hand was even more unclean looking than the Annamese maid's."[22] Yukiko thinks of the Japanese settlers as impure in contrast to the Annamese, the objects of their control: "Japanese were scattered around like trash over the beautiful land."[23] Moreover, Japanese are the "narrow and mean-spirited stray cats who walk on the soil of other people."[24] Thus the pure and sacred Yamato race, according to the state discourse of modern Japan, is associated with "trash" and "stray cats," despoiling the beautiful land of other peoples.

Furthermore, according to the state discourse, which used the Confucian ideal of holding one's proper place in social hierarchies, the Japanese, in conformance with their role as superior brothers and sisters among Asians, must lead and enlighten their inferior siblings (chapter 1). In *Ukigumo*, however, the narrator describes Japan as uncivilized: "The Japanese soldiers that one saw around here looked poverty-stricken. Wearing uniforms that did not fit them at all, their figures, with battle helmets jammed down over their big heads, looked like those of soldiers who had come from an imperfectly civilized country."[25] Thus *Ukigumo* refuses to categorize the Japanese as the sacred, superior, and central race of the Greater East Asia Co-Prosperity Sphere. Contrary to the state discourse, Yukiko "was inclined to feel a sort of racial inferiority" toward Marie, an Annamese typist.[26]

"Big heads" may be read as one of the physiological characteristics of the Japanese people. More important for this study, however, "big heads" functions as a metaphor for the men/patriarchs of individual families who represent in microcosm the emperor as the head/patriarch of the family empire. In addition, "big heads" signify the disproportionately weighty ideologies of the head compared to the weaker arms and legs of the body, which can fail to act in accordance with the grand narrative of the state. The imbalance between the soldiers' heads, which are swollen with ideology, and their "crude" bodies is symbolized by the poorly fitting helmets and uniforms that cover their bodies. In other words, the gap between the ideology and the body that enacts the ideology is signified by the ill-fitting clothes.

By depicting Japanese bodies as "crude and shabby," *Ukigumo* challenges the prescription of them adorned with wealth and power, a point celebrated in *Kokutai no hongi* (The essence of the national polity, 1937), published by the Education Ministry, and in the government slogan of a "rich nation, strong army," which had prevailed since the Meiji era. Instead of acting as the arm or leg of a Japan that is prosperous and strong, Yukiko feels like a badly crafted prosthetic in French Indochina. The narrator explains that Tomioka (Yukiko's boss and lover) and Yukiko felt "they were becoming just like the Japanese cedars that had been transplanted to the uplands of Dalat and had begun to wither."[27] In contrast, the people of Indochina make Yukiko aware of "the strength of a people that was relaxed and expansive, leisurely situated in the flow of history, [a strength] that seemed much more deeply rooted than that of her own people."[28] *Ukigumo* thus represents and re-creates the colonized with more strength and expansiveness than the colonizer.

Even more telling is the fact that the narrative stresses the disconnect between the body of a woman and the body of the empire. Reflecting on Yukiko's body during the war, the narrator explains: "Yukiko was truly happy then. . . . When the soldiers were fighting for the sake of life and death, Yukiko was wonderfully in love with Tomioka."[29] With "her body . . . young [and] fertile," Yukiko experiences the pleasure and power of "love" with Tomioka.[30] Thus the military actions are deemed to be irrelevant to her wartime experiences. The narrator even wonders at the vibrancy of Yukiko's body immediately after the war: "It was strange that the skin of a woman who had lived this kind of life should still be so velvety smooth. Even when a country had lost a war, did the skin of its young women suffer no change?"[31] The narrator emphasizes that Yukiko's physical experience is personal and unrelated to the rise or fall of the Japanese empire.

Many critics, including Noriko Mizuta, consider Yukiko's experience to be personal, apolitical, and ahistorical. Mizuta explains by highlighting "Hayashi's narrative of asymmetrical wanderings of man and women."[32] She writes: "Tomioka's move to Dalat . . . is not a personal escape from Japan but part of a national movement to colonize Asia . . . none of Tomioka's experiences would have been possible without the national power and protection of Japan."[33] In contrast, Mizuta contends that Yukiko entertains the possibility of personal freedom precisely because she is in *gaichi* and thus "outside Japanese history":[34]

The primeval forests of Indochina where Yukiko and Tomioka
fall in love are a dreamland located outside the institutions of
Japan. For Yukiko, it is a place that returns men and women to a

primitive state, and a place in which Yukiko's youth, sexual appeal, and vitality show their true strength. The chaos of wartime Japan, where the social system is moving toward destruction, makes possible Yukiko's escape, and her anarchic existence outside society gives birth to the possibility, however illusory, of woman's freedom.[35]

Mizuta is correct in her focus on gender, in that Yukiko does aspire to leave the institutionalized womanhood of Japan. I recognize that the unmarried Yukiko's wandering outside the domestic space and then moving from Tokyo to the areas colonized by Japan, the so-called outer territories (*gaichi*), may appear to signal her departure from the center to the margins, from living inside the system of the nation and its history to existing outside it. But despite Mizuta's arguments that Yukiko's wandering is indicative of her estrangement from the system in which Japanese women live, I contend that Yukiko does not exist outside the discourse of nationalism that contributed to the expansion of the empire. Indochina is not "outside" but "inside" the system of Japan, for Yukiko as well as for Tomioka. Therefore, the narrator's focus on Yukiko's freedom and independence as decentered from the state discourse demands further careful analysis.

Expanding Empire

In Hayashi's *Ukigumo,* Yukiko travels to Indochina out of her own wish (*shigan*) to leave Japan. She does so under military auspices, however, as a typist for a forestry survey at the Ministry of Agriculture and Forestry. By 1942 the Japanese empire had displaced the French empire and gained control of Indochina. Upon Yukiko's arrival, her boss Tomioka's colleague Kano says, "Let's have a toast. To Koda Yukiko, who has come all the way to Dalat on occupation duty!"[36] And as Seya, an old engineer reminds her, Yukiko's actions in Indochina are not free from the nation-state's endeavors to build the empire: "Wherever we go, the Japanese Army will be there. There's nothing to worry about. What's more, as the only Japanese woman, you will have a great many responsibilities. You will be working hand in hand with the Imperial Army."[37] Although neither Yukiko nor Tomioka is "a great patriot" like Kano, it is the imperial army that guides their actions.[38] Moreover, Yukiko's relationship with Tomioka operates within the war of invasion for the expansion of the empire. Tomioka explains that it is Japan that determines both Yukiko's and his own being: "This country has made us what we are . . . although we are like floating leaves without roots"[39] Although Yukiko and Tomioka appear to move like freely drifting clouds, without aim or direction, their presence and actions in French Indochina, and their own encounter and relationship, would be impossible were it not for the Japanese empire's militarist expansion.

In French Indochina, Yukiko feels ill suited to playing a leadership role in strengthening Japan's hold on its new territory, and remains inadequate as a subject of the Japanese empire. In stark contrast to the "poverty-stricken life [which] is suffocating" in *naichi,* however, she experiences a measure of liberation and fulfillment in *gaichi,* Indochina, owing to her participation in the expansion of the empire.[40] By traveling to Dalat and staying in a French-style mansion, Yukiko attains a sense of physical and financial freedom, comfort, and security.[41] This change occurs as a result of her physical mobility beyond the border of *naichi* but within the space of the empire of Japan.

In *Ukigumo,* the setting of the French-style mansion, and the dining room table in it, narrate Japan's identification with the Western imperial powers and with the colonization of a neighboring Asian nation—colonization in which Yukiko participates. John Dower uses the metaphor of a banquet to explain Japanese imperialism: "While most of the rest of the world fell under the control of the Western powers, Japan emulated them and joined their banquet."[42] In the novel, the dining scene at the French mansion reflects and recalls Japan's contest with Western imperial powers in the prewar era. Japanese bureaucrats, including Yukiko's boss, Tomioka, take over a mansion that members of the privileged class of French colonizers had used as a summer residence: they occupy it as the official residence of the Japanese colonizers, thus replacing the Western imperial power of France. Japanese control of "Asia" is reflected in their use of an Annamese maid, Niu.

It is true that as a marginalized woman in *naichi,* Yukiko had nothing to do with the Japanese state. In French Indochina, Yukiko works in the same low-income service sector she did in Tokyo. Yet Yukiko, who could not have associated with such bureaucrats in Tokyo, stays at this mansion as a Japanese colonizer and breaks bread with them in Dalat. She remains part of that state and its social conventions, which exploit neighboring

Asian nations, ethnicities, and races as the inferior servants of the Japanese empire. This scene clearly shows how Yukiko tastes her share of the "benefits" of Japan's colonization of "Asia." Whereas her body was economically restricted and marginalized in the homeland of Japan, Yukiko is able to experience the luxury of upper-class society in Indochina by operating within the nation-state's imperialist discourse of the Greater East Asia Co-Prosperity Sphere, which sang the freedom and empowerment of Asia with Japan at its center.

The depiction of Yukiko's mobile body in an open expanse of woods is another powerful example that her experience of freedom and power is that of an agent acting out the central discourse of the state. Yukiko spontaneously falls in love with Tomioka and accompanies him when he enters the woods to conduct a survey for the Ministry of Agriculture. Tomioka kisses her, holds her hands, and leads her into the woods. Yukiko's body leaps into the expansive space. Yukiko's body, which moves from Tokyo to Dalat and enters the woods at the hand of Tomioka, redraws the expanding body of the Japanese empire in the prewar era. It is precisely the political discourse of *kokutai,* the national body that governs Yukiko's "personal" body.

Many critics have interpreted Yukiko's freedom and strength as the experience of a woman who has moved out of the system of Japan. The Ministry of Agriculture was at the margin of the Japanese government system, in contrast to the Ministry of Education and the Home Ministry, which dominated the state discourse on women. In addition, French Indochina was on the geographic periphery of the Japanese empire. However, it was the building of an economic base through the exploitation of foodstuffs, natural resources, and labor in the occupied territories at the periphery, such as French Indochina, that made possible the expansion of *kokutai* and its "development" abroad. In this sense, the core state discourse brought about its subjects'/people's movement toward the periphery.

Conversely, people's movement toward the periphery supported the core discourse of the state. For Yukiko, the movement of her body to Indochina, at the periphery of *gaichi,* is an act of connecting to the central discourse of the state—something impossible for her to achieve in Tokyo, at the center of *naichi.* In other words, by moving to the periphery of Japanese occupied territory, Yukiko participates in the central discourse that reconstructs "Japan." Her "personal" experience and interpersonal relationships evolve in a setting created by the central discourses of the state and the geopolitical expansion of the empire in the prewar era.

Naichi after the War

After the war, the Japanese empire loses its limbs (i.e., its colonies), and Yukiko's body returns from the periphery of the occupied territory to the center of the Japanese torso (Tokyo in the postwar era). She arrives at the Atsuga Port on a returning ship (*hikiage sen*) that carries only women from Southeast Asia. Although Yukiko's body was liberated in the sunlight of the South Pacific in the prewar era, it shrinks in the severe winter weather of postwar Tokyo, just as the body of Japan shrinks after the loss of its colonies. The novel depicts contraction, chaos, and devastation as it traces Yukiko's body and its movements through the devastated spaces of postwar Japan.

In prewar *gaichi*, Yukiko had worked as a subject of the empire for the bureaucratic organization of the state. As a war returnee, however, she is unable to secure a socially and financially stable position through marriage or a job, and so must continue the life of a wanderer. Her lover, Tomioka, tells Yukiko that he is unable to abandon his wife and marry her. With no stable home, Yukiko roams through the *shitamachi* until she finally moves into the dark, confined, shabby storage room of a hardware store. Behind the store stretch the burned fields, black markets, narrow winding roads, and rundown hotels of postwar Tokyo. These devastated spaces are the backdrop for Yukiko's body and represent the immediate postwar period, when almost 60 percent of all housing in Tokyo and Osaka had been destroyed by air raids. Both Yukiko's roaming body and her body consigned to the storage space overlap with the space of postwar Tokyo under ashes and in ruins.

Yukiko's physical condition mirrors the effects of postwar national politics on women's bodies. Although she has no prospect of marrying Tomioka, she continues her uncertain relationship with him, becomes pregnant, has an abortion, and suffers repeated surgeries afterward. Her abortion takes place within the particular historical and political context of postwar Japan, which produced an intersection of national and professional interests in legalizing and liberalizing abortion. More specifically, Yukiko's abortion reflects the desire of the Japanese elites and the occupation forces led by the Supreme Commander of the Allied Powers to secure economic growth and avoid the remilitarization of postwar Japan by limiting the seemingly out-of-control population growth caused by repatriation and the baby boom.[43] At the historical junction of prewar and postwar, Tiana Norgren explains:

The national goals formulated by Japanese elites had shifted from expansionism and pronatalism to domestic retrenchment and population control. . . . However, the overarching goal of bringing individuals' reproductive lives into conformity with the national interest remained the same.[44]

Yukiko in *Ukigumo* exists outside the system of family but continues her affair with Tomioka in hopes of marrying him. Her body, which suffers from complications of abortion in postwar Tokyo, is invaded, injured, and weakened.

Yukiko's experience of physical invasion also overlaps with the history of the American occupation of Japan. Yukiko becomes a prostitute for an American soldier, Joe, and the exchange value of her body manifests itself in the products from the United States—a transistor radio, chocolates, Coca-Cola—that Joe brings to her room, which she calls her "castle" *(shiro)*. In the novel, Yukiko explains her relationship with Joe to her lover, Tomioka: "That man [Joe] needs affection, too. It's the same affectionate feeling you had for the Annamese maid."[45] Here Yukiko refers to Niu, whom Tomioka had impregnated during his mission as a Japanese colonizer in French Indochina during the war. Thus Yukiko offers her sexual services ("affection") to Joe under the American occupation in postwar Japan just as Niu served as a sexual object for Tomioka under the Japanese occupation in prewar French Indochina. By equating Joe in postwar Japan with Tomioka in prewar Indochina—and herself with the Annamese maid, Niu—Yukiko exposes the material and sexual hegemony and parallelism between the occupying American military in postwar Japan and the colonizing Japanese empire in prewar French Indochina.

Re-creation of *Gaichi* in Postwar Japan

As Yukiko lives under the American occupation in postwar Japan, she entertains the memory of war, especially nostalgia for the lost time and space of Japan's prewar colony. Bathed in the nostalgic memory of war rather than peace, she dwells in a continuum between the prewar and postwar periods. This continuity is expressed in her paradoxical conformity to the systems of marriage and bureaucracy in the prewar and postwar eras. Yukiko's wish to marry Tomioka, to have him return to the Ministry of Agriculture, and to relive their time in French Indochina reveals that she depends on the male-dominated colonial policies and actions in *naichi* and *gaichi,* both during and after the war. As the narrator in the novel explains, on the one hand Yukiko wishes to be independent of men and the system of the nation-state: "Yukiko wanted to toil by doing her own work without depending on anyone."[46] On the other hand, "she could not, now, separate herself from the scent of this man's body."[47] Indeed, "her love that is attached to all of Tomioka is the last futile attempt for a woman to make her blood flow."[48] The narrator also explains: "Remembering the wash of colors and sights that was French Indochina, Yukiko thought, I want to see that place once more."[49]

To rebuild a relationship with Tomioka and to recover the health of her body, weakened by abortion, Yukiko must re-create in postwar Japan the sense of physical freedom and empowerment her body experienced as a Japanese colonizer in prewar French Indochina. She therefore insists on accompanying Tomioka when she learns that he has been given a position at the Ministry of Agriculture on remote Yakushima, a semitropical island at the southern end of Japan. By the time she arrives there with Tomioka, however, Yukiko is bedridden. As though in accord with Yukiko's wish to re-create the old village in Dalat, the narrator explains, the village on Yakushima "was exactly like an Annamese hamlet in French Indochina."[50] Thus, desperate for life and love, Yukiko attempts to regain her personal health and happiness in the space of Yakushima, which, though at the margin, is still inside Japan. In the choices she makes at the end of her life as a migrant, Yukiko therefore seeks a final, harmonious resolution of her personal conflicts in nostalgia for the modern Japanese empire, and ultimately encapsulates the story of the modern empire in her personal story.

The last scene of the novel, however, emphasizes the collapse of the empire. The open, warm, sunlit space of the woods in French Indochina in the prewar era is replaced by the cold, dark, rain-swept woods of Yakushima in the postwar era. The space of the nightmarish fringes of postwar Japan threatens and represses Yukiko's weakened body. In the end, while Tomioka is away visiting the forestry station in the woods, Yukiko "suffers considerably," collapses, and dies alone in the official residence of the Ministry of Agriculture.[51]

In reading the death of Yukiko at the end of the novel, Hasumi Shigehiko and Nakafuru Satoshi hold that Hayashi Fumiko meant to punish Yukiko as a participant in the colonization of Asia.[52] It is known, however, that Hayashi herself made no apologies for her own activities as a war reporter at the front in China and Southeast Asia from the late 1930s into the early 1940s. W. K. Wimsatt and Monroe Beardsley reminded us in "The Intentional Fallacy" (1946) that it is impossible to know what the author meant, and I refrain here from speculating on Hayashi's intentions. However, the narrator in the novel does explicitly explain Yukiko's remorse about the Japanese colonization of French Indochina. Yukiko's nostalgia is accompanied by her reflections on the aggressive, arrogant, and irresponsible practices of former Japanese colonizers:

> How did they hope to sell off, to other parts of the world, these great forests of *merukushi,* with their beautifully shaped trunks and the fine grain of their wood? Were not the Japanese—who were suddenly rummaging about among the treasures of other people that had taken them centuries to develop—nothing but robbers? How on earth were the Japanese going to administrate so many sublime forests?[53]

With their invasion of French Indochina, the Japanese exploited the fruits of Annamese labor. Moreover, the narrator in the novel explains: "The long history of these tea fields that had been carefully managed for so many years made her [Yukiko] feel ashamed of the high-handed tactics that the Japanese had used to take over everything—even these fields—in a short amount of time."[54]

Ukigumo as a text represents not only remorse but also a sense of responsibility on the part of a sexually violated and socially marginalized woman in *naichi* who benefited from the Japanese empire's colonization of neighboring Asian nations in *gaichi.* For example, in conversation with Tomioka in the novel, Yukiko refers to the "war trial" broadcast on the radio and comments on moral "responsibility" with respect to the Japanese colonization of French Indochina: "You and I are involved too, in these trials."[55] Thus Yukiko not only notices the Japanese exploitation of natural resources and labor in French Indochina but identifies with those who were tried at the Tokyo War Crimes Tribunal. She recognizes that Japan's colonization policy and actions were due both to the dominance of male politicians, bureaucrats, and military officials and to the collaboration of low-ranking civil servants such as Tomioka at the geographical periphery of the empire—and of socially and economically marginalized women such as Yukiko herself.[56]

Kano Mikiyo has pointed out the importance of facing the paradoxical contradiction of being simultaneously victim and aggressor.[57] The realization that one can be an aggressor while also being a victim of the same system is driven home by the circumstance that Yukiko, who lives at the economic margin of society and outside the institutionalized womanhood of Japan, has paradoxically participated in the central discourse of *kokutai* that contributed to the Japanese empire's colonization of its neighboring nations. Yukiko is indeed the object of economic and sexual exploitation in *naichi,* and in that sense she is a weakling and a victim. It is important to recognize how women like Yukiko made attempts to transgress the borders of their designated roles and thus gain freedom and power outside the spaces of home and the homeland of Japan, as recent studies have done. However, in benefiting from the empire's economic and sexual invasion and exploitation of Japan's occupied territory, Yukiko stands on the side of the aggressor against French Indochina. Thus it is equally important to acknowledge that it was within the expanding *kokutai,* which mobilized all its subjects, that women like Yukiko explored the possibilities of their personal freedom and empowerment in modern Japan.

Conclusion

This chapter has examined the relationship between female migrant bodies at the margins of Japanese society and the politically significant spaces of home, factory, battlefield, and the woods in *naichi* and *gaichi* of the empire that can either suffocate or liberate and empower those bodies. When the heroine in *Hōrōki* aspires to leave Tokyo and hopes that the society that has exploited her body will explode, she nevertheless continues to imagine uncultivated land on the periphery as a utopia for socially and economically marginalized people like herself. In the war zone in China invaded by the Japanese military, the heroine in *Hokugan butai* is filled with a euphoric sense of nationalism, identifies with the Japanese soldiers who are happy to die for the emperor, and wants to look after them as a nurturing nurse. On the battleground in China she finds a home she wants to stay in and a family empire she admires. In *Ukigumo,* the heroine Yukiko's experience in *gaichi* Indochina, under the control of the Japanese army, gives her a sense of physical and material freedom and empowerment she has never experienced in *naichi.* Her yearning for Indochina as a place of promise and nostalgia reminds us of the background of migration in which some Japanese people imagined and/or experienced *gaichi* as a utopia where individual freedom would blossom.

The Japanese empire invaded vast regions of Japan's neighboring nations, encompassed them into a modern capitalist system, and violently transformed the lives and views of colonized people. Yosano Akiko, Tamura Toshiko, and Hayashi Fumiko as authors, and their literary characters as well, actively participated in the discourse that both resisted and reproduced the empire by depicting women's bodies that move through, occupy, and re-create political spaces in the contest between the Japanese and Western imperial powers.

From Literary to
Visual Memory of Empire

IN THIS FINAL CHAPTER, I demonstrate how the visual techniques and metaphors used in Naruse Mikio's film adaptations of Hayashi Fumiko's novels reframe the bodies of migrant women in the language of space and time, and how the visual narrative functions as the medium of memory to re-create the Japanese imperial past in the present.[1] I examine the visual representations of female bodies that move through the spaces of home to outside the home, and on to the periphery of the geopolitical space of the empire of Japan. Further, I explore how these representations narrate *both* women's marginalized experiences and their participation in the central discourse of the state. In particular, I problematize how Naruse Mikio's filmic adaptations of Hayashi Fumiko's novels *Meshi* (Repast, 1951, novel and film) and *Ukigumo* (Floating clouds, 1951, novel; 1955, film)—and their popular and scholarly interpretations in the postwar era—focus on the issue of gender and class in *naichi* (the inner territory), or the Japanese homeland, and gloss over the problem of women's participation in the Japanese colonization of neighboring nations in *gaichi* (the outer territory).

Most of the scholarship on Hayashi Fumiko and Naruse Mikio has created dominant narratives about single migrant women at the margin of society, portraying them either as apolitical figures or as transgressors moving and residing outside the state discourse on Japanese women. These narratives, and the ideologies underlying them, move between the literary and the visual media, and as a result they are remade and recycled in the modern age of mechanical mass production.[2] When these narratives are created in the context of the postwar era as it reconstructs Japan's imperial past, they tend to focus on the victimization of women. In *The Cinema of Naruse Mikio*, a major contribution to film and Japanese studies, Catherine Russell points out "the deep ambivalence of both [the] novel and film" *Floating Clouds,* but she does not explore the nature of this ambivalence in depth.[3] I argue that the paradox of the visual representation of migrant woman in Naruse's *Ukigumo* lies in the fact that she moves outside the state discourse on gender in *naichi.* As her body moves to the periphery of the Japanese empire, however, her ideology swings toward the central discourse of the state that contributed to the expansion of the empire and colonization of other nations, ethnicities, and races in *gaichi.*

It is the bodies of women in the prewar and postwar eras—moving between the ideologically significant spaces of home and outside the home, and from there to the fringes of Japanese empire—that serve both to disconnect and connect the time and geopolitical space of Japan in memory. In what follows, I examine how Naruse Mikio's films as visual medium negotiate with Hayashi's novels as literary medium in re-creating women's bodies moving in and occupying the spaces in the prewar and immediate postwar eras. Edward Casey's statement in *Remembering* is instructive for this study of representations of the female body:

> Places are empowered by the lived bodies that occupy them; these bodies animate places, breathe new life into them by empowering them with directionality, level, and distance—all of which serve as essential anchoring points in the remembering of place.[4]

In chapters 1 and 2, I examined not only how the organ theory of the nation-state *(yūkitai kokka ron)* and the theory of the body of the nation-state *(kokutai ron)* became the political tools used to draw and expand the borders of Japan, but also how concepts of Japan as a body and the Japanese people as its body parts shaped notions of femininity and masculinity, ethnicity and race, and social classes. By exploring some of the important concepts of Japan as a body that contributed to the formation and destruction of the empire, I provided readers with the theoretical and historical context that prescribed women as body parts of Japan.

In this conclusion, I expand on the notion of *kokutai*—the body of Japan—with different components of space and place animated by human bodies moving through and occupying them. Mariko Asano Tamanoi's statement that nostalgia for the perished empire of Japan is in some sense prevalent among the Japanese in the early twenty-first century also informs this study. She explores "how the memory of victimization has turned to nostalgia for the same past that 'victimized' the Japanese."[5] In my analysis of Naruse's film adaptations of Hayashi's novels, I explore how the memory of victimization of women in *naichi* has turned to nostalgia for the same past that also victimized Japanese women and the colonized nations and ethnicities in *gaichi*.

Before conducting a textual analysis with a focus on woman's mobile body, time, and space, we must first see how Naruse came to adapt Hayashi's novels. Naruse was known for his mastery of literary adaptation, but his subject matter was especially close to Hayashi's, and the ideologies of the critical narratives on Naruse and Hayashi share important similarities.

Naruse Mikio and His Film Adaptations of Hayashi Fumiko's Novels

Naruse Mikio (1905–69) was known as a master of film adaptation of literary works, and his choice of the subjects was similar to Hayashi Fumiko's. A year after Hayashi began to receive critical and popular recognition for *Hōrōki*, Naruse created his first film.[6] Although his works stretch from the prewar period in 1929 to the immediate postwar era in the 1940s, Naruse's career as a director is understood to have peaked in the early to mid-1950s of the postwar era. This period not only overlaps with the "golden age" of Japanese film but also coincides with the years when Naruse created film adaptations of Hayashi's novels.[7] In 1951, the year Hayashi died, Naruse produced his first film adaptation of her novel *Meshi* (Repast). Subsequently, he directed *Inazuma* (Lightning, 1952), *Tsuma* (Wife, 1953), *Bangiku* (Late chrysanthemum, 1954), *Ukigumo* (Floating clouds, 1955), and *Hōrōki* (Diary of a vagabond, 1962). All six of these films based on Hayashi's novels are representative of Naruse's works in postwar Japan. *Ukigumo*, especially, was highly praised and won the designation "best film" in *Kinema junpō* in 1955, the year it was first released. As Catherine Russell writes, "*Floating Clouds* remains Naruse's most well-known film in Japan" and "is the film that brought Naruse the greatest recognition."[8] In his lifetime, Naruse directed eighty-nine films and came to be known as a director of "women's films" because most of his protagonists are women.[9]

In the eyes of critics, it seems natural for Naruse to have adapted Hayashi's novels because of the female characters his films otherwise depict. The main female characters in Naruse's films include housewives, but the majority of his female characters are unmarried women and widows, ranging from the young to the middle-aged and elderly. They are the working-class or middle-class women who live in urban areas, especially in Tokyo. In contrast to the upper-middle-class daughters in director Ozu Yasujirō's films, many of the single women in Naruse's film are low-income, working-class women who work as office clerks, typists, tour bus guides, owners of retail shops or bars, geisha, or farmers. Their living spaces consist of simple and small houses and streets in the *shitamachi*, or lower city.

Furthermore, the subject matter of Naruse's films—single women engaged in personal struggles at the edge of society for their daily economic survival—overlaps with that of Hayashi's novels.[10] Kawamoto Saburō, for example, says of the female protagonists of Naruse's films, "Women firmly establish their own place at the periphery of society. . . . They live solely by their own power, and live through the chaotic time of the postwar era."[11] On Naruse himself, Kawamoto writes: "Unlike socialist directors, [Naruse] did not link poverty directly with social problems. He depicted poverty only at the individual level with style *(kihin)*."[12] Moreover, in the world of Naruse's films, single and low-income women are victims who nevertheless demonstrate "a stubborn perseverance."[13] In short, the dominant interpretation of Naruse's films in Japan constructs women as positioned at the bottom or on the periphery of society, engaging in personal and therefore apolitical struggles. Accordingly, Naruse's film adaptations have invited interpretations similar to those of Hayashi's works, and have often recycled the stories and ideologies of women as persevering victims who live outside the political system but survive through persistence.

The Body of a Married Woman and the Space of Home: *Meshi*

Before analyzing the ideologies of narratives on single migrant women, I first examine the representation of the bodies of married women who move in the spaces of home and *shitamachi* and who are in some significant ways constructed as the opposite of single women. Focusing on the body, space, and time, this section also exposes the continuum of gender politics from the prewar to the postwar era in Japan. When depicting married women, Naruse's films use the home, and especially the kitchen, as their designated space. For example, *Meshi* (Repast), Naruse's first film adaptation of a Hayashi novel, frequently features kitchen scenes. The main character of the film, Michiyo, left her life and family in Tokyo when she married Okamoto Hatsunosuke and moved to Osaka. Although Michiyo feels unfulfilled in the role of housewife, she dutifully engages in the daily chores of cleaning and cooking. According to Nakafuru Satoshi, the art director of many of Naruse's films, the kitchen in *Meshi* is "a privileged space for women" and "Michiyo's sacred area," containing "the god of the stove" *(kamado gami)*.[14] Considering that many male policy makers in modern Japan categorize women in diametrically opposed categories—as either sacred mothers and wives or filthy whores[15]—this division defines and privileges the kitchen as a "sacred area" where the wife prepares meals for the husband. The resulting construct conforms with and re-creates the dominant ideology of women in the prewar era.

In Naruse's films, however, the sacred home, especially the kitchen, is constructed simultaneously as a spatial metaphor for bodily confinement and repression. For example, the kitchen is designed as the area of "withdrawal" *(hikikomi)* and as a "sunken space" *(ochi-ma)* one step below the dining area.[16] In *Meshi,* the couple rarely shares the same space simultaneously, and they often converse through the sliding doors *(shōji)* that divide the kitchen occupied by the wife, Michiyo, from the dining room occupied by her husband, Hatsunosuke. Using the sliding doors as a frame, Naruse's film separates the spaces for the wife and husband and depicts Michiyo cooking meals inside and at a lower level within the house. When Naruse chooses to place Michiyo in the area occupied by Hatsunosuke, he shows her in one scene crawling to clean the floor. Wiping the floor with a cloth requires a stooped posture. By making the female body crawl in the male-dominated space, however, the film makes the visual statement that Michiyo occupies a lower stratum than Hatsunosuke in the household. This scene visually signifies Michiyo's utterance "I am a maid" in Hayashi's original novel.[17] Naruse's film depicts Michiyo paradoxically, as both the womanly ideal and household slave within the family system.

Body and space are narrated not only visually but verbally by Michiyo at the outset of the film. "My husband is sitting in front of the dining table. I bring the pot of miso soup . . . yesterday, . . . today, . . . and tomorrow . . . between the kitchen and the dining room. . . . Does woman's life eventually age and wither in vain there?"[18] Michiyo calls into question her movements between the kitchen and the dining room within the space of home. Her voice and point of view command the center of Naruse's film adaptation, in contrast to the original novel, in which the initial focus is on Hatsunosuke and Satoko (Hatsunosuke's unmarried niece) rather than on Michiyo. The narrative framework in Naruse's film is structured around the wife, whereas the narrator in the novel shifts perspective among Hatsunosuke, Satoko, and Michiyo. Thus Naruse's visualization of Hayashi's literary discourse emphasizes how the body of the wife moving within the enclosed space of the home withers while nurturing her husband. In this sense, *Meshi* can be interpreted as a social critique of the role and status imposed on the married woman in the household.

Hayashi's death prevented her from completing the novel, so the conclusion of the film adaptation demonstrates how Naruse's visual narrative, with the language of space and body, illuminates his view of the position of married women in postwar Japan. The original novel breaks off as Michiyo leaves Hatsunosuke's house in Osaka, returns to her native home in Tokyo, and interacts with her friends and relatives. To complete the unfinished novel, the film adaptation ends with Michiyo's narrative voice describing her way back to Osaka with Hatsunosuke, whom she met on the occasion of his business trip to Tokyo. Michiyo reflects on her relationship with her husband: "To live by this man and seek happiness with this man . . . may be my true happiness. . . . Isn't women's happiness such a thing?"[19]

How does this conclusion of the film adaptation negotiate with the original novel? There are several references to women's "happiness" in the novel. For example, Michiyo's friend Tomiyasu Seiko states: "All women become unhappy upon marriage in their adopted homes."[20] Michiyo reflects: "The times when just being beside him had made me happy had all disappeared after coming to Osaka."[21] Considering these utterances in the novel, the ending of the film may be a response to Hatsue, who is married to Michiyo's brother and who tells Michiyo in the novel, "In any new era, there is no place for women to rely on and return to."[22] For Michiyo, who came to know that "life in Tokyo wasn't easy,"[23] the place to return to is limited to the family she married into—that is, Hatsunosuke's household in Osaka. Furthermore, to live the experience of discontent at their married home and redefine it as "happiness" may be considered to be "women's happiness" for those who live in the system of marriage and family, and who have no other way to survive economically and socially. In other words, Naruse shows that "women's happiness" is a highly qualified kind of contentment.

Borderlines between Private Space and Public Space

To expand the argument on the spaces that married women occupy and move through, it is instructive to explore the relationship between the private space of home and the public space of *shitamachi* in *Meshi*. The lower-income class to which Michiyo belongs is narrated visually by the language of space in Naruse's film. The original novel describes Michiyo's house as follows: "At the very bottom corner of the *nagaya* [row house] of twelve houses on both sides, the letters of Okamoto Hatsunosuke can be seen."[24] This description in the novel is translated visually in Naruse's film. According to the script, the house is located at the "place that is one step below" and in the "low ground/hollow" *(kubochi).*[25] In addition, the house "has no light at all."[26] With the film setting that visualizes the script, the viewer understands that Michiyo's married home is positioned on a dark and narrow backstreet rather than a bright central one.

The world in Naruse's film can be seen to be narrow because the drama revolves around the house, especially the kitchen and the dining table.[27] However, one of the reasons a family drama becomes a social drama is the ambiguous relationship between private and public space. Russell contends that "the depiction of Tokyo as a modular extension of the home is an important means by which the family drama becomes a social drama."[28] One example of spatial ambiguity in *Meshi* is the *genkan* (entryway) that extends the structure of the house to the outside world. In contrast to the contemporary residential space, which clearly draws the line between inside and outside, Marc Menish explains that the entryway of Japanese houses in the 1950s was "formally, a part of the inside of the house, but . . . in actuality, a semi- (half) public space where outsiders can enter without the permission from the residents of the house."[29]

Thus the *genkan* was simultaneously a private realm and a public realm. The dirt or concrete floor of the *genkan* is directly linked to Michiyo's entrance to the kitchen, but it simultaneously serves as the entrance to the outside world. The script of the film *Meshi* describes the *genkan* as leading to "similar houses on both sides of the alley with the roofs connected."[30] As Russell points out, identical houses are characteristic of *nagaya* architecture, but they also reflect the postwar era of the 1950s, when indistinguishable residential living spaces were built rapidly in urban areas during the reconstruction of Japan. The extension of the frame of the private space into identical houses on the public street is further indication of the ambiguous nature of private and public spaces.[31]

The ambiguity between public and private is also created by transience and portability in the borderlines that draw, erase, and redraw public and private spaces. For example, the borderlines that delineate the sphere of a married woman in the private space move as the body moves into the public space. As a result, the private space of home expands and reappears in the public space of *shitamachi,* and thus the domestic(ated) experience of married women in the individual households is repeated outside the home.[32] A spatial metaphor of woman's confinement and suffocation is achieved by the visual technique of framing Michiyo's body in close medium-shots at tables, sliding doors (*fusuma, shōji*), and walls at home, and in similar architectural structures such as inns.[33] As with "movable/removable barriers in his films of the 1950's," the lines that draw boundaries delineating space and structure are mobile.[34]

Moreover, the fuzzy distinction between the domestic and public spaces in the early 1950s signifies that women's roles and positions within the household according to prewar policies remained unchanged in women's postwar daily experiences. In this sense, as Russell contends, the discourse in *Meshi* participates in the political debate on the issue of women's social roles and rights in the 1950s. In Hayashi's original novel, Michiyo's neighbor says that "it has been as many as six years since the war ended" but "the conventional practices (*shikitari*) of wartime still remain."[35] In addition, Michiyo's friend Suzuki Katsuko refers to a common friend, Nabei Ritsuko, who is bound to the home at all times: Although "married couples should be equal partners," "women are thinking only about home even when they are outside the home. Then the rights of men and women are not at all equal."[36] Even when a woman's body moves outside the home, the framework of the family system continues to confine her.

Furthermore, "equality between men and women" was supposed to have been guaranteed by Japan's postwar constitution (promulgated in 1946, effective in 1947).[37] But in Naruse's *Meshi,* Michiyo asks, "What is marriage about? . . . enslaving myself with laundry and cooking meals from morning to night as though I am a maid."[38] The film problematizes the perpetuation of the gender division of labor and women's unpaid domestic work. Women as nurturing wives and mothers, who engage in the daily chores of cooking and cleaning in the home space, evoke the continuity of women's roles and position from the prewar to the postwar era. Thus *Meshi* critically depicts the system of marriage and family in which married women are portrayed, paradoxically, both as the feminine ideal and as the slaves of the household. I agree with Russell, who writes: "Many forms of discrimination remained deeply entrenched in social life, language, career expectations, and public policy. In this sense, we can look at Naruse's postwar films as a complex response to the 'failed promise of democracy.'"[39]

The Bodies of Single Women and the Space of *Shitamachi: Meshi*

Naruse's *Meshi* features other spaces where women can be freed from the confinement of home. Single women are often interpreted as those who have freedom or power because they live "outside" the space of home and the system of family. Kawamoto Saburō points out that "husband and family are rather a burden on her [Michiyo]. . . . In the world of Naruse Mikio, single women are livelier [than married women]."[40] For example, when Hatsunosuke and his unmarried niece, Satoko, go sightseeing in Osaka, she occupies a position of power in the scene by standing at the top of the stairs looking down on him. The contrast between the unmarried Satoko and the housewife Michiyo becomes clear when this scene is juxtaposed with that of Michiyo crawling on the dining room floor to clean it. Marc Menish explains that the single woman "Satoko . . . is usually shot from a higher angle, further away so that her entire (unrestricted) body can be viewed."[41] Naruse's interpreters agree that his visual techniques and metaphors emphasize the idea that single women embody freedom and power outside the home, whereas married women experience confinement and repression of their bodies within the framework of home.

I have examined how the visual techniques and metaphors in Naruse's films narrate married and single women. Transience and mobility of the borderlines draw, erase, and redraw the spaces of home and *shitamachi* through which women's bodies move. Other characteristics of editing in Naruse's films prominently include discontinuity and fragmentation.[42] Although these can also be found in Ozu Yasujirō's films, Russell explains the difference between Naruse and Ozu as follows: "The fragmentation of narrative space in Naruse's cinema constitutes an aesthetic of interruption and incompletion, whereas Ozu's fragmentation is controlled within an overall harmonic and balanced system."[43] In Naruse's editing, camerawork cuts into characters' movements, and as a result creates the effects of interruption, incompletion, and discontinuity.[44] Thus the bodies and spaces are not shown as integral parts of an organic whole. Rather, the space occupied by the body and the system symbolized by the space appear as disconnected fragments in Naruse's films.

Although Naruse's film editing may be characterized by fragmentation and discontinuity, there are nonetheless spaces that are defined and created by the borderlines between nations and empires. In addition, as we shall see from my analysis of *Ukigumo*, the characters in Naruse's films fervently wish for continuity of time and space and resolution of their unresolved problems, which his cinematic technique and his structuring of the narrative consistently frustrate. But even though the characters' desire for completion is often left unfulfilled, their dreams are narrated, acts are committed, and reality is created and finally destroyed in Naruse's films.

When discontinuity is examined in the historical context, we find that time was interrupted and space was disconnected in 1945 in the transition from the prewar to the postwar era, when the Japanese empire as a space lost its colonies. Because of this historical rupture, continuity can only be restored through the medium of memory, and especially through nostalgia for the lost time and space. The following discussion of *Ukigumo* analyzes how Naruse's film visually narrates Hayashi's novel and re-creates the bodies of women in relation to the once expanded then shrunken space of the modern Japanese empire. The character Yukiko's memory in the novel and film *Ukigumo* is not only part of the text but also part of the social context in which readers of the novel and the audience of the film living in postwar Japan can remember the past—the Japanese imperial past—whether or not they experienced it firsthand.

The Migrant Female Body and the Space of Empire: *Ukigumo*

The film *Ukigumo* (1955), Naruse's most recognized work, is based on Hayashi's last complete novel, a text that is arguably one of the most important works of postwar Japanese literature. Both the novel and film describe the heroine Yukiko's perspective of continuity and discontinuity between different times—the prewar and postwar eras in particular. But they do not stop there: they also re-create the complex relationship between the female body and the space of the empire of Japan, using the narrative as the medium of memory in the postwar era. Russell contends that *Floating Clouds* is "an anomaly in [Naruse's] cinema" and "a departure from his usual model of *shōshimin-eiga*" (home drama) because it is much more of an epic, historically based work.[45] Whether or not *Ukigumo* is representative of Naruse's complete oeuvre is of no significance for this study. Rather, the following argument focuses on the fact that *Ukigumo* has become one of the most recognized of all Japanese films, and that audiences have repeatedly used it as a visual medium through which to remember or forget war and Japan's imperial past.

The film *Ukigumo* is notable for depicting the mobility of the body and malleability of spaces. As Nakafuru Satoshi points out in his interview with Hasumi Shigehiko, *Ukigumo* stands out among Naruse's films for the large number of shooting locations used.[46] Settings in the film include the spaces depicted in the novel—Tokyo, Ikaho, and Yakushima in Japan, and Dalat in French Indochina (present-day Vietnam). In these spaces, a single woman, Yukiko, is always on the move, and her body in motion disconnects and reconnects the time and space of Japan in the contexts of the rise and fall of the empire. In the novel and film, Yukiko's body moves from her native home in Shizuoka to her brother-in-law Iba's house in Tokyo in prewar *naichi* (the inner territory of Japan). As a typist for the Ministry of Agriculture, Yukiko is transferred to Dalat, in prewar *gaichi,* and falls in love with a bureaucrat, Tomioka; as a war repatriate, she returns to Tokyo in the immediate postwar era; travels to Ikaho with Tomioka; and finally moves to Yakushima with him. The story ends there after Yukiko's death.

Both Yukiko in *Ukigumo* and Satoko in *Meshi* are single, unmarried women. Unlike Satoko, however, Yukiko has no stable home or family background and so is not treated as a respectful candidate for status as a sacred wife and mother in either prewar or postwar Japan. As in the novel, Yukiko is repeatedly raped by her brother-in-law, Iba, at his house. To visually narrate Yukiko's defenseless and violated body, the camera films Iba from a low angle when he suddenly appears in Yukiko's bedroom. The script of the film explains the scene. "Iba ... rips the futon off [Yukiko] and forces himself on her. He presses her arms down on both sides."[47] After showing Iba, the camera focuses on "Yukiko's terrified face."[48] Rather than the liberation and power that Satoko as a single woman may embody, Yukiko's mobility outside the home in prewar *naichi* signifies sexual abuse by a member of her extended family.

Yukiko is freed, however, from the restrictions she experiences in the homeland of Japan when she earns a position as a typist at the Ministry of

Agriculture and the opportunity to leave the space of prewar *naichi* and enter *gaichi*, French Indochina, which had fallen under the control of the Japanese empire in 1942.[49] Yukiko's life changes from one of economic and physical repression to one of freedom, comfort, and security when she travels to Dalat, stays in a French-style mansion occupied by the Japanese bureaucrats as their official residence, and enters the open space of woods with her lover Tomioka. It is her body in motion beyond the border of *naichi* but within the space of the empire of Japan that makes the changes possible.

In Naruse's film, the space of the French-style mansion, the dining setting there, and the act of eating in it narrate visually and vividly Japan's identification with one of the Western imperial powers, France, and with the colonization of Indochina—colonization in which Yukiko participates and from which she benefits. In the film, the whiteness of the setting at the dining table—white tablecloth, white wine,[50] and Yukiko's white dress—signifies not only the freshness/newness of her experience but also the Japanese empire's initial identification with Western imperialism, its subsequent displacement of the "white" Western imperial power, and its assertion of control over the darker-skinned Annamese, symbolized by the maid, Niu, who serves the food. This scene in the film is shown as a flashback and as an object of nostalgia in the postwar era. Thus Yukiko's objects of nostalgia include the products of colonial transformation—Japanese lifestyles that put the colonized Annamese people in the role of servants.

Another sign of whiteness is also evident in the scene in the woods. Adorned in a "white, thin, silk skirt," according to the screenplay,[51] Yukiko appears in an open wooded space that is filled with bright white light. Tomioka kisses her and leads her into the woods. In the open and expansive space, her body leaps in joy. In reference to the representation of Yukiko and Tomioka in French Indochina, Russell writes that "Tomioka served as an official in the Imperial Forestry Ministry, and Yukiko was posted there as a typist, but the imagery is more that of a country retreat than a workplace."[52]

As explored in chapter 6, Yukiko's experience has been read by many critics as that of a woman at the economic and social margins whose experience in *gaichi* is personal, apolitical, and ahistorical.[53] Noriko Mizuta, for example, contends that, unlike Tomioka, Yukiko entertains the possibility of freedom because she is in *gaichi*, and thus "outside the institutions of Japan" and "outside Japanese history."[54] "The war offered her [Yukiko] an opportunity to escape the Japanese institutions of womanhood, even if it turned out to be a false hope."[55] Mizuta's point is repeated by Russell: "Dalat is a virtual escape from Japanese social conventions."[56] Because of the focus on gender and on her existence "outside" the institutionalized womanhood of Japan, Yukiko's body as part of the national and imperial body has yet to be explored in depth. Yukiko may not be as innocent as the images of her white dress and the bright white light in the woods of French Indochina might suggest.

In my analysis of the novel *Ukigumo* in chapter 6, I argued that whereas her body was economically restricted and marginalized in the homeland of Japan, Yukiko is able to experience the luxury of upper-class society by participating in the state apparatus, which exploits the natural and human resources in *gaichi*. Specifically, it is the language of space and a mobile body that create Yukiko as an agent who acts on the nation-state's imperialist discourse of the liberation, salvation, and empowerment of Japan at the center of Asia. Rather than actually retreat in any way, it is the expansion of the space of the empire that makes Yukiko's prewar experience in *gaichi* possible. This is nowhere more evident than in the depiction of Yukiko's mobile body in an open expanse of woods. Led by the hands of a bureaucrat and her lover, Tomioka, Yukiko's body redraws and expands the border of the Japanese empire. Yukiko is an integral part of the body of Japan.

Another example is the depiction of Yukiko's body in the first scene of the film, in which Yukiko arrives at the port of Atsuga from French Indochina on a returning ship *(hikiage sen)*. Naruse thus emphasizes that her body, moving through the chaotic and devastated spaces of postwar Japan, is that of an individual *hikiagesha* (war returnee). Yukiko is one of the millions of civilians and soldiers who were repatriated from the former colonies. The script explains the scene: "Returnees from South Asia are getting off the ship. Among the crowd of women, which consists only of comfort women, geisha, nurses, typists, clerks and the like, there is also Kōda Yukiko, who is not outfitted with proper winter attire."[57] In the severe weather, she shivers and contracts her body as she gets off the ship. This scene of Yukiko's body in the film visually mirrors the body of a shrunken Japan. The narrator in the original novel states: "Japan . . . has become only a torso *(dotai)*, having lost all of Korea, Taiwan, the Ryukyu Islands, Karafuto and Manchuria as a result of the last war."[58] Naruse's film draws this parallel with the visual effect in which Yukiko's body, having played its part as a subject of the Japanese empire in its expanded territory in *gaichi* in prewar Japan, tightens as she draws in her arms and legs in response to the cold, just as the body of Japan contracted into a mere torso after the loss of its colonies.

It is true that Yukiko's position as a migrant—and as a person standing outside the institutionalized, family-based womanhood of prewar *naichi*—is reestablished in postwar Tokyo. For example, when she appears at the house of her lover, Tomioka, Yukiko stands in the *genkan* (entryway), an ambiguous borderline between the private and public space, and is not allowed to enter the house. Exposed to the suspicious gaze of Tomioka's wife and mother-in-law, she realizes her own position as an outsider.[59] In this scene the contrast becomes clear between the women who live inside the framework of home and Yukiko, who is denied access.

Although Yukiko in the film *Ukigumo* is excluded from the framework of home and the system of family, including Tomioka's family, her continued relationship with him leads her to experience pregnancy, abortion, and repeated surgeries for complications resulting from the abortion. As mentioned in chapter 6, the story coincides with the legalization of abortion in Japan as part of the Japanese and Occupation authorities' efforts to promote economic growth by slowing the baby boom. Thus Yukiko's physical condition mirrors the effects of postwar national politics on women's bodies.[60] Her shrunken body that the audience sees at the beginning of the film is seen again after her abortion. The script explains the scene in the film: she "is attacked by chill and stops"; she shivers and "shrinks her body."[61] Suffering from the complications of abortion in postwar Tokyo, Yukiko's body is violated and weakened, just as the body of Japan under American occupation is.

In both the film and the novel, Yukiko becomes a prostitute for an American soldier, Joe. But deletion and focus of the film editing that evolves around the sexual and hegemonic relationship between men and women and empires results in emphasizing the suffering of the Japanese woman, Yukiko, and silencing the predicament of the Annamese woman, Niu. In the novel, Yukiko equates Joe in postwar Japan with Tomioka in prewar French Indochina, and equates herself with Niu. Just as Tomioka used Niu as a sexual object during the Japanese occupation in prewar French Indochina, so Joe takes advantage of Yukiko's sexual services under the American occupation in postwar Japan. In the novel, Tomioka impregnates Niu but leaves her behind in French Indochina and returns to his wife in Tokyo in the postwar era. Thus the novel narrates the Japanese imperial invasion and conquest that allow the male colonizer Tomioka to fulfill his economic and sexual desires in the occupied territory by exploiting and abandoning the Annamese woman. This story is deleted in the film, however. By erasing Tomioka's sexual invasion of Niu, the film *Ukigumo* makes it invisible and doubly silences the colonized Annamese woman's predicament. What is highlighted in the film is the Japanese woman Yukiko as a weakling and victim who struggles to overcome the economic exploitation and sexual invasion of her body in Japan in the prewar and postwar periods.

As Yukiko lives under the American occupation in postwar Japan, she entertains the memory of war, rather than peace, and feels nostalgia for the lost time and space of Japan's prewar colony. She thus dwells in a continuum between the prewar and postwar periods. This is expressed in her paradoxical conformity to the status quo in *naichi* and *gaichi* both during and after the war. In the film *Ukigumo*, Yukiko wants Tomioka to return to the Ministry of Agriculture, and she accompanies him when he is given a position on remote Yakushima, a semitropical island at the southern end of Japan. There, she imagines, she will be able to rebuild her relationship with Tomioka by recapturing the lost dream of colonized *gaichi*,[62] as well as the physical freedom and strength she experienced as a Japanese colonizer in prewar French Indochina. In the choices she makes at the end of her life as a migrant, Yukiko therefore seeks a final, harmonious resolution of her personal conflicts in nostalgia for the modern Japanese empire, and ultimately encapsulates the story of the modern empire in her personal story.

The last scene of the film, however, emphasizes the fall of the empire, and of Yukiko's damaged and socially marginalized body in postwar Japan. Rather than being able to leap into the woods with Tomioka, Yukiko arrives on Yakushima on a stretcher. In the end, while Tomioka is away visiting a forestry station, Yukiko collapses and dies alone in the official residence of the Ministry of Agriculture.[63]

Although Russell contends that it would be "a reactionary reading" to see "Yukiko's death [as] symbolic of a national death," I think this point deserves reconsideration.[64] Immediately before she dies, the film shows Yukiko leaving her futon and crawling across the floor in an attempt to close a window that is clattering in a storm. Until this final scene, her movement has been toward the outer world—outside the space of home and the system of family, when she left her native home in Shizuoka for Tokyo; toward the outer territory of Japan, when she left for French Indochina in the prewar era; and to the periphery of Japan, when she left for Yakushima in the postwar era. In the end, however, Yukiko attempts to close the window leading to the outside. In Naruse's film, the space expands as the body moves outside the home, and even more so as it moves outside the homeland. Yukiko's body, which has moved along with the expanding borderlines of the empire in the prewar era, withers and collapses along with the empire in the postwar era. Not only is Yukiko dead, but she is disembodied, in the sense that she is deprived of the space of French Indochina and denied the basic stance on which her experience and memory depend.[65]

In contrast to Hasumi Shigehiko, who contends that Hayashi Fumiko meant to punish Yukiko with death for her participation in the colonization of French Indochina, Russell maintains that "there is little evidence that *Floating Clouds* constituted any kind of remorse on [Hayashi Fumiko's] part."[66] She also argues that "the characters cannot be said to feel responsible for their role in the war."[67] As examined in chapter 6, however, Yukiko does express remorse about the Japanese exploitation of natural resources and labor in French Indochina; not only that, but she comments on moral "responsibility" when listening to the "war trial" broadcast on the radio, and tells Tomioka that both he and she are included in the trials.[68]

When she identifies with those who were tried at the Tokyo War Crimes Tribunal, Yukiko says, "I want to hear the facts about the war."[69] Yukiko recognizes that "the facts" of Japan's colonization policy and actions were created not only by the male-centered grand narrative created by the policy makers and military officials but also by the collaboration of low-ranking civil servants such as Tomioka at the geographical periphery of the empire—and of socially and economically marginalized women such as Yukiko herself.[70] Thus her sense of remorse and responsibility for the egotistical, reckless, and destructive policies and actions of the former . Japanese colonizers accompanies her nostalgia for the lost colony of the Japanese empire.

It is important to understand Yukiko's nostalgia, which represents not only her own longing but also the nation's yearning for the spectacles of lost empire, landscapes, and lifestyles. Tamanoi elaborates on Fred Davis's ideas on this topic:

Nostalgia enables a person (or a nation) to maintain his (or its) identity intact. Yet Davis' argument implies that the identity of such a person (or nation) has already been ruptured, and that it is the reason why he (or nation) resorts to nostalgia.[71]

Yukiko's identity is created by her moving beyond institutionalized womanhood in Japan, and also by her moving *toward* the state's institutionalized colonization of Southeast Asia. What is ruptured is the latter form of her identity, which Yukiko attempts to re-create by resorting to nostalgia. Davis also argues that nostalgia has a "tendency to eliminate from memory or, at minimum, severely to mute the unpleasant, the unhappy, the abrasive, and most of all, those lurking shadows of former selves about which we feel shame, guilt, or humiliation."[72] Yukiko's guilt revolves around the exploitation of natural resources and labor in French Indochina. This fits in with what Renato Rosaldo calls "imperialist nostalgia," felt by agents of colonialism who lament the passing of what they themselves have transformed, remember what they have destroyed, and at the same time attempt to establish their innocence.[73] Yukiko is indeed nostalgic for specific spaces and experiences connected to the "history of expansion, dominance, and downfall of the Japanese empire."[74]

Furthermore, when she comments on the ongoing trial of war criminals at the Tokyo War Crimes Tribunal, Yukiko refers to the "facts" of military aggression that supported Japanese colonization. Yet as Tamanoi points out, "The past to be remembered does not cover only facts; it also covers the images into which those facts have already been transformed. Hence the facts that do not fit in such images may have been forgotten."[75] In the film *Ukigumo*, there is one brief scene that features a military truck in the woods. The emphasis, however, is on the expansive natural space in which Yukiko walks hand in hand with Tomioka and jumps for joy. These images of nature and of dreamlike retreat encourage the audience to remember Indochina as a lush natural world, in contrast to the grating facts of Japanese military aggression, economic exploitation, and imperial expansion.

Naruse Mikio's film *Ukigumo* has been passed down to viewers as a set of images. As a medium of memory, the film has assisted audiences in remembering a past that marginalizes Yukiko. The film also represents a strategy that enables the state and people to forget the facts of the expansion and aggression of the Japanese empire. But we must also remember that the power of the Japanese state, which once dominated ordinary Annamese people and in which Japanese women participated, helped Yukiko gain a sense of freedom and power.

In the course of the film, both Yukiko and the Japanese empire live, grow, flourish, weaken, and die. As images of Yukiko in French Indochina are inserted as flashbacks into her life in postwar Japan, phenomena pass by like "a floating cloud—appearing [and] disappearing."[76] We who live today, however, continue to narrate the prewar and postwar eras—and re-create the past in memory—by interpreting such narratives. The dominant narratives about unmarried migrant Japanese women have focused on their gender- and class-specific marginalized experience as women in *naichi,* glossing over their participation in Japan's colonization of neighboring nations in *gaichi.* As one of the most recognized visual narratives in postwar Japan, Naruse's film *Ukigumo* frames Yukiko's experience of material comfort, physical freedom, and power as an occupying colonizer in French Indochina in the prewar era as something unreal. This dreamlike experience of nonreality is signaled in the film by inserting discontinuous shots of Yukiko and Tomioka in the woods in Dalat into the narrative of their lives in the postwar era. But if Yukiko's experience in French Indochina was dreamlike, the expansion of the Japanese empire was a nightmarish reality for the Annamese, who were invaded and exploited. If *gaichi* in the prewar era continues to be created and interpreted as a temporary and unrealistic dream, the question of how and why the "reality" of those who were colonized came into being may not be tackled.

With sensitivity to the visual sign of mobile female bodies that move from the space of home to the public sphere, and then to the fringes of Japan in the prewar and postwar periods, I have demonstrated how the use of visual techniques, metaphors, and effects works together to re-create the Japanese imperial past in the present. Naruse Mikio's film adaptations of Hayashi Fumiko's novels are an example of how the visual medium negotiates with the literary medium in disconnecting and reconnecting the female bodies and geopolitical spaces of Japan in the prewar and postwar periods. This concluding chapter of the book has examined the relationship between the female migrant bodies at the margin of Japanese society and the politically significant spaces that can either suffocate or liberate and empower those bodies.

Conclusion

In this study, I have defined legal and educational documents, works of literature and film, and academic critiques and popular commentaries as discourses, and focused on the bodies and borders of spaces as the site of historical and political intervention and negotiation. On the premise that it is the body of the female migrant, as the surface of inscription and enactment, that constructs the subjectivity of authors and readers, this book has examined how three writers, Yosano Akiko, Tamura Toshiko, and Hayashi Fumiko, acted in modern Japan by becoming and describing female bodies in motion.

In negotiating with the state-driven nationalist discourse on women in the empire of Japan, the three writers' depictions of migrant bodies in their texts seem to violate the boundaries imposed on women's gender, sexuality, and class and to deviate from the norms of a united, organic body of Japan. As travelers and migrants, their bodies in motion indeed freed themselves from the settled and domesticated dynamics of culture established by the Japanese nation-state, and attempted to empower themselves as the decentered and unhoused. To use Edward Said's term, Yosano, Tamura, and Hayashi, and some of the narrators and characters in their texts, can be read as "migrants in exile"—that is, as disruptive minorities who question the majority and the norm, and who carry a political mission of liberation from the settled and domesticated dynamic of the establishment. Writings of the three authors disrupt the effectiveness of the central nationalist discourse and liberate the authors from it. Their discourse seems to transcend the boundaries of national imperial domains. However, when the migrant bodies of these authors and their narrators and characters move between homes and homelands, cross national limits, and set foot on foreign soil, their discourse on race and ethnicity acts to strengthen the state discourse of the empire of Japan. Migrant bodies in their texts act as integral parts of the empire. Their bodies redraw, rather than transcend, the imperial borders.

"Migrants in exile" enable the author and reader to envision and re-enact movements that make it possible to cross the borders of the empire and become free of nationalist and imperialist confines. Our focus on liberation also enables us, however, to envision and reenact movements that help us forget that female migrants' bodies sometimes redrew the borders that violated the lives of the peoples who were invaded by the Japanese empire. Amnesia about Japan as an aggressor may no longer dominate, but it nevertheless persists in many sectors of Japanese society.[77] Although it remains in the minority, there has been scholarship on Japanese women that exposes them as active participants in Japanese aggression.[78] With this study, I propose that representations of the direction taken by the women's movement must be remembered and examined as they relate to the liberation and empowerment not only of women but also of the state of Japan, which colonized neighboring nations in the prewar era in some instances with the active participation of women. Only by acknowledging the national in the crossnational bodies that traversed the imperial borders can we begin to understand both sides of women's stories, which at once resist and re-create the Japanese empire.

Acknowledgments

The conception of this book took place in 2000, and its completion was possible because of the intellectual, moral, and financial support of many individuals and institutions. I extend special thanks to Ayako Kano, who inspired and supported me throughout my graduate studies at the University of Pennsylvania and beyond. I am profoundly indebted to the late William R. LaFleur, who opened fascinating intellectual paths for me and constantly challenged and encouraged me. I am deeply grateful to Linda Chance for her guidance and to Kathleen Uno for her support of my research and preparation of the manuscript. I also thank Cecilia Segawa-Seigle, Frederick Dickinson, G. Cameron Hurt, Frank Chance, Paul Gordon Schalow, and Susan Lindee for guidance and support.

Particular thanks go to those individuals who read and discussed with me drafts of this book. Akira Mizuta Lippit and Jan Bardsley provided invaluable critiques and constant encouragement. Friends and colleagues read my writings and made useful suggestions: Leroy Hopkins, Douglas Berger, Jeff Mellor, and David Lee. I thank my editors at the University of Minnesota Press, Jason Weidemann, Danielle Kasprzak, and Laura J. Westlund, as well as Mary Byers and Victoria Scott, for careful work vetting and preparing the manuscript.

Many people contributed ideas, suggestions for readings, thought-provoking questions, and critiques that shaped the direction of this book. I owe special thanks to Chizuko Ueno for her intellectual leadership and incredible generosity, especially during my visiting scholarship at the University of Tokyo. Noriko Mizuta's support for my research during my visiting scholarship and my visiting associate professorship at Josai University gave me valuable opportunities for the stimulating exchange of ideas and publications. Many thanks are due Wakakuwa Midori and Chino Kaori, both now deceased, and to Ayako Saitō and Ikeda Shinobu for helpful critiques and encouragement when I presented this book project at the Image and Gender Research Group in Tokyo. Hasegawa Kei at Hosei University provided very useful comments. Iwasaki Minoru, Nakano Toshio, Narita Ryūichi, and Senda Yuki of the Workshop in Critical Theory, as well as members of Cultural Studies Forum, inspired me with ideas they shared.

I benefited from the opportunities to present papers at the national meetings of the Association for Asian Studies, the Mid-Atlantic and the South Eastern Region Conferences of AAS, the University of Pennsylvania Humanities Colloquium, the University of Tokyo Graduate School of Sociology faculty meeting, the Gender Colloquium at the University of Tokyo, Image and Gender Research Group in Tokyo, the Columbia University Graduate Student Conference on East Asia, the University of Pennsylvania Graduate Student Conference on East Asia, and graduate seminars at Hosei University, Josai University, and Waseda University.

Various libraries made important texts needed for this book accessible: the Van Pelt Library at the University of Pennsylvania, the University of British Columbia Library, the Japanese American Museum in Los Angeles, the National Diet Library in Japan, the University of Tokyo Libraries, and Waseda University Libraries.

My research summers and semesters would have been impossible without the grants and fellowships I received: a visiting scholarship from the University of Tokyo; a visiting scholarship from Josai University; a research travel grant from the Northeast Asia Council of the Association for Asian Studies; professional development and research awards and a grant from the Exhibit, Performance, and Publication Expenses Fund of the College of Arts and Sciences of the University of Tennessee; and from the University of Pennsylvania an Asian and Middle Eastern Studies Departmental Fellowship, a Women's Studies Program dissertation fellowship, School of Arts and Sciences travel grants, and a Graduate Student Association Council travel grant.

I express gratitude to my senior colleagues at the University of Tennessee for their support for my research and book publication: Bruce Bursten, Carolyn R. Hodges, Erec Koch, Jon LaCure, Mary Papke, and John Zomchick. To administrative assistants Beth Cole, Linda Greene, Peggy Guinan, Ingrid McMillen, Diane Moderski, and Paula Roberts, I appreciate your careful and responsible paperwork and communications that helped me receive grants and made research trips possible. Terry and Lenny Lai, Mimi and Dan Pakenham, and Nariko Takayanagi and Steven

Heine provided me with homes during my research summers in Tokyo, Los Angeles, and Vancouver.

Many thanks to friends and colleagues for input and help: Hitomi Tonomura at the University of Michigan; Nicola Liscutin at the University of London; Olaf Berwald, Chris Holmlund, Peter Höyng, LaVinia Jennings, Miriam Levering, and my colleagues in the Department of Modern Foreign Languages and Literatures and the School of Arts and Sciences at the University of Tennessee; Bruce Baird, Yoshie Endo, Sari Kawana, Matsumoto Hideyuki, Maki Morinaga, Hiroko Kimura Sherry, Atsuko Takahashi, Tomoko Takami, Ching-Jen Wang, and Seiko Yoshinaga from the University of Pennsylvania; Marlene Arnold and Leroy Hopkins at Millersville University; Atsuta Keiko and Tomiyama Yukiko at Waseda University; and Iwakawa Daisuke at the University of Tokyo. Thanks to my junior colleagues for stimulating discussions during my visiting associate professorship at the University of Pennsylvania: Rachel Epstein, Kathryn Hemmann, Nathan Hopson, Sean Rhoads, and Jeremy Sather. I am also grateful to Ivar Andersen and Atsuko Horiguchi, Doi Satoko, Hamamoto Maki, Toyota Horiguchi, Fred Kamau, Ikuko Muroga, and Asami Segi for their encouragement.

My greatest debt is to my parents, Minoru and Reiko Horiguchi, whose enthusiasm for art and education and unconditional support have helped make my academic and professional endeavors possible. In gratitude and love I dedicate this book to them.

Notes

Introduction

1. There is a movement in the study of women's history in Japan to examine continuity rather than discontinuity in the prewar and postwar periods. See *Kōza gendai to henkaku* henshū iinkai, "Minshū ishiki ni okeru tennōsei/kokka" (The imperial system and the nation-state in the consciousness of the people), in *Kōza gendai to henkaku 2*, 211–34. Chizuko Ueno examines *danzetsu shikan* (historical view of discontinuity) and *renzoku shikan* (historical view of continuity) in the prewar and postwar periods. See Ueno, *Nationarizumu to jendā*, 16–21.

2. See Pettman, "Women, Gender and Nationalism," in *Worlding Women*, 45–63.

3. One of the earlier examples is William Elliot Griffis's "First Glimpses of Japan" and "A Ride on the Tokaido," in his *The Mikado's Empire* (1900). An interesting contemporary example is the image of Japan's Self-Defense Force as analyzed by anthropologist Sabine Fruhstuck in her *Uneasy Warriors* (2007).

4. The phrase *ryōsai kenbo* (good wife, wise mother) became the basis of women's education in Japan at the end of the nineteenth century and, eventually, the ideal and reality of Japanese women. Although it is open to question how effectively the state ideology governing the educational system permeated the everyday lives of women, both middle- and lower-class women gradually recognized and incorporated the values of a "good wife, wise mother," and this shift contributed to the building of the "rich nation, strong army." I examine this in chapter 2.

5. Examples include Raddeker, *Treacherous Women of Imperial Japan*, and Hane, *Reflections on the Way to the Gallows*.

6. See Nishikawa, *Sensō eno keisha to yokusan no fujin 5*; Suzuki, *Feminizumu to sensō*; Kanō, *Onnatachi no jūgo*.

7. See note 6.

8. Ueno, *Nashonarizumu to jendā*, 60–67 and 180–85. All English translations of Japanese texts are mine, unless otherwise stated. English translation of Ueno's *Nashonarizumu to jendā* is available in *Nationalism and Gender*.

9. Ueno, *Nashonarizumu to jenda*, 22–23.

10. By being excluded from suffrage under the Imperial Constitution, women possessed no legal rights to participate in the policy-making process of modern Japanese society.

11. Wakakuwa, *Kōgō no shōzō Myōken kōtaigō no hyōshō to josei no kokuminka,* 342.

12. A synchronic analysis of statements or enunciations in discourse derives from the methodology called archaeology, which is an elaboration of the concept of "episteme" that Michel Foucault employed in *The Order of Things.* The primary research directions Foucault took, and which also guide this work, are the rejection of a logic of representation; the view of a literary text as part of other social and political texts, institutions, and practices; and the assumption that the body is a surface of inscription and events in order to legitimize authorities. See Foucault, "What Is an Author?"; *Discipline and Punish;* and the first volume of *The History of Sexuality.* For a succinct summary of Foucault's positions, see Mark Poster, "Foucault, Michel."

13. Butler, *Bodies That Matter,* 139.

14. Satomi, *Kokutai shisōshi,* 29.

15. Butler's theory on the performativity of language (signifying practices) and of the body is politically important for my study. If the body and language are performative, they can be performed differently, create different meanings, and destabilize compulsory and oppressive social discourses, practices, and institutions. See Butler, *Bodies That Matter* (1993) and *Gender Trouble* (1990).

16. Butler, *Bodies That Matter,* 12.

17. Foucault, *Discipline and Punish,* 25–26.

18. Ibid.

19. Lois McNay notes that "despite Foucault's theoretical assertion that power is a diffuse, heterogeneous and productive phenomenon, his historical analyses tend to depict power as a centralized, monolithic force with an inexorable and repressive grip on its subject." See McNay, *Foucault and Feminism,* 38. Peter Dews points out that "Foucault's analysis of the disciplinary techniques within the penal system is skewed towards the official representatives of the institutions—the governors, the architects, etc. and not towards the voices and bodies of those being controlled" (quoted in ibid., 39).

20. Foucault, "Docile bodies," in *Discipline and Punish,* 135–69.

21. Mizuta, "Kindaika to josei hyōgen no kiseki," 12.

22. Ibid.

23. Ibid., 11.

24. Ibid.

1. Japan as a Body

1. Slaymaker, *The Body in Postwar Japanese Fiction,* 12.

2. Ishida, *Nihon kindai shisōshi ni okeru hō to seiji,* chapter 5, 161–85.

3. Furuta, *Higashi ajia ideorogī o koete,* 172.

4. Quoted in Ishida, *Nihon kindai shisōshi ni okeru hō to seiji,* 169. All English translations of Japanese texts are mine, unless otherwise stated.

5. Furuta, *Higashi ajia ideorogī o koete,* 172.

6. Ichimura Mitsue, *Kokka oyobi kokumin ron* (Studies on the nation-state and people), 93–94; quoted in Ishida, *Nihon kindai shisōshi ni okeru hō to seiji,* 177.

7. Ishida, *Nihon kindai shisōshi ni okeru hō to seiji,* 177.

8. Minobe Tatsukichi, "Defense of the Organ Theory," in Tsunoda, de Bary, and Keene, *Sources of Japanese Tradition,* 749.

9. Ibid., 749–50. The original text appears in Minobe, *Kenpō kōwa,* 24–25.

10. Minobe, "Defense of the Organ Theory," in Tsunoda, de Bary, and Keene, *Sources of Japanese Tradition,* 749.

11. Ishida, *Nihon kindai shisōshi ni okeru hō to seiji,* 173.

12. Hozumi, *Hozumi Nobushige ibunshū,* 1:449.

13. Ibid., 2:85.

14. Kaieda, *Kensei hen,* 527.

15. Katō Fusō, *Nihon kokutai ron* (1892); quoted in Ishida, *Nihon kindai shisōshi ni okeru hō to seiji,* 185.

16. Hozumi Yatsuka, *Kokumin kyōiku aikokushin* (1897); quoted in Ishida, *Nihon kindai shisōshi ni okeru hō to seiji,* 185.

17. Ishida, *Nihon kindai shisōshi ni okeru hō to seiji,* 185.

18. Oguma, *Tanitsu minzoku shinwa no kigen,* 54. An English translation is available in Oguma, *A Genealogy of "Japanese" Self-Images.*

19. Quoted in Shively, "Japanization of the Middle Meiji," 84.

20. Quoted in Oguma, *Tanitsu minzoku shinwa no kigen,* 54.

21. Quoted in ibid., 248.

22. Morris-Suzuki, *Re-Inventing Japan,* 118.

23. "Fundamentals of Our National Polity," in Tsunoda, de Bary, and Keene, *Sources of Japanese Tradition,* 787–88.

24. Ibid., 793.

25. Ibid., 787.

26. Ibid., 789.

27. Oguma, *Tanitsu minzoku shinwa no kigen,* 141.

28. Morris-Suzuki, *Re-Inventing Japan,* 88.

29. Ibid., 92.

30. "The Later Mito School," in Tsunoda, de Bary, and Keene, *Sources of Japanese Tradition,* 592–95.

31. Tsunoda, de Bary, and Keene, *Sources of Japanese Tradition,* 705–6.

32. Inoue Kaoru, *Segai Inoue Kaoru Kōden* (Official biography of Inoue Kaoru, 1934); quoted in Shively, "Japanization of the Middle Meiji," 91.

33. Fukuzawa Yukichi, *Jiji shinpō* (Current affairs news, 1882); reprinted in *Fukuzawa Yukichi zenshū,* 7–8.

34. Shively, "Japanization of the Middle Meiji," 81.

35. Ibid., 93.

36. Ibid., 82.

37. *Japan Weekly Mail,* April 30, 1887; quoted in Shively, "Japanization of the Middle Meiji," 96.

38. Sugiura Jūgō, "Nihon kyōiku no hōkō" (1887); quoted in Shively, "Japanization of the Middle Meiji," 106.

39. Watanabe Ikujirō, *Kyōiku chokugo no hongi to kanpatsu no yurai* (The fundamental meaning of the imperial rescript on education and the history of its formation, 1931); quoted in Shively, "Japanization of the Middle Meiji," 93.

40. Quoted in Shively, "Japanization of the Middle Meiji," 94.

41. Tatebe, "Teikoku no kokuze to sekai no senran" (The empire's policy and the chaotic war in the world); quoted in Oguma, *Tanitsu minzoku shinwa no kigen,* 141.

42. See Morris-Suzuki, *Re-Inventing Japan,* 28–34.

43. Taniguchi, *Tōyō minzoku no taishitsu,* 90.

44. Minami Jirō, *Jikyoku to naisen ittai* (The present situation and "Japan and Korea as one"); quoted in Oguma, *Tanitsu minzoku shinwa no kigen,* 241.

45. Kurashima, "Ketsueki no konyū," 12.

46. Morris-Suzuki, *Re-Inventing Japan,* 78–87.

47. Yasuda, *Yasuda Yojurō zenshū,* 16:42, 47.

48. See Suzuki Yūko, *Jūgun ianfu naisen kekkon* and *"Jūgun ianfu" mondai to sei bōryoku.*

49. Shimomura, "Daitōa kyōeiken," 81.

50. See Tsunoda, de Bary, and Keene, *Sources of Japanese Tradition,* 662–79.

51. Oguma, *Tanitsu minzoku shinwa no kigen,* 262.

52. Kokusai, *Academic and Cultural Organizations in Japan,* 504; quoted in Morris-Suzuki, *Re-Inventing Japan,* 96.

53. Ishihara and Satō, "Nikka konketsu jidō no igakuteki chōsa," 164.

54. Kiyono Kenji, *Sumatora kenkyū,* 569 and 575.

55. Kōseishō kenkyūjo jinkō minzokubu, *Yamato minzoku o chūkaku to suru sekai seisaku no kentō,* 303–19; Oguma, *Tanitsu minzoku shinwa no kigen,* 249–58; Morris-Suzuki, *Re-Inventing Japan,* 96.

56. Kiyono, *Nihon jinshu-ron hensen-shi,* 169.

57. Ibid.

58. Young, *Japan's Total Empire,* 366.

59. Ibid., 365–66.

60. Chin, "Colonial Medical Police and Postcolonial Medical Surveillance Systems in Taiwan, 1895–1950s," 326–38.

61. Young, *Japan's Total Empire,* 371–72.

62. Ibid., 366–70.

2. The Universal Womb

1. Uno, *Passages to Modernity*, 148.
2. Ibid.
3. Ibid., 146.
4. On the government policies toward women from 1890 to 1910, see Nolte and Hastings, "The Meiji State's Policy Toward Women, 1890–1910."
5. Nakajima, "Kokkateki bosei," 253. All English translations of Japanese texts are mine, unless otherwise stated.
6. Uno, *Passages to Modernity*, 7.
7. Ibid., 12.
8. Ibid., 7–8.
9. Ibid., 144.
10. Ibid., 145.
11. Ibid., 143–44.
12. Ibid., 141.
13. Otsubo, "Engendering Eugenics," 243.
14. Ibid.
15. Miyake, "Doubling Expectations," 268.
16. Nakajima, "Kokkateki bosei," 245.
17. Oguma, *Tanitsu minzoku shinwa no kigen*, 141.
18. Suzuki Yūko, *Jūgun ianfu naisen kekkon*.
19. Morris-Suzuki, *Re-Inventing Japan*, 114.
20. Uno, *Passages to Modernity*, 140.
21. Oguma, *Tanitsu minzoku shinwa no kigen*, 252.
22. See Pettman, *Worlding Women*, 60.
23. See Furutani, *Gendai bosei gaku*, 88. Nakajima cites a housewife whom Furutani introduces in *Gendai bosei gaku*, in the section titled "Mother of Japan," 88.
24. Suzuki Yūko, "Hirohito shi to 'Shōwa' shi to onna," 24; quoted in Morris-Suzuki, *Re-Inventing Japan*, 120.
25. Mori Yasuko, *Kokkateki bosei no kōzo*, 228.
26. Nakajima, "Kokkateki bosei," 245.
27. Ibid., 246.
28. Ibid., 251.
29. Ibid., 141.
30. Uno, *Passages to Modernity*, 140.
31. Ibid., 21.
32. Ibid., 141.
33. See Nolte, "Women's Rights and Society's Needs," 712–14.
34. Otsubo, "Engendering Eugenics," 232.

35. Uno, *Passages to Modernity*, 21.

36. Nolte, "Women, the State, and Repression in Imperial Japan," 5.

37. Tsurumi, "Female Textile Workers and the Failure of Early Trade Unionism in Japan."

38. Mackie, *Creating Socialist Women in Japan*, 76–77. By conducting the debate according to the state discourse of *bosei hogo* (motherhood protection), maternalist feminists subscribed to the notion that the state is a paternal figure under which his children, including women, live. The debate focused on the questions of the suitability of the government's definition of women's roles and of its support for women with children.

39. Fujime, "The Licensed Prostitution System and the Prostitution Abolition Movement in Modern Japan," 163.

40. See Suzuki Yūko, *Jūgun ianfu naisen kekkon, "Jūgun ianfu" mondai to sei bōryoku*, and *Nihongun ianfu kankei shiryō shūsei*; Yoshimi Yoshiaki, *Jūgun ianfu*.

41. Mori, *Youth and Other Stories*, 441.

42. Ibid.

43. See Stanlaw, "Japanese Emigration and Immigration," 46; Young, *Japan's Total Empire*, 330.

44. Young, *Japan's Total Empire*, 308–9.

45. Stanlaw, "Japanese Emigration and Immigration," 45.

46. See Garon, "Women's Groups and the Japanese State," 10. In 1890, shortly before the first session of the Imperial Diet, the government issued a new Law on Assembly and Political Association (Shūkai oyobi seishahō). This was the first law that banned women from sponsoring, attending, or joining political meetings and associations. In 1900, these provisions were implemented in the Police Law (Chian Keisatsuhō). In 1921, the Lower House passed an amendment to Article 5 that would have allowed women to sponsor and attend political discussion meetings. Despite vigorous attempts to nullify the prohibitory law against women's political rights in the 1890s and 1900s, the measure subsequently failed in the House of Peers.

47. Quoted in Nolte, "Women's Rights and Society's Needs," 706–7.

48. *Dai nihon teikoku gikai-shi*, vol. 12, 44th Diet, House of Peers (March 26, 1921), 1158–59; quoted in Garon, "Women's Groups and the Japanese State," 17.

3. Resistance and Conformity

1. Uno, *Passages to Modernity*, 12.

2. Mackie, *Creating Socialist Women in Japan*, 53–54.

3. Quoted in Bardsley, *The Bluestockings of Japan*, 94. Bardsley's translation and analysis of the writings that appeared in *Seitō* are a significant contribution to the fields of modern literature and women's studies in Japan.

4. Ibid., 94–95.

5. Ibid., 90.

6. Tomida, *Hiratsuka Raichō*, 190–91; Bardsley, *The Bluestockings of Japan*, 93.

7. Quoted in Bardsley, *The Bluestockings of Japan*, 97.

8. Quoted in Mackie, *Creating Socialist Women in Japan*, 58.

9. The essay is translated in Hiratsuka, *In the Beginning, Woman Was the Sun*, 203–4; Lowy, *The Japanese "New Woman,"* 82–83; and Tomida, *Hiratsuka Raichō*, 177–79.

10. Bardsley, *The Bluestockings of Japan*, 85.

11. Bardsley writes, "All activities confirmed the reputation of the Bluestockings as out-of-bounds New Women" (ibid., 86).

12. Silverberg, "The Modern Girl as Militant," 239–66.

13. Mackie, *Feminism in Modern Japan*, 73.

14. Ibid.

15. Ibid., 75.

16. The image is reproduced on the cover of Iwauchi Zensaku, *Jokōsan ni okuru* (Tokyo: Nihon Rōdō Sōdōmei Kantō Boshoku Rōdō Kumiai, 1926); cited in Mackie, *Creating Socialist Women in Japan*, 74–75.

17. Nihon Kirisutokyō Fujin Kyōfukai, *Nihon kirisutokyō fujin kyōfukai 100-nen-shi*, 498. See also Yoshimi Kaneko, "Baishō no jittai to haishō undō."

18. Mackie, *Feminism in Modern Japan*, 91. Takamure, "Museifu shugi no mokuhyō to senjutsu." On Takamure's life and thought, see Takamure, *Takamure Itsue Zenshū*.

19. On Itō Noe's life, thought, and writing, see Itō, *Teihon Itō Noe zenshū*.

20. Writings by and on Kaneko Fumiko include Kaneko, *Nani ga watashi o kō sasetaka*, and Yamada Shōji, *Kaneko Fumiko*.

21. Hane's *Reflections on the Way to the Gallows* is a representative work on women's rebellion against the social repression in prewar Japan.

22. Raddeker, *Treacherous Women of Imperial Japan*.

23. Quoted in Mackie, *Feminism in Modern Japan*, 89.

24. Ibid., 88.

25. Fujimura Yoshirō, *Dai nihon teikoku gikai-shi* 12, 44th Diet, House of Peers (March 26, 1921), 1158–59; quoted in Garon, "Women's Groups and the Japanese State," 17.

26. Garon, "Women's Groups and the Japanese State," 13.

27. On the New Women's Association, see Mackie, *Feminism in Modern Japan*, 58–63.

28. Mackie, *Creating Socialist Women in Japan*, 157.

29. Rodd, "Yosano Akiko and the Taisho Debate over the 'New Woman,'" 189–93.

30. Nishikawa Fumiko, "Fujin no honsei to shakai shugi," *Shūkan heimin shinbun,* 20–11 (1904); quoted in Mackie, *Creating Socialist Women in Japan,* 50. Nishikawa, "Fujin to heiwa," *Shinshin fujin: Heiwa gō,* 1–10 (1914); quoted in Mackie, ibid., 85.

31. Kōtoku Shūsui, "Fujin to seiji," *Shūkan heimin shinbun,* 22–5 (1904); quoted in Mackie, *Creating Socialist Women in Japan,* 58.

32. Mackie, *Feminism in Modern Japan,* 90.

33. See Mackie, *Creating Socialist Women in Japan,* 149–50.

34. Garon, "Women's Groups and the Japanese State," 15.

35. Mackie, *Feminism in Modern Japan,* 30–31.

36. Garon, "Women's Groups and the Japanese State," 14.

37. Mackie, *Feminism in Modern Japan,* 92.

38. Garon makes this point in "Women's Groups and the Japanese State," 9.

39. Ryang, "Love and Colonialism in Takamure Itsue's Feminism."

40. Said, *Culture and Imperialism,* 332.

41. Yosano, *Pari yori,* 351.

42. Lippit, "Negotiations of Genre," in *Topographies of Japanese Modernism,* 164.

43. Adorno, *Minima Moralia,* 81.

44. Said, *Culture and Imperialism,* 336.

4. Behind the Guns

1. Hasegawa, *Tamura Toshiko hen kaisetsu.*

2. Watanabe, *Yosano Akiko,* 7. All English translations of Japanese texts are mine, unless otherwise stated.

3. Kawade Shobō Shinsha Henshūbu, *Shinbungei tokuhon: Yosano Akiko,* 216–19.

4. Rabson, "Yosano Akiko on War," 65.

5. Beichman, *Embracing the Firebird,* 264–65.

6. Ibid., 113 and 77.

7. Matsudaira, "Hyōden Midaregami," 215.

8. Nakagawa, "Nihon shisōka ron 2," 146.

9. When discussing Yosano's free and candid expression of sexuality in *Tangled Hair,* critics emphasize how, as a young woman from a middle-class family, she rebelled against the state prescription that women should only have either the reproductive desire of a "good wife, wise mother" or the carnal desire of a prostitute. Beichman's *Embracing the Firebird* examines Yosano's emergence in poetry in the work *Tangled Hair* with a focus on her early years up to the age of twenty-two.

10. Yosano, "Hirakibumi," 19–20.

11. Nakagawa, "Nihon shisōka ron 2," 142.

12. Noda, "Akiko ni okeru sensō to shi," 92.

13. Kennan, Sunday supplement of *Yomiuri shinbun* (November 13, 1904); quoted in Rabson, "Yosano Akiko on War," 52.

14. Yosano, "Hirakibumi," 17.

15. Ibid., 19.

16. Ōmachi Keigetsu; quoted in Kawade Shobō Shinsha Henshūbu, *Shinbungei tokuhon*, 74.

17. Yosano, "Kimi shini tamōkoto nakare," 25–28.

18. Mackie, *Creating Socialist Women in Japan*, 60.

19. See Rabson, "Yosano Akiko on War," 63.

20. Ibid.

21. Yūri, "Heiwa o ai suru kokoro," 25; quoted in Rabson, "Yosano Akiko on War," 64.

22. Ibid., 23; quoted in Rabson, "Yosano Akiko on War," 64.

23. Yosano, "'Onnarashisa' to wa nanika," 334; translation by Laurel Rasplica Rodd, in Copeland, *Woman Critiqued*, 40–41.

24. Yosano, "The Day the Mountains Move"; translation by Rodd, "Yosano Akiko," 180.

25. Yosano, "'Onnarashisa' to wa nanika," 336–39; translation by Rodd, in Copeland, *Woman Critiqued*, 40–41.

26. Yosano, "Nihon fujin no tokushoku wa nanika," 94.

27. Yosano, "'Onnarashisa' to wa nanika," 341; translation by Rodd, in Copeland, *Woman Critiqued*, 40–41.

28. Yosano, "Joshi no tettei shita dokuritsu," translation by Rodd, "Yosano Akiko," 192.

29. Yosano, *Yokohama bōeki shinpō*, October 20 and 27, 1918; reprinted in Kōuchi, *Shiryō bosei hogo ronsō*, 161–68.

30. Yosano, "'Onnarashisa' to wa nanika," 339; translation by Rodd, in Copeland, *Woman Critiqued*, 40–41.

31. Yosano, "Ubuya monogatari," 34.

32. Copeland, *Woman Critiqued*, 46.

33. See Mackie, *Creating Socialist Women in Japan*, 86–90.

34. Ibid., 89. Yosano's conformity with the nation-state has been pointed out mainly in reference to her unquestioning support of the liberal and bourgeois stance. As Vera Mackie explains, Yosano conforms to the mainstream economic and political system by advocating a feminism grounded on equal, individual rights and freedom in education, employment opportunities, financial independence, and suffrage. Although there was a gradual shift in emphasis from an interest in individualism to an engagement with the issues of capitalism, Yosano paid little attention to the situation of working women, who contributed to the nation's

economy in sexually and economically exploited conditions. A contemporary of Yosano, Yamakawa Kikue, in assessing Yosano during the *bosei hogo* debate in 1918, made the point that Yosano's vigor, ideas, and efforts could only be shared by women of the middle class and above. Yosano, along with other liberal feminists, left the dominant economic system unquestioned.

35. Beichman, "The Shape of *Tangled Hair*," in *Embracing the Firebird*, 227–49.

36. Karatani, "The Discovery of Interiority," in *Origins of Modern Japanese Literature*, 45–75.

37. Beichman, "The Variety of *Tangled Hair*" and "The Shape of *Tangled Hair*," in *Embracing the Firebird*, 199–226, 227–49.

38. Quoted in Suzuki Sadami, "Utaron o megutte."

39. In Yosano, *Teihon Yosano Akiko zenshū*, 9:135.

40. Yosano, "Yamano ugoku hi kitaru" ("The Day the Mountains Move"), the first poem in the series of poems called "Sozorogoto" (Wandering thoughts), appeared in the premier issue of the journal *Seitō* in 1911; translated by Rodd, "Yosano Akiko," 180.

41. Yosano, "Daiichi no jintsū" (The first labor pain), 255.

42. Yosano, "Childbirth and Ability," *Yokohama bōeki shinpō* (April 20, 1919); translated by Rodd, "Yosano Akiko," 195.

43. Yosano, "Ubuya monogatari," reprinted in *Shinbungei tokuhon Yosano Akiko*, 209.

44. Yosano, "Ubuya monogatari," 34–35; translated by Rodd, "Yosano Akiko," 180.

45. Yosano, "Futari no onna no taiwa" ("A Dialogue between Two Women"). The essay was originally serialized in *Tokyo asahi shinbun* (November 1914); translated by Rodd in "Yosano Akiko," 184.

46. My translation. See also Tsunoda, de Bary, and Keene, *Sources of Japanese Tradition*, 94–95.

47. Yosano, "'Onnarashisa' to wa nanika," 339.

48. Yosano, "Uchū to watakushi," in Yosano, *Teihon Yosano Akiko zenshū*, 9:144–45.

49. Yosano, "Nihon fujin no tokushoku wa nanika," 98.

50. Ibid., 98.

51. Translated by Rabson, "Yosano Akiko on War," 59–60.

52. Yosano, *Tōhaku* (January 1942); translated by Rabson, "Yosano Akiko on War," 62.

53. Translated by Rabson, "Yosano Akiko on War," 62.

54. See Duus, Myers, and Peattie, *The Japanese Informal Empire*, on the process and institutions of the Japanese military takeover in Manchuria.

55. Tamanoi, *Memory Maps*, 20.

56. Ibid., 160.

57. Ibid., 15.

58. Ibid., 14.

59. Quoted in Tamanoi, *Memory Maps*, 14.

60. Ibid., 14–15.

61. Manshūkoku-shi Hensan Kankōkai, *Manshūkoku-shi*, 219–21; quoted in Tamanoi, *Memory Maps*, 16.

62. Tamanoi, *Memory Maps*, 16.

63. Yosano, *Travels in Manchuria and Mongolia*, 66. Page numbers for subsequent citations of *Travels in Manchuria and Mongolia* are given parenthetically in text.

64. Tamanoi, *Memory Maps*, 18.

65. Yosano, *Travels in Manchuria and Mongolia*, 103.

66. Robertson, *Takarazuka*, 133.

67. Tamanoi, *Memory Maps*, 16.

68. "Rosy-Cheeked Death" first appeared in the April 1932 issue of the magazine *Tōhaku* (Winter oak). Reprinted in Yosano, *Teihon Yosano Akiko zenshū*, 8:272–75; translated in Rabson, "Yosano Akiko on War," 71.

69. Tamanoi, *Memory Maps*, 15.

5. Self-Imposed Exile

1. Mizuta, "Jendā kōzō no gaibu e," 137. All English translations of Japanese texts are mine, unless otherwise stated.

2. Satō Toshiko (a pen name of Tamura Toshiko), "Goaisatsu," 151.

3. Satō Toshiko (Tamura Toshiko), "Futsuka kan," 438.

4. Watanabe, "Tamura Toshiko," 369.

5. Hasegawa, *Tamura Toshiko hen kaisetsu*, 264.

6. See Ericson, ed., Introduction to "Tamura Toshiko (1884–1945)."

7. Quoted in Yamasaki, "Miira no kuchibeni ron," 19.

8. XYZ, "Kokei bundan no ganshoku"; quoted in Mitsuishi, "Tamura Toshiko *Onna sakusha* ron," 126.

9. Ibid.

10. Ibid.

11. Kobayashi Aio, *Shin bunshō no kenkyū*; quoted in Mitsuishi, "Tamura Toshiko *Onna sakusha* ron," 129.

12. Masamune Hakuchō, "Toshiko ron"; quoted in Mitsuishi, "Tamura Toshiko *Onna sakusha* ron," 133.

13. Aozukin, "Toshiko no 'Sensei'"; quoted in Mitsuishi, "Tamura Toshiko *Onna sakusha* ron," 132.

14. Kobayashi Aio, "Inshōteki toiu koto"; quoted in Mitsuishi, "Tamura Toshiko *Onna sakusha* ron," 129.

15. Copeland, *Woman Critiqued,* 60.

16. Ibid., 55.

17. Mizuta, "Jendā kōzō no gaibu e," 133–35.

18. Enomoto, "Tamura Toshiko," 12.

19. Copeland, *Woman Critiqued,* 58.

20. Mizuta, "Jendā kōzō no gaibu e," 133–34. Mizuta contends that Tamura wrote against men and the state whose expectations concerning the roles and position of women within the family posed obstacles for women's self-expression. "The desire of Toshiko's protagonists, who live as they wish, transcends the rules of gender. . . . In order to penetrate this self-centeredness of the protagonists, there is no way but to head out beyond the husband, family, and *bundan*" (135).

21. Tamura Toshiko, *Hōraku no kei,* 66–67.

22. Yukiko Tanaka, "Tamura Toshiko," 5–10.

23. Mitsuishi, "Tamura Toshiko *Onna sakusha* ron," 133.

24. Tamura Toshiko, *Miira no kuchibeni,* 373.

25. Izu, "Onna ni totte jiritsu towa nanika," 75.

26. Ibid., 76.

27. Satō Toshiko (Tamura Toshiko), "Nihon fujin undō no nagare o miru," in Tamura, *Tamura Toshiko sakuhinshū,* 3:403–4.

28. Satō Toshiko (Tamura Toshiko), "Uchida Tamino san eno ohenji," 208.

29. Joan E. Ericson problematizes the categorization of "woman writer" in Japan. See "Reading a Woman Writer," "When Was Women's Literature?," and "Women's Journals" in her *Be a Woman,* 3–17, 18–38, and 39–56, respectively.

30. Tamura wrote a short story, "Bokuyōsha" (Shepherds), for *Tairiku nippō* on January 1, 1919.

31. Mizuta, "Jendâ kōzō no gaibu e," 140.

32. Kurosawa, "Kaisetsu," 434.

33. Kudō and Phillips, *Bankūbâ no Ai,* 238.

34. Ogata, "Tamura Toshiko to *Kagayaku*," 86.

35. On Tamura's *Josei* (Women's voice), see Watanabe, *Ima to iu jidai no Tamura Toshiko,* 21–58; Watanabe, "Tamura Toshiko *Josei* ni tsuite"; Ō, "Shanhai jidai no Tamura Toshiko."

36. Due to the limited availability of source material, I must concentrate on these writings during this period. Tamura was most active writing for *Tairiku nippō* (1908–41) from 1918 until 1924. After 1924, when her husband, Suzuki Etsu, the editor of *Tairiku nippō,* left the newspaper and became the chief editor of *Nikkan minshū* (Daily people, 1924–41), Tamura's work appeared more frequently in *Minshū* than in *Tairiku nippō. Tairiku nippō* survived in its entirety, whereas only a limited number of issues of *Minshū* is accessible: the Hino City Hall preserves issues from March 1935 until November 1936, and the British Columbia Library holds issues from May until December 1941. All these preserved

issues were published after Tamura left Vancouver in 1936, so her works in *Minshū* are no longer available.

37. In the examination of social and political texts and contexts, I draw examples from the documents written between the 1890s and 1940s to show that conflicting and changing political conditions and identities of the immigrants residing in Canada were experienced not only in a temporal dynamic—that is, diachronically over time—but also as a relation of phenomena sychronically at the time in which Tamura wrote.

38. The following anecdote from the 1890s presents a case of early immigrants' self-determination: "The . . . pioneers were mostly sailors on foreign vessels, who did not possess valid passports officially issued by the Ministry of Foreign Affairs of the Government of Japan. . . . Taking pride in having a Japanese passport, a Momozaki tried to seek friendly associations with those Japanese in Canada, but all those high spirited pioneers ridiculed him by saying, 'You are too weak-hearted! Who needs an official document of the Japanese Government!'" See Jinshirō Nakayama, "Canada and the Japanese," 275. This anecdote exemplifies the immigrants' claim of autonomy and independence from the Japanese government.

39. Gonnami, "Introduction," 9.

40. Suzuki Etsu, quoted in Kudō and Phillips, *Bankūbā no ai,* 24–25.

41. *Tairiku nippō,* October 14, 1920.

42. Ishii, *Modan toshi kaidoku tokuhon.*

43. See "Japanese Immigration," in Department of External Affairs, *Documents on Canadian External Relations, 1919–1925,* 3:706.

44. See Kudō and Phillips, *Bankūbā no ai:* "On the evening of September 7, 1907 . . . 7,000 to 8,000 people gathered to protest the increasing Asian immigration. At around midnight, a part of the excited crowd of the Asiatic Exclusion League raced through Chinatown yelling and chanting their slogans, breaking every window, and then headed to Little Tokyo on Powell Street. . . . In the meeting room of the [Vancouver City] Hall, the crowd shouted 'We don't need the Japanese. . . . Stand for White Canada,' etc." (24–25).

45. Canadians' complaints about the growing numbers of Japanese and their competitiveness in professions continued to be reflected in the votes of the parliament of British Columbia, which passed anti-Japanese regulations and laws from the 1890s to the 1940s. See "Consul General of Japan to Prime Minister," in Department of External Affairs, *Documents on Canadian External Relations 1919–1925,* 3:237–38, 703-43. See also Nakayama, "Canada and the Japanese," 281–85.

46. Shinpo, *Kanada nihonjin imin monogatari,* 69–84.

47. Nakayama, "Canada and the Japanese," 282.

48. Ibid.

49. See Yoshida, *Ningen no kagaku sōsho 2, zōhoban,* 150.

50. Quoted in Kudō and Phillips, *Bankūbā no ai,* 166.

51. Suzuki Etsu founded the Kanada Nihonjin Rōdō Kumiai (Canadian Japanese Labor Union) in 1920. On April 12, 1920, *Tairiku nippō* featured the article "Nihojin rōdōsha no tachiba" (The position of the Japanese laborers) and encouraged the Japanese to unite with "white" workers.

52. On August 15, 1914, in *Tairiku nippō*, the Canadian Japanese Association encouraged Japanese immigrants to volunteer for the Canadian army and navy in World War I.

53. See Yoshida, *Ningen no kagaku sōsho 2, zōhoban,* 178.

54. Quoted in Kudō and Phillips, *Bankūbā no ai,* 166.

55. See Jinshirō Nakayama, "Canada and the Japanese," 263.

56. Tori no ko (Baby Bird, a pen name of Tamura Toshiko; works are listed in the bibliography under Tamura Toshiko), "Kono machi ni sumu fujintachi ni."

57. Tori no ko (Tamura Toshiko), "Tabigarasu no onshin."

58. Tori no ko (Tamura Toshiko), *Tairiku nippō,* January 25, 1919.

59. Tori no ko (Tamura Toshiko), in "Shinshun no uta" (New Year's poetry).

60. Tori no ko (Tamura Toshiko), "Mizukara hatarakeru fujintachi ni."

61. Tori no ko (Tamura Toshiko), "Nikkai kaizōan tsūka ni yotte."

62. Tori no ko (Tamura Toshiko), "Bi no shōkei."

63. Tori no ko (Tamura Toshiko), "Kono machi ni sumu fujintachi ni."

64. Tori no ko (Tamura Toshiko), "Bi no shōkei."

65. Tori no ko (Tamura Toshiko), "Mizukara hatarakeru fujintachi ni."

66. Tori no ko (Tamura Toshiko), "Nikkai kaizōan tsūka ni yotte."

67. Ibid.

68. Tori no ko (Tamura Toshiko), "Saikin no Nihon fujin shisō no dōtei."

69. Ibid.

70. Tori no ko (Tamura Toshiko), "Bi no shōkei."

71. Tori no ko (Tamura Toshiko), "Mizukara hatarakeru fujintachi ni."

72. Ibid.

73. Tori no ko (Tamura Toshiko), "Kono machi ni sumu fujintachi ni."

74. Tori no ko (Tamura Toshiko), "Mizukara hatarakeru fujintachi ni."

75. Tori no ko (Tamura Toshiko), "Nikkai kaizō tsūka ni yotte."

76. Ibid.

77. Ibid.

78. By bearing children and raising the next generation of industrious workers and strong soldiers for imperial expansion, women secured the well-being of the nation's resources. Moreover, "good wives, wise mothers" and their fertile bodies became a symbol of the nation-state's power and growth. See Miyake, "Doubling Expectations," 268.

79. Tori no ko (Tamura Toshiko), "Nikkai kaizō tsūka ni yotte."

80. See Nolte, "Women, the State, and Repression in Imperial Japan," 4.

81. Tori no ko (Tamura Toshiko), "Kono machi ni sumu fujintachi ni."

82. Azuma, *Between Two Empires,* 10–11.

83. Ibid., 14.

84. Suzuki Toshiko (Tamura Toshiko), "Aru tomo e" (1).

85. Suzuki Toshiko (Tamura Toshiko), "Aru tomo e" (2).

86. Yukari (Tamura Toshiko), "Taishūsha no shujin."

87. Azuma, *Between Two Empires,* 147.

88. Suzuki Toshiko (Tamura Toshiko), "Aru tomo e" (4).

89. Yukari (Tamura Toshiko), "Kiyohara Senzō shi" (2).

90. Yukari (Tamura Toshiko), "Kiyohara Senzō shi" (3).

91. Yukari (Tamura Toshiko), "Yokota jimukan" (1).

92. Yukari (Tamura Toshiko), "Yokota jimukan" (2).

93. Ibid.

94. Azuma, *Between Two Empires,* 164.

95. Ibid., 159.

96. Wu, "Hokubei jidai to Tamura Toshiko," 261.

97. Satō Toshiko (Tamura Toshiko), "Kariforunia monogatari," 42. Anne Sokolsky analyzes this story in "Writing between the Spaces of Nation and Culture."

98. Satō Toshiko (Tamura Toshiko), "Kariforunia monogatari," 38.

99. Ibid., 32.

100. Ibid., 45.

101. Wu, "Hokubei jidai to Tamura Toshiko," 93.

102. Satō Toshiko (Tamura Toshiko), "Kariforunia monogatari," 6.

103. Azuma, *Between Two Empires,* 145.

104. Satō Toshiko (Tamura Toshiko), "Kariforunia monogatari," 10.

105. Ibid., 3.

106. Ibid., 42–43.

107. Ibid., 28.

108. See Watanabe, *Ima to iu jidai no Tamura Toshiko,* and the special issue of *U.S.–Japan Women's Journal* (no. 28, 2005) devoted to Tamura.

109. Satō Toshiko (Tamura Toshiko), "Hitotsu no yume," 264.

110. Satō Toshiko (Tamura Toshiko), "Futsuka kan," 438; also in Tamura, *Tamura Toshiko sakuhinshū,* 3:407–16.

111. Satō Toshiko (Tamura Toshiko), "Dōsei o mamoru," 92–93.

112. Satō Toshiko (Tamura Toshiko), "Nihon fujin undō no nagare o miru"; originally appeared in *Miyako shinbun* (Miyako newspaper), June 1937, 17–19. Reprinted in Tamura, *Tamura Toshiko sakuhinshū,* 3:398–406.

113. Satō Toshiko (Tamura Toshiko), "Warera wa nani o subekika."

114. Satō Toshiko (Tamura Toshiko), "Jogakusei seikatsu no kaikaku"; quoted in Watanabe, *Ima to iu jidai no Tamura Toshiko,* 246.

115. See note 35.

6. Wandering on the Periphery

1. Brown's *I Saw a Pale Horse* and Ericson's *Be a Woman* include detailed biographical information of Hayashi Fumiko.

2. Brown, *I Saw a Pale Horse*, 3.

3. Ericson, *Be a Woman*, 88.

4. Brown, *I Saw a Pale Horse*, 15, 17.

5. Komata, "Gyokai," 120. All English translations of Japanese texts are mine, unless otherwise stated.

6. Mizuta, "Hayashi Fumiko no miryoku," 26.

7. Ericson, *Be a Woman*, 82.

8. Ibid., 83.

9. Kawamoto, "'Akarui sengo' no nakano 'kurai sensō,'" 143.

10. Ibid., 141–51.

11. See also "Hayashi Fumiko no jūgunki." Kawamoto ("'Akarui sengo' no naka no 'kurai sensō'") and Takahashi *(Senjō no joryū sakka tachi)* have also pointed out and questioned Hayashi's cooperation with the Japanese government's war efforts.

12. Hayashi, *Hōrōki*, 390 (page numbers for subsequent citations are given parenthetically in text). All translations from *Hōrōki* are mine, unless otherwise indicated. Joan Ericson's translation is available in *Be a Woman*.

13. Ericson, *Be a Woman*, 71.

14. Here I use Lippit's translation in his *Topographies of Japanese Modernism*, 159.

15. Hayashi, *Hōrōki*, 276.

16. Takahashi, *Senjō no joryū sakka tachi*, 165.

17. Hayashi, *Hokugan butai*, 101 (page numbers for subsequent citations are given parenthetically in text). All translations from *Hokugan butai* are mine.

18. Among others, Noriko Mizuta evaluates *Ukigumo* as follows: "*Drifting Clouds* captures the spirit of Japan after its defeat, and it is a masterpiece of postwar literature" (Mizuta, "In Search of a Lost Paradise," 346).

19. My translation. The original is "chōsen ya taiwan ya ryūkyū rettō karafuto manshū kono haisen de subete o ushinatte dōtai dake ni natta nihon" (Hayashi, *Ukigumo*, 362). Lane Dunlop chooses not to translate *dōtai* ("torso"): "In this defeat, Japan had lost Korea, Taiwan, the Ryukyu Islands, Sakhalin, and Manchuria, and had been reduced to its four main islands" (Hayashi, *Floating Clouds*, 288).

20. Although discourse on the nation-state as the body could already be seen in the early-modern period (1603–1868) in Aizawa Seishi's *Shinron* (New theses, 1825), Japan as a body in the modern era (1868–1945) has its source in the organ theory of the nation-state *(yūkitai kokka ron)* that was imported from Germany. I explore *yūkitai kokka ron* and *kokutai ron* in detail in chapter 1.

21. Hayashi, *Gendai nihon bungaku eiyaku senshū*, 86.

22. Hayashi, *Floating Clouds*, 22.

23. Hayashi, *Ukigumo*, 125.

24. Ibid., 124–25.

25. Hayashi, *Floating Clouds*, 14.

26. Ibid.

27. Ibid., 39.

28. Ibid., 163.

29. The original goes as follows: "ano toki wa hontō ni kōfuku datta. . . . heitai no minna ga seishi o kakete tatakatte iru toki ni, yukiko dake wa tomioka to fushigina koi ni toritsukarete ita noda kara" (Hayashi, *Ukigumo*, 210). Lane Dunlop omits this part in his translation.

30. Hayashi, *Ukigumo*, 191.

31. Hayashi, *Floating Clouds*, 61.

32. Mizuta, "In Search of a Lost Paradise," 348.

33. Ibid., 340.

34. Ibid., 346.

35. Ibid., 338.

36. Hayashi, *Floating Clouds*, 30.

37. Ibid., 19.

38. Ibid., 176.

39. My translation. The original appears in Hayashi, *Ukigumo*: 307-8: "kono kunigara ga oretachi o tsukuru yōni nattanda yo . . . . Ne no nai ukigusa mitai na wareware daga" (307–8).

40. Hayashi, *Floating Clouds*, 163.

41. Ibid., 254.

42. Dower, *Embracing Defeat*, 21.

43. Norgren, *Abortion before Birth Control*, 36–37, 43.

44. Ibid., 40.

45. Hayashi, *Ukigumo*, 117. My translation of the original: "ano hito [Joe] mo sabishii no yo. Anata ga Niu o kawaigatteta kimochi to onaji yo." Lane Dunlop translates the original in this way: "He's lonely, too. It's the same feeling you had for Niu" (Hayashi, *Floating Clouds*, 94).

46. Lane Dunlop omits the translation of the original: "dare nimo tayorazu dare nimo awanaide korekara jibun dake no shigoto o shite hatarakitai to omotta." Hayashi, *Ukigumo*, 236.

47. Hayashi, *Floating Clouds*, 250.

48. My translation. The original reads: "Tomioka no subete ni hikasareru aijō ga jibun no ketsueki o tsukuru tame no onna no saigo no agaki no yōna ki mo shite kite" (Hayashi, *Ukigumo*, 291). Lane Dunlop translates as follows: "She even had the sense that her love for him was something instinctual, primal, in the blood" (Hayashi, *Floating Clouds*, 227).

49. Hayashi, *Floating Clouds,* 163.

50. Ibid., 283.

51. Ibid., 298.

52. In their dialogue, Hasumi and Nakafuru maintain that Yukiko deserves to die in this manner because of the material and physical advantages she enjoyed as a former colonizer in French Indochina. See Naruse and Nakafuru, *Naruse Mikio no sekkei,* 199–200.

53. Hayashi, *Floating Clouds,* 38.

54. Ibid., 98.

55. Ibid., 286.

56. Historiographical research on the empire of modern Japan (1868–1945) has shifted focus from the emperor, state bureaucracy, and military to the Japanese people themselves. In the field of "people's history" *(minshūshi),* scholars tackle questions about the relationship between the ideology of the state and that of the people, as indicated in the roles the populace played in building and expanding the empire. *Minshū-shi* scholars such as Yasumaru Yoshio, Irokawa Daikichi, and Kano Masanao have been active since the 1970s.

57. Kanō Mikiyo, *Tennōsei to jendā,* 52.

Conclusion

1. This chapter is based on Horiguchi, "Migrant Women, Memory, and Empire." Some scholars have pointed out the impossibility of knowing the past as it occurs and instead have emphasized the narrative as the means to know the past. Mariko Asano Tamanoi reminds us of this point in the introduction to her *Memory Maps,* 5. See also Fujitani, White, and Yoneyama, "Introduction."

2. See Walter Benjamin, "The Work of Art in the Age of Mechanical Reproduction" ("Das Kunstwerk im Zeitalter seiner technischen Reproduzierbarkeit"; originally published in *Zeitschrift für Sozialforschung* in 1936 and included in *Illuminations*). As James Naremore explores, comparative analyses of the original novel and the film adaptation often take one of four different positions: (1) some point out the inferiority of the film adaptation as a copy of the original work of literature; (2) other studies judge the success or failure of fidelity of the film adaptation to the original novel; (3) still others analyze the film adaptation as a digest of the original novel; and finally, (4) some analyze the narratives and ideologies that traverse different media. See Naremore, "Introduction." By relying on Jacques Derrida's deconstruction of the dichotomy and hierarchy of the original and copy, I avoid the judgment of the superiority or inferiority of literature to film adaptation. See Derrida, "Signature Event Context," 185. On the relationship between semiotics and ideology, see Roland Barthes, *Mythologies;* on intertextuality of narratives and ideologies, see Barthes, *S/Z.*

3. Russell, *The Cinema of Naruse Mikio,* 280.

4. Casey, *Remembering,* 197.

5. Tamanoi, *Memory Maps,* 6.

6. Naruse's first film was a short comedy titled *Chanbara kappuru* (A sword fight couple), made in 1929 and released in January 1930.

7. Hasumi and Nakafuru, *Naruse Mikio no sekkei,* 197 and 249. All English translations of Japanese texts are mine, unless otherwise stated.

8. Russell, *The Cinema of Naruse Mikio,* 10–11.

9. Ibid.; see also by Russell, "Too Close to Home," 88.

10. Kawamoto, "Ima hitotabi no sengo nihon eiga dai nana kai," 339.

11. Ibid., 338.

12. Ibid., 336.

13. Russell, "Too Close to Home," 90.

14. Hasumi and Nakafuru, *Naruse Mikio no sekkei,* 150.

15. For example, Mori Ōgai—a civil and military medical doctor who wrote a blueprint for the factory law in 1911, as well as a literary authority who wrote, among others, the novella *Youth* in the same year—re-created the discourse on two types of women in modern Japan. According to *Youth,* the "prostitute type" appears in opposition to the "maternal type." It is important to promote the maternal type because these women contribute not only to the continuation of human kind in general but also to the sovereign state. "The maternal type [who] desires only to breed" contributes to society because such women reproduce sources of national strength. According to *Youth,* it is crucial to educate and expand the number of women of the maternal type because the nation contains the anti-social force—the prostitute type—as well. They are antisocial because "the prostitute type has only carnal desire" and no desire for reproduction. Ōgai, *Youth,* 441.

16. Hasumi and Nakafuru, *Naruse Mikio no sekkei,* 146.

17. Hayashi, *Meshi,* 69.

18. Tanaka and Ide, Film script *Meshi* (1959), 61.

19. Naruse, *Meshi* (film, 1951).

20. Hayashi, *Meshi,* 45.

21. Ibid., 119.

22. Ibid., 197.

23. Ibid., 204.

24. Ibid., 38.

25. Hasumi and Nakafuru, *Naruse Mikio no sekkei,* 157 and 152.

26. Ibid., 158.

27. Russell, "Too Close to Home," 95.

28. Ibid., 107.

29. Menish, "Representation of Space in the Films of Mikio Naruse," 34.

30. Tanaka and Ide, *Meshi,* 60.

31. Russell, "Too Close to Home," 107.

32. Menish contends that Michiyo finds no respite from spatial confinement even when she leaves the space of home for a gathering with friends at a restaurant; see Menish, "Representation of Space," 28.

33. Ibid.; Russell, "Too Close to Home," 95.

34. Menish, "Representation of Space," 37.

35. Hayashi, *Meshi,* 27 and 90.

36. Ibid., 27 and 41.

37. As a member of the offices of the Supreme Commander of the Allied Powers during the U.S. occupation, Beate Sirota Gordon (1923–) played an important role in writing articles 14 and 24 into the postwar Japanese Constitution. Article 14 outlaws discrimination based on "race, creed, sex, social status or family origin." Article 24 guarantees equality between the sexes in marriage. Therefore, the new constitution ensured women's liberation and rights in postwar Japan, and the 1950s witnessed vigorous debates and movements to promote equality between men and women in the area of labor.

38. Tanaka and Ide, Film script *Meshi,* 68.

39. Russell, *The Cinema of Naruse Mikio,* 28.

40. Kawamoto, "Ima hitotabi no sengo nihon eiga dai nana kai," 341.

41. Menish, "Representation of Space," 28.

42. Russell, "Too Close to Home," 95.

43. Ibid., 101.

44. Ibid.; Menish, "Representation of Space," 18.

45. Russell, *The Cinema of Naruse Mikio,* 10–15.

46. Hasumi and Nakafuru, *Naruse Mikio no sekkei,* 215.

47. Mizuki, Screenplay *Ukigumo,* 83.

48. Ibid.

49. The occupation policy of the Ministry of Agriculture of the Japanese government aimed to secure French Indochina's natural resources, specifically wood and rice.

50. Mizuki, Screenplay *Ukigumo,* 80.

51. Ibid., 81.

52. Russell, *The Cinema of Naruse Mikio,* 280.

53. Mizuta, "In Search of a Lost Paradise," 348.

54. Ibid., 346.

55. Russell, *The Cinema of Naruse Mikio,* 281.

56. Ibid., 280.

57. Mizuki, Screenplay *Ukigumo,* 79.

58. My translation. The original is "chōsen ya taiwan ya ryūkyū rettō karafuto manshū kono haisen de subete o ushinatte dōtai dake ni natta nihon" (Hayashi, *Ukigumo,* 362).

59. Menish, "Representation of Space," 34.

60. Norgren, *Abortion before Birth Control,* 43, 36–37.

61. Mizuki, Screenplay *Ukigumo,* 93-94.

62. Hayashi, *Floating Clouds,* 270.

63. Ibid., 298.

64. Russell, *The Cinema of Naruse Mikio,* 283.

65. Edward Casey contends that "to be disembodied is not only to be deprived of place, *unplaced;* it is to be denied the basic stance on which every experience and its memory depend." quoted in Tamanoi, *Memory Maps,* 160.

66. Russell, *The Cinema of Naruse Mikio,* 280.

67. Ibid.

68. Hayashi, *Floating Clouds,* 286.

69. Ibid.

70. See chapter 6, note 56.

71. Tamanoi, *Memory Maps,* 6; see Davis, *Yearning for Yesterday.*

72. Davis, *Yearning for Yesterday,* 37.

73. Rosaldo, "Imperialist Nostalgia."

74. Gao, "Kioku sangyō to shite no tsūrizumu"; quoted in Tamanoi, *Memory Maps,* 159.

75. Tamanoi, *Memory Maps,* 20.

76. Hayashi, *Floating Clouds,* 303.

77. Yoneyama, "Memory Matters."

78. Suzuki Yūko investigates female intellectuals' activities during prewar and postwar periods by challenging the long-established framework that has uncritically vindicated the responsibility of the aggressors. See Suzuki, *Feminizumu to senso̅.* Hasegawa et al. examine women's responsibility for the Fifteen-Year War (1931–45) in their *Onna tachi no senso̅ sekinin.*

Bibliography

Ackroyd, Joyce. "Women in Feudal Japan." *Transactions of the Asiatic Society of Japan* 3rd ser. 7 (1959): 31–68.

Adachi, Nobuko. *Japanese Diasporas: Unsung Pasts, Conflicting Presents, and Uncertain Futures.* New York: Routledge, 2006.

Adorno, Theodor. *Minima Moralia: Reflections on a Damaged Life.* London: Verso, 1951.

Aizawa Seishi. *Shinron* (New theses). Tokyo: Iwanami, 1941.

Anderson, Benedict. *Imagined Communities: Reflections on the Origin and Spread of Nationalism.* New York: Verso, 1991.

Aozukin. "Toshiko no Sensei" (Toshiko's teacher). *Shinchō* 19, no. 1 (1913): 81.

Arai Tomiyo. *Chūgoku sensen wa dō egakareta ka: Jūgunki o yomu* (How was the Chinese battlefront described? Reading war correspondents). Tokyo: Iwanami Shoten, 2007.

———. "Hayashi Fumiko no jūgunki" (Hayashi Fumiko's war correspondence). *Ōtani daigaku bungei ronshū* 53 (September 1999): 1–21.

Azuma, Eiichiro. *Between Two Empires: Race, History, and Transnationalism in Japanese America.* New York: Oxford University Press, 2005.

Bardsley, Jan. *The Bluestockings of Japan: New Woman Essays and Fiction from "Seitō," 1911–16.* Ann Arbor: Center for Japanese Studies, University of Michigan, 2007.

———. Introduction to "Chapter 2: The Essential Woman Writer." In *Woman Critiqued: Translated Essays on Japanese Women's Writing,* edited by Rebecca L. Copeland, 53–60. Honolulu: University of Hawai'i Press, 2006.

Barthes, Roland. *Mythologies.* Translated by Annette Lavers. New York: Hill and Wang, 1972.

———. *S/Z.* Translated by Richard Miller. New York: Hill and Wang, 1974.

Beasley, W. G. *Japanese Imperialism 1894–1945.* New York: Oxford University Press, 1987.

Beichman, Janine. *Embracing the Firebird: Yosano Akiko and the Birth of the Female Voice in Modern Japanese Poetry.* Honolulu: University of Hawai'i Press, 2002.

Bernstein, Gail Lee, ed. *Recreating Japanese Women, 1600–1945.* Berkeley: University of California Press, 1991.

Boehmer, Elleke. *Colonial and Postcolonial Literature.* Oxford: Oxford University Press, 1995.

Boudaghs, Michael Kevin. *The Dawn That Never Comes: Shimazaki Toson and Japanese Nationalism.* New York: Columbia University Press, 2003.

Bourdieu, Pierre. *The Logic of Practice.* Translated by Richard Nice. Cambridge: Polity, 1990.

Brown, Janice. "The Celebration of Struggle: A Study of the Major Works of Hayashi Fumiko." PhD diss., University of British Columbia, 1985.

————, trans. *I Saw a Pale Horse (Aouma wo mitari) and Selected Poems from Diary of a Vagabond (Hōrōki).* Ithaca, N.Y.: Cornell University East Asia Program, 1997.

Butler, Judith. *Bodies That Matter: On the Discursive Limits of "Sex."* New York: Routledge, 1993.

————. *Gender Trouble: Feminism and the Subversion of Identity.* New York: Routledge, 1990.

Casey, Edward. *Remembering: A Phenomenological Study.* 2nd ed. Bloomington: Indiana University Press, 2000.

Chin, Hsien-Yu. "Colonial Medical Police and Postcolonial Medical Surveillance Systems in Taiwan, 1895–1950s." *Osiris.* Vol. 13, *Beyond Joseph Needham: Science, Technology, and Medicine in East and Southeast Asia,* edited by Morris Low, 326–38. Chicago: University of Chicago Press, 1998.

Chow, Rey. *Writing Diaspora: Tactics of Intervention in Contemporary Cultural Studies.* Bloomington: Indiana University Press, 1993.

Chu, Patricia P. *Assimilating Asians: Gendered Strategies of Authorship in Asian America.* Durham, N.C.: Duke University Press, 2000.

Copeland, Rebecca L., ed. *Woman Critiqued: Translated Essays on Japanese Women's Writing.* Honolulu: University of Hawai'i Press, 2006.

Crowley, James B. "A New Asian Order: Some Notes on Prewar Japanese Nationalism."

In *Japan in Crisis: Essays on Taishō Democracy,* edited by Bernard S. Silberman and H. D. Harootunian, 279–298. Ann Arbor: University of Michigan Press, 1999.

Davis, Fred. *Yearning for Yesterday: A Sociology of Nostalgia.* New York: Free Press, 1979.

Department of External Affairs. *Documents on Canadian External Relations, 1919–1925.* Vol. 3, edited by Lovell C. Clark. 23 vols. Ottawa: Crown, 1970.

Derrida, Jacques. "Signature Event Context." *Glyph* 1 (1977): 172–97.

Doak, Kevin M. "What Is a Nation and Who Belongs? National Narratives and the Ethnic Imagination in Twentieth-Century Japan." *American Historical Review* 102, no. 2 (1997): 283–309.

Dower, John W. *Embracing Defeat: Japan in the Wake of World War II*. New York: W. W. Norton, 1999.

———. *Japan in War and Peace: Essays on History, Culture and Race*. London: HarperCollins, 1995.

———. *War without Mercy: Race and Power in the Pacific*. New York: Pantheon Books, 1987.

Dreyfus, Hubert L., and Paul Rabinow. *Michel Foucault: Beyond Structuralism and Hermeneutics*. Chicago: University of Chicago Press, 1983.

During, Simon. *Foucault and Literature: Towards a Genealogy of Writing*. London: Routledge, 1992.

Duus, Peter, Raymond Myers, and Mark R. Peattie. *The Japanese Informal Empire in China, 1895–1937*. Princeton, N.J.: Princeton University Press, 1991.

Enomoto Takashi. "Tamura Toshiko." *Kokubungaku kaishaku to kanshō* (National literature: Interpretation and appreciation) 50, no. 10 (1985): 10–13.

Ericson, Joan E. *Be a Woman: Hayashi Fumiko and Modern Japanese Women's Literature*. Honolulu: University of Hawai'i Press, 1997.

———, ed. "Tamura Toshiko (1884–1945)." Special issue, *U.S.–Japan Women's Journal*, no. 18 (2005).

Feng, Peter X. *Identities in Motion: Asian American Film and Video*. Durham, N.C.: Duke University Press, 2002.

Field, Norma. "War and Apology." *Position: East Asia Cultures Critique* 5, no. 1 (Spring 1997): 1–49.

Forsythe, Ruth Hyland. "Songs of Longing: The Art of Hayashi Fumiko." PhD diss., University of Minnesota, 1988.

Foucault, Michel. *The Birth of the Clinic*. New York: Pantheon Books, 1973.

———. *Discipline and Punish: The Birth of the Prison*. Translated by Alan Sheridan. New York: Vintage Books, 1995.

———. *The History of Sexuality*. Vol. 1. Translated by Robert Hurley. New York: Pantheon Books, 1978.

———. *The Order of Things: An Archaeology of the Human Sciences*. New York: Pantheon, 1970.

———. "What Is an Author?" In *Textual Strategies: Perspectives in Post-Structuralist Criticism*, edited by Josué V. Harari, 101–20. Ithaca, N.Y.: Cornell University Press, 1969.

Franck, Frederick, ed. *The Buddha Eye: An Anthology of the Kyoto School*. New York: Crossroad, 1982.

Fruhstuck, Sabine. *Uneasy Warriors: Gender, Memory, and Popular Culture in the Japanese Army*. Berkeley: University of California Press, 2007.

Fujime, Yuki. "The Licensed Prostitution System and the Prostitution Abolition Movement in Modern Japan." *Positions: East Asia Cultures Critique* 5, no. 1 (1997): 135–70.

Fujitani, T. *Splendid Monarchy: Power and Pageantry in Modern Japan*. Berkeley: University of California Press, 1996.

Fujitani, T., Geoffrey White, and Lisa Yoneyama, eds. "Introduction." *Perilous Memories: The Asia–Pacific War(s)*, 1–29. Durham, N.C.: Duke University Press, 2001.

Fukuda Kiyoto and Endō Mitsuhiko. *Hayashi Fumiko: Hito to Sakuhin* (Hayashi Fumiko's personality and works). Tokyo: Shimizu Shoin, 1966.

Fukuzawa Yukichi. *Fukuzawa Yukichi on Japanese Women*. Tokyo: University of Tokyo Press, 1988.

———. *Fukuzawa Yukichi zenshū* (Complete works of Fukuzawa Yukichi). Vol. 8. Tokyo: Iwanami Shoten, 1960.

———. "Jiji taisei ron" (On general trends of the times). Tokyo: Keiō Gijuku Zōhan, 1882.

Furuta Hiroshi. *Higashi ajia ideorogī o koete* (Transcending East Asian ideology). Tokyo: Shinshokan, 2003.

Furutani Tsunatake. *Gendai bosei gaku* (Studies of contemporary motherhood). Tokyo: Tokyo Gakugeisha, 1942.

Gao Yuan. "Kioku sangyō to shite no tsūrizumu" (Tourism as memory industry). *Gendai shisō* 29, no. 4 (2001): 219–29.

Garon, Sheldon. "Women's Groups and the Japanese State: Contending Approaches to Political Integration, 1890–1945." *Journal of Japanese Studies* 19, no. 1 (Winter 1993): 5–41.

Gluck, Carol. *Japan's Modern Myths: Ideology in the Late Meiji Period*. Princeton, N.J.: Princeton University Press, 1985.

Gonnami, Tsuneharu. "Introduction." In *Historical Materials of Japanese Immigration to Canada: Supplement Kanada Iminshi shiryō: Bessatsu* (Sources on immigrant history, supplementary volume), edited by Norman Amor and Tsuneharu Gonnami, 5–13. Tokyo: Fuji Shuppan, 2001.

Gordon, Andrew. *Labor and Imperial Democracy in Prewar Japan*. Berkeley: University of California Press, 1991.

Griffis, William Elliot. "First Glimpses of Japan" and "A Ride on the Tōkaidō." In *The Mikado's Empire*. 2 vols., 9th ed., 327–62. New York: Harper & Brothers, 1900.

Hall, Robert King, ed. *Kokutai no hongi: Cardinal Principles of the National Entity of Japan*. Translated by John Owen Gauntlett and edited with an introduction by Robert King Hall. Cambridge, Mass.: Harvard University Press, 1949.

Hane, Mikiso. *Rebels, Peasants, and Outcasts: The Underside of Modern Japan*. New York: Pantheon, 1982.

———, trans. and ed. *Reflections on the Way to the Gallows: Rebel Women in Prewar Japan*. Berkeley: University of California Press, 1988, 1993.

Harootunian, Harry. *Overcome by Modernity: History, Culture, and Community in Interwar Japan*. Princeton, N.J.: Princeton University Press, 2000.

Hasegawa Kei. "Kaidai" (Analysis). Vol. 1 of Tamura Toshiko, *Tamura Toshiko sakuhinshū* (Collected works of Tamura Toshiko), edited by Hasegawa Kei and Kurosawa Ariko, 435–46. Tokyo: Orijin Shuppan Sentā, 1987–88.

———. "Kaidai" (Analysis). Vol. 2 of Tamura Toshiko, *Tamura Toshiko sakuhinshū* (Collected works of Tamura Toshiko), edited by Hasegawa Kei and Kurosawa Ariko, 438–57. Tokyo: Orijin Shuppan Sentā, 1988.

———. *Tamura Toshiko hen kaisetsu* (Commentaries on Tamura Toshiko). Hasegawa Kei, Iwabuchi Hiroko, Miyake Kaho, and Watanabe Sumiko, eds. *Shinpen Nihon josei bungaku zenshū* (Comprehensive collection of Japanese women's literature: new edition), 1. Tokyo: Seishidō, 2007.

Hasegawa Kei, Kitada Sachie, Okano Sachie, and Watanabe Sumiko, eds. *Onna tachi no sensō sekinin* (Women's responsibility for war). Tokyo: Tōkyōdō Shuppan, 2004.

Hasumi Shigehiko and Nakafuru Satoshi. *Naruse Mikio no sekkei: Bijutsu kantoku wa kaisō suru* (Naruse Mikio's planning: The art director's reflections). Tokyo: Chikuma Shobō, 1990.

Hayashi Fumiko. *Floating Clouds*. Translated by Lane Dunlop. New York: Columbia University Press, 2006.

———. *Gendai nihon bungaku eiyaku senshū: Ukigumo* (Selected works of modern Japanese literature in English translation). Vol. 9, *Floating Clouds*, translated by Yoshiyuki Koitabashi and Martin C. Collcutt. Tokyo: Hara Shobō, 1965.

———. *Hatō* (Rough seas). Volume 2 of *Senjika no josei bungaku* (Women's literature during the war). Tokyo: Yumani Shobō, 2002.

———. *Hayashi Fumiko zenshū* (Complete works of Hayashi Fumiko). 23 vols. Tokyo: Shinchōsha, 1951–53.

———. *Hokugan butai* (Northern bank platoon). Vol. 12 of *Hayashi Fumiko zenshū* (Complete works of Hayashi Fumiko). Tokyo: Bunsendō, 1977.

———. *Hōrōki* (Diary of a vagabond). Tokyo: Shinchōsha, 1979, 2000.

———. *Meshi* (Repast). Tokyo: Shinchōsha, 1954.

———. *Sensen* (Battlefront). Tokyo: Chuō kōron shinsha, 2006.

———. *Ukigumo* (Floating clouds). Tokyo: Shinchōsha, 1953.

Heisig, James W., and John C. Maraldo, eds. *Rude Awakenings: Zen, the Kyoto School, and the Question of Nationalism*. Honolulu: University of Hawai'i Press, 1994.

Hirabayashi Taiko. *Hayashi Fumiko*. Tokyo: Shinchōsha, 1969.

Hiratsuka Raichō, translated with an introduction and notes by Teruko Craig. *In the Beginning, Woman Was the Sun: The Autobiography of Hiratsuka Raichō, Japanese Feminist*. New York: Columbia University Press, 2006.

Horiba Kiyoko. *Seitō no jidai: Hiratsuka Raichō to atarashii onna tachi* (The age of bluestockings: Hiratsuka Raichō and new women). Tokyo: Iwanami, 1988.

Horiguchi, Noriko. "The Body, Migration, and Empire: Tamura Toshiko's Writing in Vancouver from 1918 to 1924." In "Tamura Toshiko (1884–1945)," ed. Joan E. Ericson, special issue, *U.S.–Japan Women's Journal*, no. 28 (2005): 49–75.

———. "The Body Politic in Modern Japanese Women's Literature: Bodies of Women and of the Japanese National Empire in Yosano Akiko, Hayashi Fumiko, and Tamura Toshiko's Writings." PhD diss., University of Pennsylvania, 2003.

———. "Idōsuru shintai: Hayashi Fumiko gensaku Naruse Mikio honan eiga o megutte" (Bodies in motion: Naruse Mikio's film adaptations of Hayashi Fumiko's novels). In *Nihon eigashi soshō: Shintai, jendā, sekushuariti* (Japanese film history series: The body, gender, sexuality), 6:211–66. Tokyo: Shinwasha, 2006.

———. "Migrant Women, Memory, and Empire in Naruse Mikio's Film Adaptations of Hayashi Fumiko's Novels." *U.S.–Japan Women's Journal*, no. 36 (2009): 42–72.

Howell, David L. "Ainu Ethnicity and the Japanese State." *Past and Present* 142 (1994): 69–93.

Hozumi Nobushige. *Hozumi Nobushige ibunshū* (Literary estate of Hozumi Nobushige). Tokyo: Iwanami, 1932.

Hozumi Yatsuka. *Hozumi Yatsuka hakase ronbun shū* (Collection of Dr. Hozumi Yatsuka's essays). Tokyo: Yūhikaku, 1943.

Ichikawa Hiroshi. "Karada wa bunka o naizō suru" (The body encompasses culture). In Jitao Dai, Ichikawa Hiroshi, and Takeuchi Yoshimi, *Nihonron* (Treatise on Japan). Tokyo: Shakai Shisōsha, 1972.

Ichioka, Yōji. "Japanese Immigrant Nationalism: The Issei and the Sino-Japanese War, 1937–1941." *California History*, Fall 1990, 260–75.

———. "The Meaning of Loyalty: The Case of Kazumaro Buddy Uno." *Beyond National Boundaries: The Complexity of Japanese-American History* 23, no. 3 (Winter 1997–98): 45–72.

Ienaga, Saburō. *The Pacific War, 1931–45*. New York: Pantheon Books, 1978.

Igarashi, Yoshikuni. *Bodies of Memory: Narratives of War in Postwar Japanese Culture, 1945–1970*. Princeton, N.J.: Princeton University Press, 2000.

Irigaray, Luce. *This Sex Which Is Not One*. Ithaca, N.Y.: Cornell University Press, 1985.

Iriye, Akira. "Imperialism in East Asia." In *Modern East Asia: Essays in Interpretation*, edited by James B. Crowley, 122–49. New York: Harcourt, Brace & World, 1970.

Irokawa, Daikichi. *The Culture of the Meiji Period*. Translated by Marius B. Jansen. Princeton, N.J.: Princeton University Press, 1985.

Ishida Takeshi. *Meiji seiji shisōshi kenkyū* (Studies on the history of the political thought in Meiji). Tokyo: Miraisha, 1954.

———. *Nihon kindai shisōshi ni okeru hō to seiji* (Law and politics in the history of modern Japanese thought). Tokyo: Iwanami Shoten, 1976.

Ishihara Fusao and Satō Hifumi. "Nikka konketsu jidō no igakuteki chōsa" (A medical survey of Japanese-Chinese half-breed children). *Minzoku eisei* (Ethnic hygiene) 9, no. 3 (1941).

Ishii Shinji, ed. *Modan toshi kaidoku tokuhon* (A reader for deciphering modern cities). Tokyo: JICC, 1988.

Itagaki Naoko. *Hayashi Fumiko no shōgai: Uzushio no jinsei* (Hayashi Fumiko's tumultuous life). Tokyo: Yamato Shobō, 1965.

Itō Hirobumi. *Kenpō gikai* (Exposition of the constitution of the empire of Japan). Tokyo: Iwanami Bunko, 1940.

Itō Noe. *Teihon Itō Noe zenshū* (The standard edition of the complete works of Itō Noe). 4 vols. Edited by Ide Fumiko and Horikiri Toshitaka. Tokyo: Gakugei Shorin, 2000.

Izu Toshihiko. "Onna ni totte jiritsu to wa nanika: Tamura Toshiko to Miyamoto Yuriko" (What does independence mean for women? Tamura Toshiko and Miyamoto Yuriko). *Kokubungaku kaishaku to kyōzai no kenkyū* 25, no. 15 (1980): 72–78.

Joseishi Sōgō Kenkyūkai, ed. *Nihon joseishi: Kindai* (History of Japanese women: The modern era). Vol. 4. Tokyo: Tokyo Daigaku Shuppankai, 1982.

Kaibara, Ekken. *Women and Wisdom of Japan*. London: Murray, 1905.

Kaieda Nobunari. *Kensei hen* (Kensei edition). Vol. 4. of *Meiji bunka zenshū* (Complete collection of works on Meiji culture), edited by Meiji Bunka Kenkyūkai. Tokyo: Nihon Hyōronsha, 1929.

Kamei Shōichirō. "Unmei eno fukai nageki" (Profound lament on fate). *Nihon dokusho shinbun* (Japan newspaper on reading), May 2, 1951.

Kaneko Fumiko. *Naniga watashi o kō sasetaka: Gokuchū shuki* (What made me do what I did: A prison diary). Tokyo: Shunjūsha, 2005.

Kanneh, Kadiatu. "Feminism and the Colonial Body." In *The Post-Colonial Studies Reader*, edited by Bill Ashcroft, Gareth Griffiths, and Helen Tiffin, 346–48. New York: Routledge, 1995.

Kano, Ayako. *Acting Like a Woman in Modern Japan: Theater, Gender, and Nationalism*. New York: Palgrave, 2001.

———. "Japanese Theater and Imperialism: Romance and Resistance." *U.S.-Japan Women's Journal* 12 (1996): 17–47.

Kanō, Mikiyo. "Takamure Itsue to Kōkoku Shikan" (Takamure Itsue and historical views of the imperial nation). In *Takamure Itsue ronshū* (Collected essays of Takamure Itsue), edited by Kōno Nobuko et al. Tokyo: Takamure Itsue Ronshū Henshū Iinkai, 1979.

———. *Tennōsei to jendā* (The emperor system and gender). Tokyo: Inpakuto Shuppankai, 2002.

Karatani, Kōjin. *Origins of Modern Japanese Literature*. Translation edited by Brett de Bary. Durham, N.C.: Duke University Press, 1993.

Kasza, Gregory J. *The State and the Mass Media in Japan, 1918–1945*. Berkeley: University of California Press, 1988.

Kawade Shobō Shinsha Henshūbu, ed. *Shinbungei tokuhon: Yosano Akiko* (New reader for literary works: Yosano Akiko). Tokyo: Kawade Shobō Shinsha, 1991.

Kawai Hayao. *Shūkyō to Kagaku* (Religion and science). Tokyo: Iwanami Shoten, 1994.

Kawamoto Saburō. "'Akarui sengo' no naka no 'kurai sensō'" (The dark war within the bright postwar). *Daikōkai* (Grand navigation) 34 (June 2000): 141–51.

———. "Ima hitotabi no sengo nihon eiga dai nana kai: Binbō no sukina Naruse Mikio" (The seventh installment: Postwar films once again: Naruse Mikio who loved poverty). *Sekai* (The world). Tokyo: Iwanami Shoten, 1992.

Keene, Donald. *Dawn to the West: Japanese Literature of the Modern Era*. New York: Holt, Rinehart, and Winston, 1984.

———. "Tekkan, Akiko, and the Myōjyō Poets." In *Dawn to the West: Poetry, Drama, Criticism*. New York: Holt, Rinehart and Winston, 1984.

Kiyono Kenji. *Nihon jinshu-ron hensen-shi* (History of shifting debates on Japanese race). Tokyo: Koyama Shoten, 1944.

———. *Sumatora kenkyū* (Sumatran studies). Edited by Taiheiyō Kyōkai. Tokyo: Kawade Shobō, 1944.

Kohira Maiko. "Onna ga onna o enjiru—Meiji 40 nendai no keshō to engeki—Tamura Toshiko 'Akirame' ni furete." (Women enacting women: Makeup and theater in the fourth decade of the Meiji era: On Tamura Toshiko's "Resignation"). *Saitama Daigaku kiyō* (The bulletin of Saitama University) 47, no. 2 (1998): 66–53.

Kokusai Bunka Shinkōkai. *Academic and Cultural Organizations in Japan*. Tokyo: Kokusai Bunka Shinkōkai, 1939.

Kokushi Daijiten Henshū Iinkai, ed. *Kokushi daijiten* (Great dictionary of national history). 15 vols. Tokyo: Yoshikawa Kobunkan, 1983.

Komata Yūsuke. "Gyokai." *Kokubungaku kaishaku to kanshō* (National literature: Interpretation and appreciation) 63, no. 2 (1998): 117–20.

Kōseishō kenkyūjo jinkō minzokubu. *Yamato minzoku o chūkaku to suru sekai seisaku no kentō* (An examination of global policy centered on the Yamato nation). Tokyo: Kōseishō, 1943.

Kōuchi Nobuko. *Shiryō bosei hogo ronsō* (Sourcebook for the motherhood protection debates). Tokyo: Domesu Shuppan, 1984.

Kōza gendai to henkaku henshū iinkai. Ed. *Kōza gendai to henkaku. 2: Gendai Nihon no shihai kōzō* (Lectures on the modern period and changes. 2: The structure of control in modern Japan). Tokyo: Shinchiheisha, 1984.

Kudō Miyoko and Susan Phillips. *Bankūbā no ai: Tamura Toshiko to Suzuki Etsu* (Vancouver love: Tamura Toshiko and Suzuki Etsu). Tokyo: Domesu Shuppan, 1982.

———. *Tabibitotachi no bankūbā: Waga seishun no Tamura Toshiko* (Departure for Vancouver: Tamura Toshiko in my youth). Tokyo: Shōeisha, 1991.

Kurashima Itaru. "Ketsueki no konyū" (Mixture of blood). In *Zenshin suru Chōsen* (Korea making progress). Seoul: Chōsen Sōtokufu Jōhōka, 1942.

Kuroda Hideo. *Ō no shintai, ō no shōzō* (The body of the king, the portrait of the king). Tokyo: Heibonsha, 1993.

Kurosawa Ariko. "Kaisetsu" (Commentary). In Tamura Toshiko, *Tamura Toshiko sakuhinshū* (Collected works of Tamura Toshiko), vol. 2, edited by Hasegawa Kei and Kurosawa Ariko, 427–37. Tokyo: Orijin Shuppan Sentā, 1987–88.

LaFleur, William R. "Body." In *Critical Terms for Religious Studies,* edited by Mark C. Taylor, 36–54. Chicago: University of Chicago Press, 1998.

———. "An Ethics of AS-IS: State and Society in the Rinrigaku of Watsuji Tetsuro." In *La société civile face à l'état dans les traditions chinoise, japonaise, coréenne et vietnamienne,* edited by Léon Vandermeersch. Paris: École française d'Extrême-Orient, 1994.

Larson, Phyllis Hyland. "Yosano Akiko: The Early Years." PhD diss., University of Minnesota, 1985.

Lebra, Takie Sugiyama. *Japanese Women: Constraint and Fulfillment.* Honolulu: University of Hawai'i Press, 1984.

Lee, Nachiko Miyagi. "Yosano Akiko: A Study on Her Feminism and Selected Translations of Her Essays." MA thesis, California State University, Long Beach, 1986.

Lindee, M. Susan. *Suffering Made Real: American Science and the Survivors at Hiroshima.* Chicago: University of Chicago Press, 1994.

Lippit, Seiji M. *Topographies of Japanese Modernism.* New York: Columbia University Press, 2002.

Lock, Margaret. "Protests of a Good Wife and Wise Mother: The Medicalization of Distress in Japan." In *Health, Illness, and Medical Care in Japan: Culture and Social Dimensions,* edited by Edward Norbeck and Margaret Lock, 130–57. Honolulu: University of Hawai'i Press, 1987.

Lowy, Dina B. *The Japanese "New Woman": Images of Gender and Modernity.* New Brunswick, N.J.: Rutgers University Press, 2007.

Mackie, Vera. *Creating Socialist Women in Japan: Gender, Labour and Activism, 1900–1937.* Cambridge: Cambridge University Press, 1997.

———. *Feminism in Modern Japan: Citizenship, Embodiment and Sexuality.* Cambridge: Cambridge University Press, 2003.

Manshūkoku-shi Hensan Kanōkai. *Manshūkoku-shi: Sōron* (The history of Manchukuo: Overview). Tokyo: Manshūkoku-shi Hensan Kanōkai, 1970.

Maruyama, Masao. "Nationalism in Japan: Its Theoretical Background and Prospects." In *Thought and Behavior in Modern Japanese Politics,* edited by Ivan Morris, 135–56. New York: Oxford University Press, 1966.

Matsubara Shinichi. *Sengo no bungaku* (Postwar literature). Tokyo: Yūhikaku, 1978.

Matsudaira Meiko. "Hyōden Midaregami" (A critical bibliography of *Tangled Hair*). *Midaregami* (Tangled hair). Tokyo: Shinchōsha, 2000.

McNay, Lois. *Foucault and Feminism: Power, Gender, and the Self.* Boston: Northeastern University Press, 1993.

Menish, Marc. "Representation of Space in the Films of Mikio Naruse (1951–1960)." *Choiki bunka/kagaku kiyo.* Tokyo Daigaku/Komaba, April 1999.

Mies, Maria. "Colonization and Housewifization." In *Patriarchy and Accumulation on a World Scale: Women in the International Division of Labour.* Atlantic Highlands, N.J.: Zen Press, 1999.

Minami Jirō. *Jikyoku to naisen ittai* (The present situation and "Japan and Korea as one"). Keijō: Kokumin Sōryoku Chōsen Renmei, 1942.

Minichiello, Sharon A. *Japan's Competing Modernities: Issues in Culture and Democracy, 1900–1930.* Honolulu: University of Hawai'i Press, 1998.

Minobe Tatsukichi. *Kenpō kōwa* (Commentaries on the constitution of the empire of Japan). Tokyo: Yūhikaku, 1912.

Mitsuishi Ayumi. "Tamura Toshiko *Onna sakusha* ron: Egaku onna to egakareru onna" (An essay on Tamura Toshiko's "The Woman Writer": Woman who describes and woman who is described). *Yamaguchi kokubun* (Yamaguchi national literature), 21:124–36. Yamaguchi: Yamaguchi Daigaku Jinbungaku Kokugo Kokubun Gakkai, 1998.

Miwa, Hatsuse, and Ryū Inshun. "Tamura Toshiko: Feminizumu bungaku no senkusha" (Tamura Toshiko: The pioneer of feminist literature). In *Seitō to Nihon Joshi Daigaku dōsōsei nenpu* (*Bluestocking* and alumni of Japan Women's University, a biographical sketch), edited by Tokyo Joshi Daigaku Daigakuin Bungaku Kenkyūka Nihonbungaku Senkō nai Iwabuchi Kenkyūshitsu (Japan Women's University Graduate School, Literature Studies, Japanese Literature Major, Iwabuchi Seminar), 9–32. Tokyo: Japan Women's University Graduate School, 2002.

Miyake, Yoshiko. "Doubling Expectations: Motherhood and Women's Factory Work under State Management in Japan in the 1930s and 1940s." In *Recreating Japanese Women, 1600–1945,* edited by Gail Lee Bernstein, 267–295. Berkeley: University of California Press, 1991.

Miyoshi Masao and Harry Harootunian, eds. *Postmodernism and Japan.* Durham, N.C.: Duke University Press, 1989.

Mizuki Yōko. Screenplay *Ukigumo. Kinema junpō bessatsu.* Supplementary volume 106. Tokyo: Kinema junpō sha, 1954.

Mizuta, Noriko. "Hayashi Fumiko no miryoku" (The appeal of Hayashi Fumiko). *Kokubungaku kaishaku to kanshō* (National literature: Interpretation and appreciation) 63, no. 2 (1998): 10–15.

———. "In Search of a Lost Paradise: The Wandering Woman in Hayashi Fumiko's *Drifting Clouds*." In *The Woman's Hand: Gender and Theory in Japanese Women's Writing,* edited by Paul Gordon Schalow and Janet A. Walker, 329–51. Stanford, Calif.: Stanford University Press, 1996.

———. "Jendā kōzō no gaibu e" (Aspiring to go beyond the gender structure). In *Ima to iu jidai no Tamura Toshiko: Toshiko shinron* (Tamura Toshiko in the contemporary age: New studies on Toshiko), edited by Watanabe Sumiko, 132–40. *Kokubungaku kaishaku to kanshō bessatsu* (National literature: Interpretation and appreciation, supplementary volume). Tokyo: Shibundō, 2005.

———. "Kindaika to josei hyōgen no kiseki" (Tracing modernization and women's expression). *Joseigaku* (Women's studies) 7 (1999): 8–22.

Molony, Barbara, and Kathleen Uno. *Gendering Modern Japanese History.* Cambridge, Mass.: Harvard University Press, 2005.

Mori Eiichi. *Hayashi Fumiko no keisei: Sono sei to hyōgen* (The formation of Hayashi Fumiko: Her sexuality and expression). Tokyo: Yūseidō, 1992.

Mori Ōgai. *Youth and Other Stories.* Edited by Thomas Rimer. Honolulu: University of Hawai'i Press, 1994.

Mori Yasuko. *Kokkateki bosei no kōzō* (The structure of nationalist motherhood). Tokyo: Sanseidō, 1945.

Morris-Suzuki, Tessa. *Re-Inventing Japan: Time, Space, Nation.* New York: M. E. Sharpe, 1998.

Muramatsu Sadataka. "Hayashi Fumiko no dansei henreki" (Hayashi Fumiko's relationship with men). In *Sakka no kakei to kankyō* (The author's family background and environment), 202–17. Tokyo: Shibundō, 1964.

Myers, Ramon H., and Mark R. Peattie, eds. *The Japanese Colonial Empire, 1895–1945.* Princeton, N.J.: Princeton University Press, 1984.

Nagy, Margit. "Middle-Class Working Women During the Interwar Years." In *Recreating Japanese Women, 1600–1945,* edited by Gail Lee Bernstein, 199–216. Berkeley: University of California Press, 1991.

Najita, Tetsuo. *Japan: The Intellectual Foundations of Modern Japanese Politics.* Chicago: University of Chicago Press, 1974.

Nakagawa Yatsuhiro. "Nihon shisōka ron 2: Yosano Akiko to han feminizumu" (Studies on Japanese thinkers 2: Yosano Akiko and antifeminism). *Seiron,* no. 319 (March 1999): 136–50.

Nakajima Kuni. "Kokkateki bosei: Senjika no josei kan" (Nationalist motherhood: Views of women during wartime). In *Kōza joseigaku 1: Onna no imēji* (Lectures in women's studies 1: Images of women), edited by Joseigaku Kenkyūkai, 235–63. Tokyo: Keiso Shobō, 1984.

Nakajima Kuni et al. *Taishō no joshi kyōiku* (Women's education in the Taishō era). Tokyo: Kokudosha, 1975.

Nakamura Miharu. "Tamura Toshiko aiyoku no jiga" (Tamura Toshiko's self in love and lust). *Kokubungaku kaishaku to kyōzai no kenkyū* (The national literature: Research on interpretation and learning materials) 37, no. 13. (November 1992): 72–77.

Nakayama, Jinshirō. "Canada and the Japanese: In Commemoration of the 2600th Anniversary of the Japanese Imperial Calendar. Vancouver: Kanada Nihonjinkai, 1940." In *Historical Materials of Japanese Immigration to Canada: Supplement,* edited by Norman Amor and Tsuneharu Gonnami, translated by Tsuneharu Gonnami, 189–285. Tokyo: Fuji Shuppan, 2001.

Nakayama Makiko. *Shintai o meguru seisaku to kojin* (Policies on the body and the individual). Tokyo: Keisō Shobō, 2001.

Naremore, James. "Introduction: Film and the Reign of Adaptation." In *Film Adaptation,* edited by James Naremore, 1–18. Rutgers, N.J.: Rutgers University Press, 2000.

Naruse Miko. *Meshi* (Repast). Film of Hayashi Fumiko's novel *Meshi.* 1951.

———. *Ukigumo* (Floating clouds). Film of Hayashi Fumiko's novel *Ukigumo.* 1955.

Nihon Kirisutokyō Fujin Kyōfukai. *Nihon Kirisutokyō Fujin Kyōfukai 100-nen-shi* (One hundred year history of Christian women's missionary work in Japan). Tokyo: Domesu Shuppan, 1986.

Nishida, Kitarō. *An Inquiry into the Good.* Translated by Masao Abe and Christopher Ives. New Haven, Conn.: Yale University Press, 1990.

Nishikawa Yūko, *Sensō eno keisha to yokusan no fujin 5* (The turn to war and women's assistance for the imperial rule 5), ed. Joseishi Kenkyūkai (General study group of women's history). Tokyo: Tōkyō Daigaku Shuppankai, 1982.

Nishitani, Keiji. *The Self-Overcoming of Nihilism.* Translated by Graham Parkes and Setsuko Aihara. Albany: State University of New York Press, 1990.

Noda Utarō. "Akiko ni okeru sensō to shi: Futatsu no shi ni tsuite" (War and death in Akiko). In *Shinbungei tokuhon: Yosano Akiko* (New literary works reader: Yosano Akiko), 90–94. Tokyo: Kawade Shobō Shinsha, 1991.

Nolte, Sharon. "Women, the State, and Repression in Imperial Japan." *Working Paper* 33 (1983): 1–11.

———. "Women's Rights and Society's Needs: Japan's 1931 Suffrage Bill." *Comparative Studies in Society and History* 28 (1986): 690–714.

Nolte, Sharon H., and Sally Ann Hastings. "The Meiji State's Policy toward Women, 1890-1910." In *Recreating Japanese Women, 1600–1945,* edited by Gail Lee Bernstein, 151–74. Berkeley: University of California Press, 1991.

Norgren, Tiana. *Abortion before Birth Control: The Politics of Reproduction in Postwar Japan.* Princeton, N.J.: Princeton University Press, 2001.

Ō Kō. "Shanhai jidai no Tamura Toshiko: Chūgokugo no zasshi *Josei* o chūshin ni" (Tamura Toshiko during her time in Shanghai: With a focus on the Chinese journal *Josei* [Women's voice]). *Chūgoku joseishi kenkyū* (Studies of Chinese women's history), no. 8 (June 1998): 4–16.

Ogata Akiko. "Tamura Toshiko to *Kagayaku*" (Tamura Toshiko and *Kagayaku* [Shine]), In *Ima to iu jidai no Tamura Toshiko: Toshiko shinron* (Tamura Toshiko in the contemporary age: New studies on Toshiko), edited by Watanabe Sumiko, 78–86. *Kokubungaku kaishaku to kanshō bessatsu* (National literature: Interpretation and appreciation, supplementary volume). Tokyo: Shibundō, 2005.

Ogitari Hideo. "Kaisetsu" (Commentary). In Tamara Toshiko, *Tamura Toshiko sakuhinshū* (Collected works of Tamura Toshiko), edited by Hasegawa Kei and Kurosawa Ariko, 1:425–34. Tokyo: Orijin Shuppan Sentā, 1987–88.

Oguma Eiji. *Tanitsu minzoku shinwa no kigen: "Nihonjin" no jigazō no keifu* (A genealogy of "Japanese" self-images). Tokyo: Shinyōsha, 1995.

———. *A Genealogy of "Japanese" Self-Images.* Translated by David Askew. Melbourne: Trans Pacific Press, 2002.

Oki Motoko. "Meiji shakai shugi undō to josei" (The Meiji socialist movement and women). In *Nihon joseishi kindai* (Modern Japanese women's history), edited by Joseishi Sōgō Kenkyūkai, 4:115–48. Tokyo: Tokyo Daigaku Shuppankai, 1982.

Ōkubo Norio. "Sengo bungakushi no naka no jyoryū bungaku: Hayshi Fumiko *Ukigumo* no ichi" (Women's literature wihtin the history of postwar literature: The position of Hayashi Fumiko's *Ukigumo*). *Kokubungaku kaishaku to kanshō* (National literature: interpretation and appreciation) 37, no. 3. (March 1972): 47–52.

Otsubo, Sumiko. "Engendering Eugenics: Feminists and Marriage Restriction Legislation in the 1920s." In *Gendering Modern Japanese History*, ed. Barbara Molony and Kathleen Uno, 255–56. Cambridge, Mass.: Harvard University Press, 2005.

Pettman, Jan Jindy. *Worlding Women.* London and New York: Routledge, 1996.

Poster, Mark. "Foucault, Michel." In *The Johns Hopkins Guide to Literary Theory*, 277–79. Baltimore: The Johns Hopkins University Press, 1997.

Rabson, Steve. "Yosano Akiko on War: To Give One's Life or Not; A Question of Which War." *Journal of the Association of Teachers of Japanese*, special issue "Yosano Akiko (1878–1942)," 25, no. 1 (April 1991): 45–74.

Raddeker, Hélène Bowen. *Treacherous Women of Imperial Japan: Patriarchal Fictions, Patricidal Fantasies.* London and New York: Routledge, 1997.

Robertson, Jennifer. *Takarazuka: Sexual Politics and Popular Culture in Modern Japan.* Berkeley: University of California Press, 1998.

Rodd, Laurel Rasplica. "Yosano Akiko and the Taisho Debate over the 'New Woman.'" In *Recreating Japanese Women, 1600-1945,* edited by Gail Lee Bernstein, 175–98. Berkeley: University of California Press, 1991.

Rosaldo, Renato. "Imperialist Nostalgia." *Representations* 26 (1989): 107–22.

Rubin, Gayle, and Judith Butler. "Sexual Traffic." *Differences: A Journal of Feminist Cultural Studies* 6, no. 2–3 (1994): 62–99.

Russell, Catherine. *The Cinema of Naruse Mikio: Women and Japanese Modernity.* Durham, N.C.: Duke University Press, 2008.

———. "Too Close to Home: Naruse Mikio and Japanese Cinema of the 1950s." In *Global Cities: Cinema, Architecture, and Urbanism in a Digital Age,* edited by Linda Krause and Patrice Petro, 87–114. Rutgers, NJ: Rutgers University Press, 2003.

Ryang, Sonia. "Love and Colonialism in Takamure Itsue's Feminism: A Postcolonial Critique." *Feminist Review,* no. 60, Feminist Ethnics and the Politics of Love (Autumn 1998): 1–32.

Saeki Shōichi and Matsumoto Kenichi, eds. *Sakka no Jiden 87: Shirīzu Ningen Toshokan* (Autobiography of the author 87: The library of human beings series). Tokyo: Nihon Tosho Sentā, 1994.

Said, Edward W. *Culture and Imperialism.* New York: Vintage Books, 1993.

———. *Orientalism.* New York: Random House, 1979.

———. *Representation of the Intellectual.* New York: Vintage Books, 1994.

Saitō Tomiichi. *Watakushi no Hayashi Fumiko* (Hayashi Fumiko in me). Chiba: Rinshobō, 1997.

Sakai, Naoki. *Translation and Subjectivity.* Minneapolis: University of Minnesota Press, 1997.

———. *Voices of the Past: The Status of Language in Eighteen-Century Japanese Discourse.* Ithaca, N.Y.: Cornell University Press, 1991.

Salazar, Ruben Dario. "Midaregami: Original Composition, Akiko Yosano, Poetry, Song Cycle, Japan." PhD diss., University of Cincinnati, 1998.

Sankei Shinbun. *"Nihonjin no ashiato" shuzaihan* (The Sankei newspaper: "Traces of Japanese"). Tokyo: Fusōsha, 2001.

Sasaki Toshiji and Gonnami Tsuneharu. *Kanada iminshi shiryō* (Historical materials of Japanese immigration to Canada). Vol. 8. Tokyo: Fuji Shuppan, 2000.

Satō, Barbara Hamill. "The Moga Sensation: Perceptions of the Modern Gāru in Japanese Intellectual Circles During the 1920s." *Gender and History* 5, no. 3 (1993): 363–81.

———. *The New Japanese Woman: Modernity, Media, and Women in Interwar Japan.* Durham, N.C.: Duke University Press, 2003.

Satō Toshiko [a pen name of Tamura Toshiko]. "Dōsei o mamoru" (Protecting the same sex). *Fujin kōron* (Women's review). January 1937, 92–93.

————. "Futsuka kan" (Two days). *Kaizō* (Reshuffle). April 1938, 437–43.

————. "Goaisatsu" (Greetings). *Kagayaku* (Shine). (April 1936): 151.

————. "Hitotsu no yume" (One dream: For a certain young, proletarian female writer). *Bungei shunjū* (Literary works in all seasons). June 1936, 264–69.

————. "Jogakusei seikatsu no kaikaku" (Improvements of the lives of female students). *Nihon hyōron* (Japan's critiques). November 1938, 109–13.

————. "Jūgun bunjin ni okuru chikara no bungaku o!" (To war correspondents: Power to literature!). *Teikoku daigaku shinbun* (Imperial university newspaper), September 12, 1938.

————. "Kariforunia monogatari" (California story). *Chūō kōron* (Central review), July 1938. *Sōsaku* (Creation), 1–45.

————. "Nihon fujin undō no nagare o miru" (Observing the flow of the Japanese women's movements). *Miyako shinbun* (Miyako newspaper), June 1937, 17–19.

————. "Uchida Tamino san eno ohenji" (My response to Ms. Uchida Tamie). In *Tamura Toshiko Sakuhinshū*, 3:392–406. Tokyo: Orijin shuppan sentā, 1988.

————. "Warera wa nani o subekika" (What should we do?). *Shinnyoen* (New women's circle), January 1938, 89–90.

Satomi Kishio. *Kokutai shisōshi* (Intellectual history of national polity). Vol. 2 of *Nihon kokutai gaku* (Studies of Japan's national polity). Tokyo: Nihon Kokutai Gakkai, 1992.

Sawicki, Jana. *Disciplining Foucault: Feminism, Power and the Body.* London and New York: Routledge, 1991.

Setouchi Harumi. *Tamura Toshiko.* Tokyo: Kōdansha, 1993.

Sheets-Johnstone, Maxine. *Giving the Body Its Due.* Albany: State University of New York Press, 1992.

Shimomura Hiroshi. "Daitōa kyōeiken" (Greater East Asia Co-Prosperity Sphere). *Kyōwakai kankei shiryō shū* (Collection of Co-Prosperity Association–related materials). Vol. 2, 1941, edited by Higuchi Yūichi. Tokyo: Ryokuin Shobō, 1991.

Shinbungei tokuhon Yosano Akiko. Tokyo: Kawade Shinbō Shinsha, 1991.

Shinpo Mitsuru. *Kanada Nihonjin imin monogatari* (Stories of Japanese immigrants in Canada). Tokyo: Tsukiji Shokan, 1986.

Shively, Donald H. "Japanization of the Middle Meiji." In *Tradition and Modernization in Japanese Culture.* Princeton, N.J.: Princeton University Press, 1971.

Sievers, Sharon. *Flowers in Salt: The Beginnings of Feminist Consciousness in Modern Japan.* Stanford, Calif.: Stanford University Press, 1983.

Silverberg, Miriam. "The Modern Girl as Militant." In *Recreating Japanese Women, 1600–1945,* edited by Gail Lee Bernstein, 239–66. Berkeley: University of California Press, 1991.

Sivin, Nathan. "State, Cosmos, and Body in the Last Three Centuries B.C." *Harvard Journal of Asiatic Studies* 55, no. 1 (June 1995): 5–37.

Slaymaker, Douglas N. *The Body in Postwar Japanese Fiction.* London and New York: Routledge, 2004.

Smith, Robert J., and Ella Lury Wiswell. *The Women of Suye Mura.* Chicago: University of Chicago Press, 1982.

Sokolsky, Anne. "Writing between the Spaces of Nation and Culture: Tamura Toshiko's 1930s Fiction about Japanese Immigrants." In "Tamura Toshiko (1884–1945)," ed. Joan E. Ericson, special issue, *U.S.–Japan Women's Journal,* no. 28 (2005): 76–108.

Sontag, Susan. *Illness as Metaphor.* New York: Farrar, Straus, and Giroux, 1978.

Spivak, Gayatri Chakravorty. *In Other Worlds: Essays in Cultural Politics.* New York: Methuen, 1987.

Stanlaw, James. "Japanese Emigration and Immigration: From the Meiji to the Modern." In *Japanese Diasporas: Unsung Pasts, Conflicting Presents, and Uncertain Futures,* edited by Nobuko Adachi, 35–51. London and New York: Routledge, 2006.

Suzuki Etsu. "Nichijō seikatsu no kaizen: Tokuni fujingata ni nozomukoto" (Improvement of daily life: Especially what I ask of women). *Tairiku nippō* (The continental daily news), June 30, 1922.

Suzuki Masakazu. "Hōkō suru ai no yukue: Tamura Toshiko 'Ikichi' o yomu" (Heading of the wandering love: A reading of Tamura Toshiko's "Lifeblood"). *Kindai bungaku kenkyū* (Studies of modern literature), 13 (February 1996): 1–16.

———. "Tamura Toshiko 'Onna sakusha' ron: 'Onna' no tōsōkatei o yomu" (Essay on Tamura Toshiko's "The Woman Writer": A reading of the process of a woman's struggle). *Nihon bungaku kenkyū* (Studies of Japanese literature), 33 (January 1994): 65–74.

Suzuki Sadami. "Utaron o megutte: Yosano Akiko to Taishō seimei shugi" (On the discourse on poetry: Yosano Akiko and Taishō life centrism). *Yuriika: Shi to hihyō* (Poetry and criticism: Eureka) 8 (2000): 114–25.

Suzuki Toshiko [Tamura Toshiko]. "Aru tomo e: Rosuanjirusu no inshō" (To a friend: My impression of Los Angeles) (1). *Rafu shinpō,* December 19, 1933.

———. "Aru tomo e: Rosuanjirusu no inshō" (To a friend: My impression of Los Angeles) (2). *Rafu shinpō,* December 20, 1933.

———. "Aru tomo e: Rosuanjirusu no inshō" (To a friend: My impression of Los Angeles) (4). *Rafu shinpō,* December 22, 1933.

Suzuki Yūko. *Feminizumu to sensō: Fujin undōka no sensō kyōryoku* (Feminism and war: Women's movement activists' cooperation with the war). Rev. ed. Tokyo: Marujusha, 1997.

———. *Feminizumu to sensō: Fujin undōka no sensō kyōryoku* (Feminism and war: Women's movement activists' cooperation with the war). Tokyo: Marujusha, 1986.

———. "Hirohito shi to 'Shōwa' shi to onna" (The history of Hirohito, the history of Shōwa, and women). In *Onna, tennōsei, sensō* (Women, the emperor system, and war), edited by Suzuki Yūko, 7–37. Tokyo: Orijin sentā, 1989.

———. *Josei: Hangyaku to kakumei to teikō to; Shisō no umi e [kaihō to henkaku]* (Women: Rebellion, revolution, and resistance; Toward the sea of thoughts [liberation and change]). Tokyo: Shakai Hyōronsha, 1990.

———. *"Jūgun ianfu" mondai to sei bōryoku* (Problems of the "military comfort women" and sexual violence). Tokyo: Miraisha, 1993.

———. *Jūgun ianfu naisen kekkon: Sei no shinryaku sengo sekinin o kangaeru* (Military comfort women and marriage between Japanese and Koreans: Sexual invasion and postwar responsibility). Tokyo: Miraisha, 1992.

———. *Nihongun ianfu kankei shiryō shūsei* (Compilation of materials related to Japanese military comfort women). Vols. 1–2. Tokyo: Akashi Shoten, 2006.

———. "Sensō to josei: Josei no 'sensō kyōryoku' o kangaeru" (War and women: Rethinking women's "war cooperation"). In *Kindai nihon no tōgō to teikō 4* (Unity and resistance in modern Japan 4), edited by Kano Masanao and Yui Masaomi, 167–202. Tokyo: Nihon Hyōronsha, 1982.

Tachi Kaoru. "Ryōsai kenbo" (Good wife, wise mother). In *Kōza joseigaku 1: Onna no imēji* (Lectures in women's studies 1: Images of women), edited by Joseigaku Kenkyūkai, 184–209. Tokyo: Keisō Shobō, 1984.

Tachikawa Shōji. "Inochi eno rekishi kankaku" (Historical sensitivity toward life). In *Yamai to ningen no bunkashi* (Cultural history of illness and human beings). Tokyo: Shinchōsha, 1984.

Takahashi Takaharu. *Senjō no joryū sakka tachi* (Women writers in the battle-ground). Tokyo: Ronsōsha, 1995.

Takamure Itsue. "Museifu shugi no mokuhyō to senjutsu: Genka museifu shugi sensen no seiri ni kansuru shiken" (Purpose and strategies of anarchism: An examination on organizing the battlefront of contemporary anarchism). *Fujin sensen* (Women's battlefront), April 1930, 30–36.

———. *Takamure Itsue Zenshū*. Edited by Hashimoto Kenzō. 10 vols. Tokyo: Rironsha, 1965–67.

Tamanoi, Mariko Asano. *Memory Maps: The State and Manchuria in Postwar Japan*. Honolulu: University of Hawai'i Press, 2009.

Tamura Norio. *Suzuki Etsu: Nihon to Kanada o musunda jânarisuto* (Suzuki Etsu: A journalist connecting Japan and Canada). Tokyo: Riburopoto, 1992.

Tamura Toshiko. *See also the works listed under her pen names Satō Toshiko, Suzuki Toshiko, and Yukari.*

———. "Bi no shōkei" (Yearning for beauty). *Tairiku nippō* (The continental daily news), August 16, 1919.

———. *Bunmei sōsho* (Series on civilization). Tokyo: Uetake Shoin, 1915.

———. "Fujin yo" (Attention, women). *Tairiku nippō* (The continental daily news), January 1, 1924.

———. *Gendai nihon bungaku zenshū* (Complete collection of modern Japanese literature). Vol. 70. Tokyo: Chikuma Shobō, 1957.

———. *Gendai nihon shōsetsu taikei* (System of modern Japanese novels). Vol. 17. Tokyo: Kawade Shobō, 1956.

———. *Hōraku no kei* (Burning at the stake). In *Tamura Toshiko sakuhinshū* (Collected works of Tamura Toshiko), vol. 2, edited by Hasegawa Kei and Kurosawa Ariko, 23–83. Tokyo: Orijin Shuppan Sentā, 1988.

———. "Jiko no kenri" (The rights of the self). *Tairiku nippō* (The continental daily news), August 30, 1919.

———. "Jūgun bunjin ni okuru chikara no bungaku o!" (To war correspondents: Power of literature!). *Teikoku daigaku shinbun* (Imperial university newspaper), September 12, 1938.

———. "Kono machi ni sumu fujintachi ni" (For the women who reside in this town). *Tairiku nippō* (The continental daily news), August 2, 1919.

———. *Miira no kuchibeni* (Lip rouge on a mummy). In *Tamura Toshiko sakuhinshū* (Collected works of Tamura Toshiko), vol. 1, edited by Hasegawa Kei and Kurosawa Ariko, 307–74. Tokyo: Orijin Shuppan Sentā, 1987.

———. "Mizukara hatarakeru fujintachi ni" (For the women who work on their own). *Tairiku nippō* (The continental daily news), August 9, 1919.

———. "Nikkai kaizōan tsūka ni yotte" (On the occasion of the passage of a proposal for reorganization of the Canadian Japanese Association). *Tairiku nippō* (The continental daily news), December 7, 1921.

———. "Saikin no Nihon fujin shisō no dōtei" (Passages in recent Japanese women's thought). *Tairiku nippō* (The continental daily news), September 13, 1919.

———. "Shin no hokori" (True pride). *Tairiku nippō* (The continental daily news), August 23, 1919.

———. "Shinshun no uta" (New Year's poetry). *Tairiku nippō* (The continental daily news), January 1, 1919.

———. "Tabigarasu no onshin" (Correspondence of a traveling crow). *Tairiku nippō* (The continental daily news), December 14, 1918.

———. *Tamura Toshiko sakuhinshū* (Collected works of Tamura Toshiko). Edited by Hasegawa Kei and Kurosawa Ariko. 3 vols. Tokyo: Orijin Shuppan Sentā, 1987–88.

———. "Totsukuni no haru" (Spring in a foreign country). *Tairiku nippō* (The continental daily news), April 19, 1919.

Tanabe Seiko. "'Midaregami' no onna" (Woman with tangled hair). *Shinbungei tokuhon: Yosano Akiko 23* (A reader for new literary works: Yosano Akiko 23). Tokyo: Kawade Shobō Shinsha, 1991.

Tanaka, Stephan. *Japan's Orient: Rendering Pasts into History.* Berkeley: University of California Press, 1993.

Tanaka Sumie and Ide Toshio. Film script *Meshi* (Repast). "Sengo kessaku shinario shū" (Collection of masterpieces of postwar film scripts). *Kinema junpō bessatsu* (Kinema seasonal report, supplementary volume), vol. 9. Tokyo: Kinema junpō sha, 1959.

Tanaka, Yukiko. "Tamura Toshiko." In *To Live and to Write: Selections by Japanese Women Writers 1913–1938,* edited by Yukiko Tanaka, 3–10. Seattle: Seal Press, 1987.

———. *Women Writers of Meiji and Taishō Japan: Their Lives, Works and Critical Reception, 1868–1926.* Jefferson, N.C.: McFarland, 2000.

Taniguchi Kōnen. *Tōyō minzoku no taishitsu* (Oriental peoples and physical constitution). Tokyo: Yamagabō, 1942.

Tomida, Hiroko. *Hiratsuka Raichō and Early Japanese Feminism.* Leiden: Brill, 2004.

Treat, John Whittier. "Beheaded Emperors and the Absent Figure in Contemporary Japanese Literature." *PMLA* 109, no. 1 (1994): 100–15.

Tsubota Jōji. *Tamura Toshiko, Takebayashi Musōan, Ogawa Mimei, Tsubota Jōji shū.* Tokyo: Chikuma Shobō, 1957.

Tsunoda Ryūsaku, Wm. Theodore de Bary, and Donald Keene, comps. *Sources of Japanese Tradition,* vol. 2. New York: Columbia University Press, 1958.

Tsurumi, E. Patricia. "Female Textile Workers and the Failure of Early Trade Unionism in Japan." *History Workshop* 18 (1984): 2–27.

Turner, Terence. "Social Body and Embodied Subject: Bodiliness, Subjectivity, and Sociality among the Kayapo." *Cultural Anthropology* 10, no. 2 (1995): 143–70.

Ueda, Makoto. "Yosano Akiko." In *Modern Japanese Poets and the Nature of Literature.* Stanford, Calif.: Stanford University Press, 1983.

Ueno, Chizuko. "Are the Japanese Feminine? Some Problems of Japanese Feminism in Its Cultural Context." In *Broken Silence: Voices of Japanese Feminism,* edited and translated by Sandra Buckley, 293–301. Berkeley: University of California Press, 1997.

———. "'Kokumin kokka' to 'jendā'" (The "nation-state" and "gender"). *Gendai shisō,* October 1996.

———. *Nationalism and Gender.* Translated by Beverley Yamamoto. Melbourne: Trans Pacific Press, 2004.

———. *Nashonarizumu to jendā* (Nationalism and gender). Tokyo: Seidosha, 1998.

———. "Orientarizumu to jendā" (Orientalism and gender). In *Nyū feminizumu rebyū* (New feminism review), edited by Kanō Mikiyo, 6:108–31. Tokyo: Gakuyō Shobō, 1995.

Umehara Takeshi. "The Role of Oriental Civilization in World History." In *Nihon Bunkaron* (Studies on Japanse culture). Tokyo: Kōdansha, 1976.

Uno, Kathleen S. "One Day at a Time: Work and Domestic Activities of Urban Lower-Class Women in Early Twentieth-Century Japan." In *Japanese Women Working*, edited by Janet Hunter, 37–68. London and New York: Routledge, 1993.

———. "The Origins of 'Good Wife, Wise Mother' in Modern Japan." In *Japanische Frauengeschichte(n)*, edited by Erich Pauer and Regine Mathias, 31–46. Marburg: Förderverein Marburger Japan Reihe, 1995.

———. *Passages to Modernity: Motherhood, Childhood, and Social Reform in Early Twentieth Century Japan.* Honolulu: University of Hawai'i Press, 1999.

———. "Women and Changes in the Household Division of Labor." In *Recreating Japanese Women, 1600–1945,* edited by Gail Lee Bernstein, 17–41. Berkeley: University of California Press, 1991.

Vernon, Victoria. "Between Osan and Koharu: The Representation of Women in the Works of Hayashi Fumiko and Enchi Fumiko." In *Daughters of the Moon: Wish, Will, and Social Constraint in Fiction by Modern Japanese Women,* 137–69. Berkeley: University of California Press, 1988.

Wakakuwa Midori. *Kōgō no shōzō Myōken kōtaigō no hyōshō to josei no kokuminka* (The portrait of the empress: Representations of Empress Myōken and nationalization of women). Tokyo: Chikuma Shobō, 2001.

Wakita Haruko. *Bosei o tou: Rekishiteki hensen* (Questioning motherhood: Historical changes). Kyoto: Jinbun shoin, 1985.

Watanabe Sumiko. "Hayshi Fumiko to Hirabayashi Taiko" (Hayshi Fumiko and Hirabayashi Taiko). *Kokubungaku kaishaku to kanshō* (National literature: Interpretation and appreciation) 63, no. 2 (1998): 66–71.

———. "Satō (Tamura) Toshiko to *Josei*" (Satō [Tamura] Toshiko and the journal *Women's Voice*). In *Shōwa bungaku kenkyū* (Studies of *Shōwa* literature), 17:58–71. Tokyo: Shōwa Bungakukai, 1988.

———. "Satō (Tamura) Toshiko to *Josei*" (Satō [Tamura] Toshiko and the journal *Women's Voice*, continued). In *Shōwa bungaku kenkyū* (Studies of *Shōwa* literature), vol. 18. Tokyo: Shōwa Bungakukai, 1989.

———. "Tamura Toshiko." In *Gendai bungaku kenkyū* (Studies of modern literature), edited by Hasegawa Izumi, 369–70. Tokyo: Shibundō, 1987.

———. "Tamura Toshiko *Josei* ni tsuite" (About Tamura Toshiko's journal *Women's Voice*). *Bungaku* (Literature) 56, no. 3 (March 1988): 94–98.

———. *Yosano Akiko.* Tokyo: Shintensha, 1998.

————, ed. *Ima to iu jidai no Tamura Toshiko: Toshiko shinron* (Tamura Toshiko in the contemporary age: New studies on Toshiko). *Kokubungaku kaishaku to kanshō bessatsu* (National literature: interpretation and appreciation, supplementary volume). Tokyo: Shibundō 2005.

Watsuji Tetsurō. *Rinrigaku* (Studies of ethics). Tokyo: Iwanami Shoten, 1937.

Wiener, Michael. *Race and Migration in Imperial Japan.* New York: Routledge, 1994.

Wimsatt, William K., and Monroe Beardsley. "The Intentional Fallacy." *Sewanee Review* 54 (1946): 468–88. Revised and republished in Wimsatt and Beardsley, *The Verbal Icon: Studies in the Meaning of Poetry.* Lexington: University Press of Kentucky, 1954.

Wolfe, Patrick. "History and Imperialism: A Century of Theory, from Marx to Postcolonialism." *American Historical Review* 102, no. 2 (1997): 388–420.

Wu Peichen. "Hokubei jidai to Tamura Toshiko" (Tamura Toshiko during her time in North America). In *Ima to iu jidai no Tamura Toshiko: Toshiko shinron* (Tamura Toshiko in the contemporary age: New studies on Toshiko), edited by Watanabe Sumiko, 87–94. *Kokubungaku kaishaku to kanshō bessatsu* (National literature: Interpretation and appreciation, supplementary volume). Tokyo: Shibundō, 2005.

Yamada Keiko. "Atarashii onna" (New women). In *Kōza joseigaku 1: Onna no imêji* (Lectures in women's studies 1: Images of women), edited by Joseigaku Kenkyūkai, 210–34. Tokyo: Keisō Shobō, 1984.

Yamada Shōji. *Kaneko Fumiko: Jiko, tennōsei kokka, chōsenjin* (Kaneko Fumiko: Self, the imperial nation-state, Koreans). Tokyo: Kage Shobō, 1996.

Yamanouchi Yasushi, J. Victor Koschmann, and Ryuichi Narita. *Total War and "Modernization."* Cornell East Asia Series, Number 100. Ithaca, N.Y.: Cornell University, East Asia Program, 1998.

Yamasaki Makiko. "Miira no kuchibeni ron" (A treatise on "Rouge-lipped mummies"). In *Tamura Toshiko sakuhin no shosō* (Aspects of the works of Tamura Toshiko), 19-37. Tokyo: Senshū Daigaku Daigakuin Bungaku Kenkyūka Hata Kenkyūshitsu, 1990.

————. "Tamura Toshiko sakuhin sono gensetsu kūkan no henyō" (Changes in discursive space in the works of Tamura Toshiko). *Senshū jinbun ronshū* (Studies in the Humanities: A Journal of the Senshu University Research Society) 63 (1998): 83–91.

Yasuda Yojurō. *Yasuda Yojurō zenshū* (Complete works of Yasuda Yojurō). Tokyo: Kōdansha, 1985–89.

Yoneyama, Lisa. "Memory Matters: Hiroshima's Korean Atom Bomb Memorial and the Politics of Ethnicity." *Public Culture* 7, no. 3 (1995): 499–527.

Yōrō Takeshi. *Shintai no bungakushi* (Literary history of bodies). Tokyo: Shinchōsha, 1997.

———. "Shintai to wa nanika" (What is the body?). In *Nihonjin no shintaikan no rekishi* (History of the Japanese perspectives on bodies). Kyoto: Hōzōkan, 1996.

Yosano Akiko. "Daiichi no jintsū" (The first labor pain). In *Teihon Yosano Akiko zenshū* (Complete works of Yosano Akiko), 9:249–52.

———. "Hirakibumi" (Open letters). In *Yosano Akiko hyōronshū* (Collected essays of Yosano Akiko), edited by Kano Masanao and Kōuchi Nobuko, 19–20. Tokyo: Iwanami, 1999.

———. "Joshi no tettei shita dokuritsu" (Women's complete independence). *Fujin kōron* (Women's review).

———. "Kimi shini tamōkoto nakare" (Brother, do not offer your life). In *Yosano Akiko hyōronshū* (Collected essays of Yosano Akiko), edited by Kano Masanao and Kōuchi Nobuko, 25–28. Tokyo: Iwanami, 1999.

———. "Nihon fujin no tokushoku wa nanika" (What are the characteristics of Japanese women?). In *Gendai nihon no essei: Ai, risei, oyobi yūki* (Essays in modern Japan: Love, reason, and courage). 94–101. Tokyo: Kōdansha, 1993.

———. "Nihon kokumin asa no uta" (Citizens of Japan, a Morning Song" in *Nihon josei* (Japanese women), a separate volume of *Nihon kokumin* (Japanese people). June 1932.

———. "'Onnarashisa' towa nanika" ("What Is 'Womanliness'?"). In *Yosano Akiko hyōronshū* (Collected essays of Yosano Akiko), edited by Kano Masanao and Kōuchi Nobuko, 334–45. Tokyo: Iwanami, 1985, 1999. Translated by Laurel Rasplica Rodd in Copeland, *Woman Critiqued*, 40–41.

———. *Pari yori* (From Paris). In *Yosano Akiko hyōronshū* (Collected essays of Yosano Akiko), edited by Kano Masanao and Kōuchi Nobuko. Tokyo: Iwanami, 1999.

———. *River of Stars: Selected Poems of Yosano Akiko*. Translated by Sam Hamill and Keiko Matsui Gibson. Boston: Shambhala, 1996.

———. "Sensō" (War). *Yomiuri shinbun*, August 17, 1914.

———. *Teihon Yosano Akiko zenshū* (Complete works of Yosano Akiko). 20 vols. Tokyo: Kōdansha, 1979–81.

———. *Travels in Manchuria and Mongolia: A Feminist Poet from Japan Encounters Prewar China*, translated by Joshua A. Fogel. New York: Columbia University Press, 2001.

———. "Ubuya monogatari" (Tales of the delivery room). "In *Yosano Akiko hyōronshū* (Collected essays of Yosano Akiko), edited by Kano Masanao and Kōuchi Nobuko, 32–41. Tokyo: Iwanami Shoten, 1985.

———. *Yokohama bōeki shinpō*, October 20 and 27, 1918.

Yoshida Tadao. *Ningen no kagaku sōsho 2, zōhoban: Kanada nikkei imin no kiseki* (Series on the humanities, 2, supplementary edition: Traces of Japanese immigrants in Canada). Tokyo: Ningen no Kagaku Shinsha, 2003.

Yoshimi Kaneko. "Baishō no jittai to haishō undō" (The reality of prostitution and the abolishment movement). In *Nihon joseishi kindai* (Modern Japanese women's history), edited by Joseishi Sōgō Kenkyūkai, 4:223–58. Tokyo: Tokyo Daigaku Shuppankai, 1982.

Yoshimi Yoshiaki. *Jūgun ianfu* (The military comfort women). Tokyo: Iwanami Shoten, 1995.

Yoshimoto, Mitsuhiro. "The Difficulty of Being Radical: The Discipline of Film Studies and the Postcolonial World Order." In *boundary 2* 18, no. 3 (1991): 242–57.

Young, Louise. *Japan's Total Empire: Manchuria and the Culture of Wartime Imperialism.* Berkeley: University of California Press, 1998.

Yuasa, Katsuei. *Kannani and Document of Flames: Two Japanese Colonial Novels.* Translated by Mark Driscoll. Durham, N.C.: Duke University Press, 2005.

Yuasa Yasuo. *Kindai nihon no tetsugaku to jitsuzon shisō* (Philosophy and existentialism in modern Japan). Tokyo: Sōbunsha, 1970.

———. *The Body: Toward an Eastern Mind-Body Theory.* Edited by T. P. Kasulis. Translated by Nagatomo Shigenori and T. P. Kasulis. Albany: State University of New York Press, 1987.

Yukari [a pen name of Tamura Toshiko]. "Kiyohara Senzō shi" (Mr. Kiyohara Senzō) (2), "Kariforunia no hitosumi kara: Hito ni au" (From a corner of California: Meeting with people [41]). *Rafu shinpō* (Los Angeles Japanese daily news), July 9, 1935.

———. "Kiyohara Senzō shi" (Mr. Kiyohara Senzō) (3), "Kariforunia no hitosumi kara: Hito ni au (42)." *Rafu shinpō,* July 10, 1935.

———. "Yokota jimukan" (Officer Yokota) (1), "Kariforunia no hitosumi kara: Hito ni au (29)." *Rafu shinpō,* June 24, 1935.

———. "Yokota jimukan" (Officer Yokota) (2), "Kariforunia no hitosumi kara: Hito ni au (30)." *Rafu shinpō,* June 25, 1935.

———. "Taishūsha no shujin" (Master of Taishū Co.) (2). *Rafu shinpō,* June 3, 1935.

Yūri Kaoru. "Heiwa o aisuru kokoro" (A heart that loved peace). In *Akiko no shōgai* (Life of Akiko). Tokyo: Hanka shobō, 1948.

Index

abortion: liberalization of, 151, 170
adoption: in colonialism, 13, 24; for
  household survival, 24
Aikoku fujin (journal), 45
Ainu people: control of, 12
Aizawa Seishisai: *Shinron,* xix, 1, 196n20
Amaterasu (Sun goddess), 46
ancestry, Japanese: emperor's
  embodiment of, 6, 7, 26; in poetry,
  61; shared, 23; in Shinto, 16
Anglo-Japanese Alliance Agreement
  (1902–20), 93, 94
Annamese people: colonization of,
  149, 154, 168, 171, 174; Japanese
  body and, 145–46
Anti-Oriental Act (Canada, 1924),
  92, 93
Aozukin, 84–85
Arai Tomiyo: *Chūgoku sensen wa dō
  egakareta ka,* 127
archaeology (discourse), 182n12
Asahi shinbun: Hayashi's contributions
  to, 127, 137
Azuma Eiichiro, 114, 116

Bardsley, Jan, 37, 85, 186n3; on New
  Women, 187n11
Beardsley, Monroe, 154
Beichman, Janine: *Embracing the
  Firebird,* 53, 60; on *Tangled Hair,*
  61, 188n9
Bluntschli, J. C.: *Allgemeines
  Staatsrecht,* xix, 2, 4

body: as analytical site, 1–17;
  Foucault's theory of, xvi, xvii;
  performative, 182n15; in power
  relations, xvi; as productive force,
  xvi; as surface of inscription,
  182n12; in Western literature, 1.
  See also Japanese body; migrant
  bodies; women's bodies,
  Japanese
bosei hogo ronsō. See motherhood:
  protection debate on
British Columbia: anti-Japanese
  regulations in, 193n45
Brown, Janice, 124, 125
bundan (literary establishment), xiv;
  Hayashi and, 125; on Tamura, 84,
  85, 87, 89, 98
Butler, Judith, xv, 182n15

California: Japanese immigration to,
  70, 79. *See also* immigrants,
  Japanese (United States)
Canada: in Anglo-Japanese Alliance
  Agreement, 93, 94; anti-Japanese
  sentiments in, 90, 91–94, 193nn44–
  45; Anti-Oriental Act (1924), 92,
  93; civilization of, 99; female
  migrant workers in, 96, 100, 104,
  108; in Tamura's writings, 96–100.
  See also immigrants, Japanese
  (Canada); Vancouver
Casey, Edward: on disembodiment,
  201n65; *Remembering,* 158

children, Japanese: education of, 23, 25, 26; mixed-blood, 15. *See also* sekishi

China: dichotomy with Japan, 70, 77, 140; in *Hokugan butai,* 140–42; under Japanese colonialism, 71; resistance to Japanese Empire, 72, 75–76, 78–79; Tamura in, 120

Chūō Kōronsha: Tamura's contributions to, 82

Civil Code (Japan, 1897), xiii; household in, 30, 86, 130; women under, 32, 38, 44

class: in *Hōrōki,* 132–37; in Japanese Empire, 50, 107; among Japanese women, 20, 27, 28, 29, 31, 103; in *naichi,* 42, 157; in postwar era, 157; in Tamura's writings, 120; in Western imperialism, 107

colonialism: nostalgia for, 173

colonialism, Japanese: 17; adoption in, 13, 24; anticolonialism in, 75; assimilation in, 13–14, 15, 24; benefits for *naichi,* 154; discourse of hierarchy in, 79; ethnicity in, 43; feminist support for, 46; in French Indochina, 148–50, 152–55, 167, 168, 170–73, 198n52; in Manchuria, 69–79, 113, 114, 140; marginalization of women in, 172; medical care in, 17; modernization in, 9–10; and *naichi,* 153, 154; nostalgia for, 155, 171, 172–73; power relations of, 73; progress through, 141; race in, 43; socio-economic benefits of, 17, 31; in Southeast Asia, 173; strength of colonized in, 147; in Taiwan, 12; women's relationship to, vii, 176. *See also* imperialism, Japanese; Japanese Empire

Copeland, Rebecca: *Woman Critiqued,* 84

daijōsai (Shinto ceremony), 7

Derrida, Jacques: on original and copy, 198n2

discourse: archaeology method of, 182n12; creation of identity, xvi; Foucault's concept of, xiv; performative, xvi; women's bodies as, xiv–xix

division of labor: gendered, 45; in Japanese homes, 22; for middle-class women, 27

Dunlop, Lane, 196n19, 197n46, 197n48

Edo period: *kokutai* in, 2

Educational Rescript, Imperial, 184n39; homogeneous bloodline in, 14

emperor, Japanese: as ancestral site, 6, 7, 26; connection to Japanese people, 6; in Constitution of 1889, 3, 14; continuous succession of, 6, 14; embodiment of *kokutai,* 7; identification with nation, 3–4, 146; Korean origin theory of, 13; organ theory of, 3–4, 136; Western dress of, 11. *See also* sekishi

Ericson, Joan, 127, 129

ethnicity: constitution of Japanese body, xx; effect of organ theory on, xx; in *gaichi,* 159; in *Hōrōki,* 131; in Japanese colonialism, 43; Manchurian, 71, 74, 75; state definition of, viii; superiority in, 71

eugenics: in Japanese Empire, 14–15, 25–26, 28

Factory Law (Japan, 1911), women under, 29, 30

factory workers, female, 29, 30, 41; in *Hōrōki*, 134. *See also* laboring bodies, women's; women workers, Japanese

family: Japanese empire as, 8, 14, 19–20, 21, 36, 137, 139, 140

femininity, Japanese, 58–59; biological determinants of, 58; effect of organ theory on, xx; elevation to humanity, 65

feminists, Japanese, 33; maternalist, 44–45, 46, 63, 68, 186n39; of postwar era, xxi; relationship with state, 44–45; socialist, 40, 41, 44–45; support for imperialism, x–xi, 46; Yosano as, 52, 60, 63, 189n34

Fifteen-Year War (1931–45): women's responsibility for, 201n78

film adaptations: comparative analyses of, 198n2; of Hayashi's works, xxv, 157–58, 159, 174

Fogel, Joshua, 69

Foucault, Michel: *The Order of Things*, 182n12; on power relations, xvi, xvii, 35, 182n19; on representation, xiv; theory of the body, xvi, xvii

French Indochina: Japanese colonization of, 136, 148–50, 152–55, 167, 168, 170–75, 198n52; in Naruse's *Ukigumo*, 167, 168, 169, 173–74; natural resources of, 200n49

Fruhstuck, Sabine, 181n3

Fujime Yuki, 29–30

Fujimura Yoshirō, 33, 43

Fujitani Takashi, xx

Fukuda Hideko, 43

Fukuzawa Yukichi, 10; on status of women, 101–2

Furutani Tsunatake, 185n230

gaichi (outer territory), vii; colonial policies in, 153; "comfort stations" in, 31; estrangement from system in, 148; ethnicities in, 159; expansion of empire in, 158; in Hayashi's works, xxiv, 126, 128, 130, 136, 142–43, 152–55, 169; immigration to, 17; impurity in, 138; Japanese bodies in, 8; Japanese culture in, 73–74; migrant bodies in, xx, 48, 137–44, 155; moving bodies in, 144, 150; multiethnicity in, 74; in Naruse's *Ukigumo*, 168–69; nurses in, 45; in postwar era, 152–55; prostitution in, 134; as utopia, 155; women's bodies in, viii, xii, xxiv, 69, 124, 136; women's freedom in, 147–48; women's political rights in, 32; women's role in, xii, xxv; Yosano on, 69

Garon, Sheldon, 188n39

gender: equality issues, 102; hierarchy of, xv; in Japanese Empire, 107; Japanese state discourse on, 50; in *naichi*, xii, xxv, 42, 157, 158; performative, xvi; in postwar era, 157, 160; in social relations, xiv; in Tamura's writings, 90, 101, 104, 109, 120, 192n20; transgression of roles, vii; in Western imperialism, 107

Germany: organ theory in, 2, 196n20

"good wife, wise mother" ideology, xiv, 37, 181n4; in growth of empire, 194n78; household services in, 109; in Japanese Empire, 21–22; in multiethnic Japan, 24; in 1940s, 27; politics of, 39; versus prostitution, 59; subversion of, 38, 40; in women's education, 21

Gordon, Beate Sirota, 200n37
Greater East Asia Co-Prosperity
    Sphere, 16, 146, 150; eugenics of,
    15
Greater Japan Women's Association
    for National Defense, 26
Great Kantō Earthquake (1923), 42,
    103
Griffis, William Elliot, 181n3

Hasumi Shigehiko, 153, 167, 172,
    198n52
Hatō (Hayashi), 127
Hayashi Fumiko, vii; acclaim for,
    xxiii–xxiv; activism of, xi; affinity
    with state discourse, 46–47;
    apoliticalness of, 125, 126, 128; and
    bundan, 125; challenges to state,
    xviii; critical reception of, 124, 125–
    27, 159; crossing of borders, 47;
    death of, 129, 162; discourse of
    empire, 155; the everyday in, 125,
    127; experience of poverty, 124;
    female migrants in, 49, 50, 123,
    128–29, 137–44, 175; film adapta-
    tions of, xxv, 157–58, 159, 174;
    gaichi in, xxiv, 126, 128, 130, 169;
    gender politics of, xxiv; illegitimacy
    of, 124; journalism of, 126–27;
    members of empire in, 128; as
    migrant, xxi, 124, 125; *naichi* in, xii,
    xxiv, 128, 129–31, 138, 139,
    142,145; narratives about, 124–27;
    and nation-state discourse, 128; in
    Onomichi, 124; as outsider, 125;
    overseas travel of, 48–49; rejection
    of state mandates, xxi–xxii;
    resistance by, xii, 125, 145–48; role
    in nation building, xii; subjectivity
    of heroines, 124; themes of
    movement, 49; as victim, xi; war

correspondent duties of, 120, 126–
    27; wartime writings of, 137–38,
    153–54; on Yosano, 51. *See also*
    Hatō; Hokugan butai; Hōrōki;
    Meshi; Sensen; Ukigumo
Higuchi Ichiyō, 51; death of, 82
Hirabayashi Taiko, 125
Hiratsuka Raichō, 28; on housework,
    38; lesbianism of, 39–40; maternal
    feminism of, 44, 46, 59; on New
    Woman, 83; *Seitō* manifesto, 36–
    37, 38, 39, 44, 46; sexuality of, 37,
    38; support for imperialism, x; "To
    My Parents on Becoming Inde-
    pendent," 37; transgressive acts of,
    39–40
Hokugan butai (Hayashi), xxiv, 127;
    battlefield in, 143; China in, 140–
    42; family empire in, 137, 139, 140;
    gaichi in, 136, 142–43; and *Hōrōki*,
    138; imperialism in, 143; Japanese
    soldiers in, 138–43; moving bodies
    in, 128, 137–44
Home Ministry: banning of women's
    works, 33; state discourse of, 40,
    150; Women's Alliance of, 33
Hōrōki (Hayashi), xxiv, 43, 124, 125;
    boundaries in, 131; challenges to
    state discourse, 136; class in, 132–
    37; cloud imagery of, 129; com-
    modified bodies in, 139; creativity
    in, 133; critical reception of, 159;
    degraded body in, 132–33, 134;
    ethnicity in, 131; expansion of state
    in, 136; family in, 136–37; female
    laboring body in, 133–34; film
    adaption of, 159; and *Hokugan*
    butai, 138; moving bodies in, 143;
    naichi in, 129–31, 134–36, 138,
    139, 142; nationalist discourse
    in, 129; physicality in, 132–33;

prostitution in, 134; sequels to, 129; sickness in, 132; success of, 128

households, Japanese: adoption in, 24; as battlegrounds, 86; in Civil Code, 30, 86, 130; *genkan* (entryway) of, 163, 170; as microcosm of empire, 30, 32, 145; in Naruse's films, 161; public/private space of, 31, 163–64; as public sphere, 44, 109; survival of, 24; violence in, 88; women's duties in, 28–29, 38, 109, 161

Hozumi Nobushige, 5

Hozumi Yatsuka: *Kokumin kyōiku aikokushin*, 5, 6

Ichikawa Fusae, x

Ichimura Mitsue, 2–3

identity: creation through discourse, xvi; role of nostalgia in, 173

identity, Japanese: essentialized, xv; immigrants' construction of, 90–91, 92–95; nation-state's control of, xix, 48; physicality of, 141; Tamura on, 96

immigrants, Japanese, 17, 31–32; affinities with West, 116, 117; ideology of racial empowerment, 116; in Manchuria, 79; relationship with Japanese Empire, 108–10, 116, 117; surveillance of, 110, 111; Tamura's writings on, 79

immigrants, Japanese (Canada): allegiance to Canada, 94; assimilation efforts of, 100; construction of identity, 90–91, 92–95; education policy for, 94; gender equality for, 104; independence from Japanese government, 193n38; living conditions of, 91, 92, 94; role in Japanese Empire, 93–94, 95, 110; self-determination of, 193n38; sense of community, 90–91; temporal dynamics of, 95, 193n37; violence against, 92, 93

immigrants, Japanese (United States), 110–17; service to empire, 111; social/racial status of, 116, 117

Immigration Act (United States, 1924), 42

Imperial Constitution (Japan, 1889), xiii; emperor in, 3, 14; homogeneous bloodline in, 14; *kokutai* in, 5–6; women under, 32, 181n10

imperialism, Japanese: banquet metaphor for, 149; extension of kinship, 16; feminist support for, x–xi, 46; in *Hokugan butai*, 143; nostalgia for, 144, 166, 171; re-creation in memory, 174; as sacred mission, 16; social, 32, 66; Tamura on, 82; visual recreation of, 157, 158; women's discourse in, xii. *See also* colonialism, Japanese; Japanese Empire

individualism, Western, 7

Inoue Kaoru, 10

intellectuals as migrants, 48. *See also* women intellectuals, Japanese

Irokawa Daikichi, 198n56

Ishida Takeshi, xx, 4

Ishigaki Eitarō: *Ude*, 40–41

Issei (first-generation immigrants): in Canada, 92; conflict with Nisei, 114–15; connections to Japan, 116, 117; Japanese government's surveillance of, 111; of Los Angeles, 111; nationalism of, 114; racial empowerment of, 117; in Tamura's works, 112–17; tourism for, 113

Itō Nobuyoshi, 54

Itō Noe, 42, 187n20
Iwakura Tomomi, 5
Izu Toshihiko, on Tamura, 87–88

Japan: association with beauty, ix; as body, vii, xv, xix–xx, 1–17, 83, 110, 136, 158, 196n20; body/border of, viii, 10, 123, 131, 175; competition for power, 8; dichotomy between China and, 70, 77, 140; dichotomy between West and, 99; eternal spirit of, 6; as family, 8, 19; foreigners' knowledge of, 113; gender associations of, ix; homogeneity/hybridity in, 9; interracial marriage in, 11–12; Kinki region, 13; national autonomy of, 10; people's history of, viii, 198n56, 201n70; shogunate, ix; U.S. tourists in, 113; Westernization of, 9–12. *See also kokutai;* nation-state, Japanese

Japan, postwar: American occupation of, 152, 170–71; class in, 157; constitution of, 164, 200n37; discontinuity in, 166; economic growth of, 151–52, 170; empowerment of body in, 153; failed democracy in, 165; female migrant bodies in, 144; *gaichi* in, 152–55; gender in, 157, 160; marriage in, 160–62; *nagaya* architecture of, 163; *naichi* in, 151–52, 157; as torso, 169–70, 196n19; in *Ukigumo,* 144, 145, 151–55; urban space of, 163–64; view of prewar women, xxi; women's bodies in, 144, 153; women's rights in, 200n37; women's status in, 164–65

Japan Association of Racial Hygiene, 14

Japanese Association (Canada), 94; "Canada and the Japanese," 93, 95; in World War I, 194n52

Japanese body: as boundary, xvi; discourse of, xiv–xv; and female migrant body, 175; and foreign body, 100, 107; in *gaichi,* 8; homogeneity of, 14–17; hybrid, 12; as interethnic, 12; liberation of, 8; during Meiji era, 9–10; as metaphor, 2–4; multiethnic/multiracial, 8–14, 23–24; in *naichi,* 8; as nature, 4–7, 14; pathogens of, 91; postwar, 151, 170–71; purity of, 23, 26; state control over, xvii; strength of, 8, 14; unbroken lineage of, 61; universality of, viii; Westernization of, 9–12, 14; in Yosano's poetry, 61. *See also kokutai* (body of nation-state)

Japanese Empire: assimilation of foreign elements, 9; blood kinship in, 16, 17; body imagery of, viii, xiv, 14, 83, 110, 123, 131, 145–47, 158; borders of, vii, viii, xix, xxv, 110, 123, 131, 175; Canadian immigrants in, 93–94, 95, 110; Chinese growth under, 71; Chinese resistance to, 72, 75–76, 78–79; class in, 50, 107; collapse of, 153; competition with West, 8, 101, 107, 109–10, 155; economic development of, 31, 74, 155; eugenics in, 14–15, 25–26, 28; expansionist discourse of, 77–78; expansion of, xii, xx, 14, 34, 69, 109–10, 123, 131, 136, 148–50, 158; exploitation of natural resources, 154, 173, 200n49; as family, 8, 14, 19–20, 21, 36, 137, 139, 140; gender in, 107; homogeneous, 25–26; hybridity of,

70, 71, 77, 78; identification with Western imperialism, 149, 168; immigrants' dependence on, 116; inscription on women's bodies, 131; modernization of, 10–11; multiethnic, 74; nostalgia for, 144, 158, 166, 171; people's role in, viii, 198n56; racial hierarchy in, 145–46, 147, 150; racial purges in, 42; re-creation in memory, 157, 158, 173–74, 175–76; relationship to peripheries, 69; role of immigrant women in, 108–10; role of *kokutai* in, 1; sexual slavery in, 31, 139; sickness in, 132; in Tamura's writings, 79, 90; unity of, 9, 12, 22; universality of, xxi, 64; wartime actions of, x, 17; wise mothers of, 21–22; womb of, xv, 19–34, 118, 121, 145; women's marginalization in, 154–55, 172; women's participation in, vii–viii, 144, 150; women's resistance to, vii–viii, 35, 36–50. *See also* colonialism, Japanese; imperialism, Japanese

Japanese Labor Union (Canada), 194n51

Japanese people: common bloodline of, 6; connection to emperor, 6; ethnic superiority beliefs, 71; intermarriage with non-Japanese, 11–12, 13, 23–24; role in empire, viii, 198n56, 201n70. *See also* Yamato people

Japanese Women's Christian Temperance Union, 41, 43

Japan Hygiene Association, 15

Josei (journal), 82, 89, 120, 192n35

jyoryū sakka. See women writers, Japanese

Kaieda Nobunari, 5

Kaneko Fumiko, 42

Kanno Suga, 42

Kano Masanao, 198n56

Karatani Kōjin, 61

Katō Hiroyuki: *Kokuhō Hanron*, xix, 2

Kawabata Yasunari: "Japan, the Beautiful, and Myself," ix

Kawamoto Saburō, 127; on Naruse, 160, 165

kazoku kokka (family nation-state), 19

kenjinkai (regional associations), 90, 93

Kennan (poet), 53

Key, Ellen, 44

Kiyono Kenji, 15

Kobayashi Aio, 85

kodakara butai (childbearing corps), xiv, 25

Kōda Rohan, 83

kokutai (body of nation-state), xv; Aizawa's theory of, 1; in Constitution of 1889, 5–6; in Edo period, 2; emperor's embodiment of, 7; as family, 8; in Hayashi's works, xxiv, 150; as literal body, 5; marginalized women in, 155; of Meiji era, 4–5; Ministry of Education on, 6–7; in modern era, 2; and multiethnicity, 9; state discourse on, xxii; women's bodies in, 34, 36, 123

kokutai ron (theory of nation-state body), 1, 158; in competition for power, 8; in expansion of empire, 14; women's role in, 19

kōminka undō (assimilation effort), 13–14

Konoe Atsumaro, 45

Korea: immigration to, 70, 79; Japanese colonization of, 12

Korean people: intermarriage with Japanese, 13, 23–24; Japanization of, 12–13

Kōtoku Shūsui, 38–39, 45; antiwar rhetoric of, 54

Kudō Miyoko: *Love in Vancouver,* 89

kunmin ittai (emperor and people as one body), 21

Kurashima Itaru, 13

labor force, Japanese: lower-class women in, 28, 29, 31. *See also* women workers, Japanese

laboring bodies: male imagery of, 40–41

laboring bodies, women's: class in, 29; commodification of, 134; health of, 29; in *Hōrōki,* 133–34; maternal, 41; as prostitutes, 41; service to empire, 19, 27–30; as site of resistance, 40–44; as womb of Japan, 118, 121. *See also* productive bodies, Japanese women's; women workers, Japanese

language: performativity of, 182n15

Law on Assembly and Political Association (Japan, 1890), 43, 186n47

literature, Japanese: creation of women's roles, xiii; determinants of meaning in, xiv; institutional scrutiny of, xiii; naturalism in, 84–85; postwar, 144; Romanticism in, 52–53; of Tokyo, 83–89. *See also bundan;* women's literature, Japanese

Los Angeles: migrant women's bodies in, 111; Tamura's residence in, 110–17

Mackie, Vera, 29, 42, 189n34; on female workers, 40–41

Manchuria: Chinese resistance in, 72, 75–76, 78–79; culture of, 74, 75; ethnic diversity in, 71, 74, 75; immigration to, 70; Japanese colonization of, 69–79, 113, 114, 140; Japanese residents in, 70, 71, 79; Japanese technology in, 72, 73–74, 76; landscape of, 73, 140; as travel destination, 70

Manchurian Youth League (Manshū Seinen Renmei), 71

Manshū Teikoku Kyōwa kai (society): on Japanese unity, 6

Masamune Hakuchō, 84

Masugi Shizue, 137

maternal bodies, Japanese, 22, 36–40, 108–9, 120–21; in homogeneous Japan, 25–26; in multiethnic Japan, 23–24; versus prostitutes, 30, 59; and spirit of Japan, 26–27; state protection for, 59; in Yosano's writings, 59

Matsudaira Meiko, 53

McNay, Lois, 182n19

meaning: social constitution of, 90

Meiji era: hygiene programs of, 91–92; Japanese body during, 9–10; organ theory during, 4–5; policy on women, 185n4; prostitution during, 29–30

Menish, Marc, 163, 200n32

Meshi (Hayashi), 157; film adaptation of, 159, 160–66

migrant bodies: discourse of, xix, 35, 121; in *gaichi,* xx, 48; in Japanese empire, xxiii, 34; in modern Japan, xxii; in *naichi,* xx, 48

migrant bodies, female, 19, 47–50; effect on Japanese borders, xxv, 123; in *gaichi,* xx, 48, 137–44, 155; in Hayashi, 49, 50, 123, 128–29,

137–44, 175; and Japanese body, 175; in Los Angeles, 111; in *naichi*, xx, 48, 130, 155; in Naruse's *Ukigumo*, 166–74; in political space, 174; in postwar Japan, 144; and space of empire, 166–74; as subjects of empire, 123; as surface of inscription, 175; in Tamura, 49, 50, 81, 89–90, 96, 175; violation of boundaries, 175; visual narratives of, 157; workers, 96, 100, 104, 108; in Yosano, 49, 50, 175

migrants: disruptive, 47–48; mission of liberation, 48, 49. *See also* immigrants, Japanese

Mikawa Kiyo, 137

Minami Jirō, 12

Ministry of Education: discourse on women, 37, 150; *Kokutai no hongi*, 6–7, 64, 146–47

Minobe Tatsukichi: on body-state, 2–3; *Gikai seiji no kentō*, 3, 4

Minshū (journal): Tamura's contributions to, 192n36

Mitsuishi Ayumi, 84, 87

Miyake Yoshiko, 23

Miyake Yuriko, 125

Miyamoto Yuriko, 125

Mizuta, Noriko, xviii, 47, 88; on Hayashi's *Ukigumo*, 126, 147–48, 196n18; on Naruse's *Ukigumo*, 168–69; on Tamura, 192n20

Modern Girls, 40, 103

Mori Arinori, 20

Morikawa Shirō, 94

Mori Ōgai: *Youth*, 30, 199n15

Mori Yasuko, 26–27

Morris-Suzuki, Tessa, xx; on adoption, 24; on multiethnicity, 9

motherhood: protection debate on, 44, 59, 186n39, 190n34; relation to state, 59–60; sacred, viii, 140, 161; state control over, xviii, 21, 68. *See also* maternal bodies, Japanese

naichi (inner territory): class in, xii, 42, 157; colonial policies in, 153, 154; gender in, xii, xxv, 42, 157, 158; in Hayashi's works, xii, xxiv, 128, 129–31, 134–36, 138, 139, 142, 145; immigration from, 31–32; impurity in, 138; Japanese bodies in, 8; loss of stability in, 124; marginalized women of, 154; migrant bodies in, xx, 48, 130, 155; moving bodies in, 144; in Naruse's *Ukigumo*, 169–70; nation building in, vii; in postwar era, 151–52, 157; prostitution in, 134; race in, 42; sexual exploitation in, 154, 155, 167; women in, 51, 69, 102–5, 119, 123, 124; women's agency in, xii, 32; women's bodies in, xxiv; women's status in, 43; women's victimization in, 159

naisen ittai (Japan and Korea as one body), 12–13, 24

Nakafuru Satoshi, 153, 167, 198n52

Nakagawa Yatsuhiro, 53

Nakajima Kuni, 21, 26, 27, 185n23

Naremore, James, 198n2

narrative: in knowledge of past, 198n1

Naruse Jinzō, 22, 28

Naruse Mikio, xxv; critical narratives on, 159–60; depiction of households, 161; discontinuity in, 165–66; film adaptations of Hayashi, 157–58, 159, 174; language of space, 163–65; narrative space in, 165; *shōshimin-eiga* model of, 167; visual techniques of, 165; women characters of, 159–60, 165 nationalism, Chinese, 75–76

nationalism, Japanese: freedom from, 175; women's bodies in, vii; and women's progress, 50; women's support for, x; women's transgression of, xi

nationalim, U.S., 110, 111

nations: feminine metaphors for, viii–ix; as natural bodies, viii–ix

nation-state: control of identity, 48; organ theory of, xix–xx, 196n20

nation-state, Japanese: adoption metaphors of, 24; as body, xv, xix, 196n20; as family, 19; female migrant bodies in, 175; feminists' relationship with, 44–45; filial piety in, 7; formation of identity, xix; masculine values of, 44–45; organ theory of, xiv, xx, 1, 3–4, 19, 20, 36, 136, 158; women outside of, 123; in Yosano's poetry, 64

New Woman, 103, 187n11; in "The Seitō Manifesto," 39; Tamura as, xiii, 83, 87, 89; transgressive acts of, 40

New Woman's Association, 43–44

nikkan dōso (Japan and Korea with a common ancestry), 23

nikkan dōtai (Japan and Korea as one body), 12, 13

Nisei (second-generation immigrants): in Canada, 92; conflict with Issei, 114–15; independence for, 117; of Los Angeles, 111; mediating role of, 114; in Tamura's works, 112–17; tourism for, 113; transcendence of borders, 114–15

Nishikawa Fumiko, 44–45

Nolte, Sharon, 29

Norgren, Tia, 151–52

Oguma Eiji, 13; on ethnic homogeneity, 8–9

Okumura Hiroshi, 37

Ōmachi Keigetsu, 54

Ōtake Kōkichi, 39–40

Otsubo Sumiko, 22, 28

Ozu Yasujirō, 160; film techniques of, 165

Pacific War (1941–45): Hayashi's support for, 127; middle-class women in, 27; nostalgia for, 152, 154; Yosano on, 68

Patriotic Women's Society (Aikoku Fujinkai), 45, 130; ideology of, 139; nationalism of, 46

Pen Squadron (wartime journalists), 126–27

personal experience: politics of, 128

Pettman, Jan Jindy, viii

poetry, Japanese: ancestry in, 61; new form, 61; Yosano's innovations in, 52–53, 60

Police Law (Japan, 1900), 43, 186n47

power: disciplinary forms of, xvii

power relations: body in, xvi; over female body, xvii; Foucault on, xvi, xvii, 35, 182n19; gender in, xiv; of Japanese colonialism, 73

procreational bodies. See reproductive bodies, Japanese

productive bodies, Japanese women's, xvii; abuse of, 29; role in empire, xviii, 19, 20; socialists' view of, 41; and spirit of Japan, 27; state control of, 33

prostitution: versus "good wife, wise mother" ideology, 59, 161, 199n15; in Hōrōki, 134; legality of, 31, 41; link to empire, 134; in Meiji period, 29–30; in postwar Japan, 152 public sphere: Japanese households as, 44, 109; Japanese women in, 101, 102

Rabson, Steve, xxii, 55–56; "Yosano Akiko on War," 52
race: constitution of Japanese body, xx; effect of organ theory on, xx; hierarchy in, 145–46, 147, 150; immigrants' ideology of, 116; in Japanese colonialism, 43; in *naichi*, 42; state definition of, viii
Raddeker, Hélène Bowen, 42
Rafu shinpō (newspaper): Tamura's contributions to, 110
renzoku shikan (historical view of continuity), 181n1
representation: Foucault on, xiv; logic of, 182n12
reproductive bodies, Japanese, xii, xvii; agency through war, 66; in domestic space, 30–31; in *gaichi*, 69; in growth of empire, 46; in homogeneous Japan, 25–26; and literary creativity, 62; in multiethnic Japan, 23; production of peace, 64; service to empire, xviii, 19, 20; as source of production, 37; and spirit of Japan, 27; state discourse on, 64; state protection of, 33, 59, 60; superiority of, 62–63; in Yosano's works, xxii, 51, 60, 62–65, 78, 120
Robertson, Jennifer, 75
Rōdō fujin (journal), 41
Rokumeikan (Deer Cry Pavilion, Tokyo), 11, 112
Rosaldo, Renato, 173
Russell, Catherine: *The Cinema of Naruse Mikio*, 157–58; on *Meshi*, 164; on Naruse's narrative, 165; on postwar discrimination, 165; on *Ukigumo*, 159, 166–67, 168, 169, 171
Russo-Japanese War (1904–5): economic hardship following, 30; Japanese victory in, 74
ryōsai kenbo. See "good wife, wise mother" ideology
Ryukyuan people: control of, 12

Said, Edward: on exile, 49; on the migrant, 47, 48
Sata Ineko, 125, 137
Satomi Kishio, xv
Schmidt, Carl, 4
Seitō (feminist journal), 33, 186n3; discourse of sexuality in, 40; manifesto of, 36–37, 38, 39, 44, 46; Tamura's contributions to, 36, 83, 98; Yosano's contributions to, 36, 59, 190n40
sekishi (emperor's babies): bearing of, 23, 27, 34; women's nurturing of, 21, 22, 39, 130
Self-Defense Force (Japan), 181n3
Sensen (Hayashi), 127, 128, 138
sexuality, female: exploitation of, 154, 155, 167; Japanese state ideology of, 40, 50; objectification of, 30; in Tamura's works, 84–85, 120; transgressive, vii
sexual slavery: in Japanese Empire, 139
Shimazaki Tōson: *Hakai*, 84
shintaishi (new form poetry), 61
Shinto, 7; Amaterasu in, 46; divine ancestry ideology of, 16
shitamachi (lower city): in *Meshi*, 163–66; women in, 160
Shively, Donald H., 11
Silverberg, Miriam, 40

Sino-Japanese Wars, 12, 45; nationalism following, 20; women workers
in, 118
Slaymaker, Douglas, 1
society, Japanese: hierarchies of, 17,
146; as organic matter, 5
Sokolosky, Anne, 195n97
soldiers, Japanese: abuse of women,
31; as arms of emperor, xiv–xv;
atrocities by, 17; in *Hokugan butai*,
138–43; spirit of Japan in, 26; in
Ukigumo, 146
South Manchuria Railway Company
(SMRC), 69, 70; technology of, 72,
73–74, 76
subject, literary: construction of, xiv,
175
Sugiura Jūgō, 9–12
Suzuki Etsu, 81, 88, 95; on Canadian
discrimination, 94; and Canadian
Japanese Labor Union, 194n51;
death of, 110; on Japanese immigrants, 91; journalistic career of,
192n36
Suzuki Yūko, x, 201n78

Tairiku nippō (newspaper): Tamura's
contributions to, 90, 98, 192n36
Taiwan: Japanese colonization of, 12
Takahashi Yoshio, 11–12
Takamure Itsue, 41–42; anarchism
of, 46; on motherhood, 45, 46;
support for imperialism, x
Tamanoi, Mariko Asano, 158, 172–
73; *Memory Maps*, 70, 71, 198n1
Tamura Shōgyo, 81, 85–86
Tamura Toshiko, vii; acclaim for, 82;
activism of, xi; affinity with state
discourse, 46–47; autobiographical
works of, 89; as "Baby Bird," 96,
98–99, 100–101; *bundan* on, 84, 85;

87, 89, 98; challenges to state, xviii;
class in, 120; contributions to
Minshū, 192n36; contributions to
newspapers, xxiii; contributions
to *Rafu shinpō*, 110; contributions
to *Seitō*, 36, 83, 98; contributions to
Tairiku nippō, 90, 98, 192n36;
critical reception of, 83–89; crossing of borders, 47; death of, 82,
120; departure from Japan, xxiii;
discourse of empire, 82, 155;
discursive cultivation of, 49; female
body in, 83–90; female migrant
bodies in, 49, 50, 81, 89–90, 96,
175; on gender, 90, 101, 104, 109,
120, 192n20; on Japanese identity,
96; journalism in China, 120;
journalism in Los Angeles, 110–17;
journalism in Vancouver, 96–97,
98–105; journalism of, 82, 88,
137; literary feminism of, 82; Los
Angeles residence, 110–17;
marriages of, 81, 85–86, 89; as
migrant, xxi, xxiii, 95–100, 109,
120; mother of, 86; as New
Woman, xxiii, 83, 87, 89; North
American residences of, 79, 81,
88; overseas travel of, 48, 49, 81;
participation in war discourse, 119;
pen names of, 96, 98, 100, 114, 118;
prestige of, xxii, 82; promotion of
tourism, 113–14; re-creation of
Japanese Empire, 79; rejection of
state mandates, xxi–xxii; residence
in China, 81; resistance by, xii, 84,
86, 120; return to Japan, 89, 118–
20; role in *naichi*, xii; search for
freedom, 88; self-imposed exile of,
81, 92; sensual descriptions of, 84–
86; stories about, 82–83; support
for state, 120; transcendence in

works of, 114–15; transnationalism
of, 88; in Vancouver, 88, 89–90,
95–105; as victim, xi; on women
immigrants, 79, 98–117, 121;
on women in *naichi*, 102–5, 119; on
women's movements, 107; on
women's rights, 43; women workers in, xxiii, 100, 104, 108, 118–19;
writings in Tokyo, 82; writings
on Canada, 96–100
Tamura Toshiko, works of: "Attention, Women," 105–7; *Burning at
the Stake*, 86–87; "Correspondence of a Traveling Crow," 99;
"Kariforunia monogatari," 114–17,
195n97; *Lifeblood*, 83; *Lip Rouge
on a Mummy*, 87; "Spring in a
foreign country," 97; "To War
Correspondents," 119
Taniguchi Kōnen, 12
Tatebe Tongo, 12
Tayama Katai: *Futon*, 84
tennō kikansetsu (organ theory of
emperor), 3–4, 136
texts, Japanese: creation of Japanese
women, xvi; women in, xiii. *See also*
literature, Japanese
Tokyo: as extension of home, 163;
female bodies in, 83–89; literature
in, 83–89; postwar, 151–52; as
space of confinement, 132; as torso,
145
Tōkyo nichi nichi shinbun (newspaper): Hayashi's contributions
to, 137
Tokyo War Crimes Tribunal, 173
tourism: between Japan and United
States, 113
Travels in Manchuria and Mongolia
(Yosano), 56, 69–79; belly
metaphors in, 72, 73; celebration of

empire in, 70; Chinese resistance
in, 75–76, 78–79; depiction of
Chinese in, 75–77; *gaichi* in, 69;
Japanese Empire in, 73–74, 78–79;
Manchurian landscape in, 73, 140
Tsurumi, Patricia, 29

Ueno Chizuko, x–xi, 181n1
Ukigumo (Hayashi), xxiv, 124; body
of empire in, 145–47; colonialism
in, 136, 148–50, 153–54, 169, 170–
73, 198n52; critical reception of,
147, 196n18; expanding empire in,
148–50; film adaptation of, 157,
158, 159, 166–74; *gaichi* in, 136,
152–55, 169; Japanese soldiers in,
146; *kokutai* in, 150; malleability of
space in, 144; moving bodies in,
144; *naichi* in, 145; postwar era in,
144, 145, 151–55; publication of,
144; racial hierarchy in, 145–46,
150; resistance to state discourse
in, 145–48
umeyo fuyaseyo (give birth and
increase), 25
United States: Japanese tourism in,
113; nationalism of, 110, 111;
occupation of Japan, 152,
170–71
Uno, Kathleen, xx; on Japanese
motherhood, 22, 28; on state
power, 35

Vancouver (Canada): female Japanese
bodies in, 89–90; Japanese immigrants in, 90–93; riots (1907), 92,
93, 193n44; sociopolitical contexts
of, 90–92; Tamura in, 88, 89–90,
95–105
villages, Japanese: women's role in,
41–42

Wakakuwa Midori, xii

Watanabe Sumiko, 51, 89

Wimsatt, W. K., 154

wives, Japanese: bodies of, 36–40; duties to nation, 28–30; household duties of, 161; in Naruse's *Meshi,* 160–62; in postwar era, 162; public/private borders of, 164; in *shitamachi,* 160. *See also* "good wife, wise mother" ideology

womanhood, Japanese: institutionalization of, xxv; truth of, 84–85

women, Japanese: abuse of, 29, 31; agency of, viii, ix, x, xii, 32, 35; anarchists, 41–42, 46; artists, viii, 35; under Civil Code, 32, 38, 44; class differences among, 20; conformity with state discourse, 44–47; division of labor for, 27; education for, 20–21; education of children, 23, 25, 26; effect of eugenics laws on, 25–26; empowerment of, xxv, 63, 176; essentialized identity of, xv; experience of freedom, 144, 147–48, 155; filial piety of, 29, 31, 116, 117; happiness of, 162; household duties of, 28–29, 109, 161; liberation through knowledge, 102–3; lower-class, 28, 29, 31; marginalization of, xiv, xxv, 154–55, 160, 172; materialism of, 103; maternal/prostitute dichotomy of, 161, 199n15; middle-class, 27, 103; as Modern Girls, 40, 103; in *naichi,* 51, 69, 102–5, 123, 124; in Naruse's films, 159–60; nationalist discourse on, 50; nationalization of, 60; as New Women, 103; nurturing role of, ix, x, 21, 22, 130, 164; as outsiders, 123, 124–27; participation in

aggression, 175–76; participation in colonialism, vii, 176; participation in state discourse, xxv; as passive, viii, ix, x, xii, xvii, xxi, 35, 36, 51, 181n3; physical education for, 22–23; place in the world, 100–102, 105, 107; political disenfranchisement of, 32–33, 43, 118, 181n10, 186n47; postwar status of, 164–65, 200n37; poverty of, 160; in public sphere, 101, 102; reproductive choices of, xviii; as resilient strugglers, viii; resistance by, vii–viii, ix, x, 35, 36–50; role in Japanese unity, 22; as sacred mothers, viii, 140, 161; in *shitamachi,* 160; single, 165–66; spiritual powers of, 38; state censorship of, 32–33, 40; state control over, xvii–xviii, 20, 21; state discourses on, xiii–xiv, 33, 38, 44, 58–60, 136; texts' creation of, xvi; transgression of nationalism, xi; victimization of, ix–xi, xii–xiii, xxi, 157, 159, 160; as victims/aggressors, xi, 155; violence against, 88; as womb of empire, xv, 19–34, 118, 121, 145

women activists, Japanese: and discourse of women's bodies, 35; resistance by, viii

women immigrants, Japanese, vii, 43; and expansion of empire, xii; in labor force, xxiii, 100; transgressiveness of, xix; visual representations of, 158

women immigrants, Japanese (Canada): constraints on, 107; dichotomies of, 109; empowerment of, 104; gender equality for, 102; living conditions of, 92;

mothers, 108–9; power of, 108; progress for, 101–5; in public sphere, 102; role in empire, 108–10; status of, 104; Tamura on, 98–110; and women in *naichi*, 102–5

women immigrants, Japanese (United States): in Tamura's works, 110, 112, 114–17, 121

women intellectuals, Japanese: on construction of self, xiii; on Japanese aggression, 201n78; role in empire, xiii; support for imperialism, x–xi; as victims, x–xi; wartime actions of, xi

Women's Alliance (feminist organization), 33

women's bodies: association with creativity, 85; in memory, 158

women's bodies, Japanese: as battleground, 64, 66, 120; and body/border of empire, viii, 83, 123, 131, 158, 175; borders for, 30–34, 123; as boundaries, xv; commodified, 139; disciplinary power over, xvi; disconnection from empire, 147; as discourse, xiv–xix, xviii; discourses about, vii, 20–21, 34, 35, 51, 60, 120; in domestic space, 30–31; effect of ethnic policies on, 19, 20; exploitation of, 135; fertile, 23, 25, 65–66; and foreign bodies, 100, 107; formulation of humanity, 65; in *gaichi*, viii, xii, xxiv, 124, 136; in homogeneous Japan, 25–26; inner truth of, 84; in Japanese family empire, 19–20, 21–22; in *kokutai*, 34, 36, 123; and mobility, 69; mothers', 36–40, 108–9, 120–21; in *naichi*, xxiv; personal, 123; in postwar era, 144, 153; power relations of, xvii; publicly prescribed roles

for, xx; reproduction of empire, 63–64, 128; reproduction of truth, 62; role in empire, vii, xx–xxi, 19, 105, 144; role in nationalism, vii; in *Seitō* manifesto, 37; service to empire, 19, 26–27, 32, 33–34, 120; as sexual objects, 30; single women's, 165–66; as site of inscription, xv–xvi, xviii, xix, 131, 139, 175; as site of political conquest, 121; state discourse on, 20–21, 34, 35, 64; subjugation of, xviii; in Tamura's writings, 83–90; in Tokyo, 83–89; transgression of borders, 123; transnational, 81, 176; in Vancouver, 89–90; visual recreation of, 158; wives', 36–40; in women's literature, xviii, xix; as world, 64; in Yosano's texts, 51, 60. *See also* migrant bodies, female; reproductive bodies, Japanese

women's discourse: power of, xi

women's history, Japanese: accusation in, x, xi; continuity in, 181n1

women's literature, Japanese: national duty in, 119–20; state discourses in, xiii; women's bodies in, xviii, xix

women's movements, Japanese, 176; maternalist, 44; nationalism of, 47; Tamura on, 107

women's organizations, Japanese, 33; cooperation with state, 45

women's suffrage, Japanese, 44

women workers, Japanese: in Canada, 96, 100, 104, 108–9; exploitation of, 189n34; lower-class, 28, 29, 31; mothers, 108–9, 120–21; in Second Sino-Japanese War, 118; Tamura on, xxiii, 100, 104, 108, 118–19. *See also* laboring bodies, women's

women writers, Japanese: cultural duties of, 119; essentializing of, 85; evaluative system for, 84; extra-textualities of, xiii; intratextuality among, xiii; resistance by, xvii; role in empire, xi–xiii; war correspondents, 119
Wu Peichen, 114–15

Yamada Waka, 46
Yamakawa Kikue, 190n34; "Racial Prejudice, Sexual Prejudice, and Class Prejudice," 42–43
Yamato people: global role of, 15; state discourse on, 145, 146. See also Japanese people
Yasuda Yojurō, 13
Yasumaru Yoshio, 198n56
Yosano Akiko, vii; acclaim for, xxii, 51; activism of, xi; affinity with state, 46, 189n34; animosity toward Chinese, 75–76; autobiography of, 53; call for women's movements, 57–58; challenges to state, xviii, 58–60, 77; on childbirth, 62; concept of mobility, 56–57, 60, 69; contributions to Seitō, 36, 59, 190n40; discourse of empire, 155; discourse of women's bodies, 51, 60, 120; on emigration, 66; engagement with capitalism, 189n34; family of, 51; female migrants in, 49, 50, 175; on femininity, 58; feminism of, 52, 60, 63, 189n34; genres of, 49; independence of, 51; Japanese body in, 61; as lady warlord, 75; on maternal body, 59; as migrant, xxi; militarism of, xxii; on motherhood, 59–60, 68; multiple voices of, 60; narratives on, 51–56; nationalism of, 65, 68, 69; originality of, xxii, 51, 56; overseas travel of, 48, 52; pacifism of, 52, 55–56; participation in national discourses, 56; poetic innovations of, 52–53, 60, 68; as political writer, 52, 53–54; promotion of women's progress, 57; rejection of state mandates, xxi–xxii; reproductive bodies in, xxii, 51, 60, 62–65, 78, 120; repudiation of maternalism, 63, 68; resistance by, xii, 54, 55; role in naichi, xii; role in nation building, xii; Romanticism of, 52, 65, 78; tanka on Pacific War, 68; validation of war, 66–69; as victim, xi; women's empowerment in, 63; on women's rights, 43
Yosano Akiko, works of, 51–52; "Brother, Do Not Offer Your Life," 53–56; "Citizens of Japan, a Morning Song," 66–67; "The Day the Mountains Move," 57–58, 61–62, 105; "The First Labor Pain," 62; "How to Compose Poems," 61; "Open Letter," 64, 66; "Poetry of the Greater East Asia War," 68; "Rosy-Cheeked Death," 76–77; "Self-Reflection," 61; Tangled Hair, 52, 53, 61, 188n9; "The Universe and I," 65; "War," 63–65; "What Is 'Womanliness'?," 56–57, 58. See also Travels in Manchuria and Mongolia
Yosano Tekkan, 69
Yoshiya Nobuko, 126–27, 137–38
Young, Louise, 17, 31; Japan's Total Empire, 16
Yūkitai kokka ron. See nation-state, Japanese: organ theory of
Yūri Kaoru, 55–56

Zhang Huanxiang, 76

NORIKO J. HORIGUCHI is associate professor of modern Japanese literature at the University of Tennessee.